CAPTURING EICHMANN

CAPTURING EICHMANN

THE MEMOIRS OF A MOSSAD SPYMASTER

RAFI EITAN

Introduction by

Anshell Pfeffer

Translated and Abridged by

Galina Vromen

Greenhill Books

Capturing Eichmann
This English-language edition
first published in 2022 by
Greenhill Books,
c/o Pen & Sword Books Ltd,
47 Church Street, Barnsley,
S. Yorkshire, S70 2AS

www.greenhillbooks.com
contact@greenhillbooks.com

ISBN: 978–1–78438–757–0

Originally published in Hebrew as *The Secret Man*

CIP data records for this title are available from the British Library

Printed and bound in England by CPI Books

Typeset in 11.5/15.2 pt Minion Pro

Contents

Plates

Black and White Plates

Rafi Eitan during a hike to the historical site of Masada in 1946.
Rafi Eitan's parents, Noah and Yehudit Hantman, 1922.
Rafi with friends at Givat Hashlosha, 1942.
Rafi's brothers and their parents in a family group from the later 1950s.
Rafi and his brother Oded.
On holiday in Cyprus.
Rafi with Avrum Shalom.
Rafi, Zvika Malchin and Avrum Shalom socialising.
The team who captured Eichmann, with David Ben-Gurion.
Amos Manor, Paula Ben-Gurion, Zvika Malchin, and Rafi at the Ben-Gurion family home. (*Moshe Friedman for Itim*)
'General' Morris Cohen. (*Uri Dan*)
Rafi at his Tropi Fish business.
Mock trial of Josef Mengele. (*Herard Reogorodetzki for Itim*)
Amiram Nir, Rafi and Gideon Mahnayimi. (*Herzl Consari for DPA*)
Ariel Sharon, Rafi and potash factory director Arieh Shahar. (*Focus, Ramat Gan*)
Rafi with Lily Sharon at the Sharon family home. (*Anat Saragusti for HaOlam Hazeh*)

Colour Plates

Miriam and Rafi Eitan celebrate their fiftieth wedding anniversary in 2011.

Rafi the sculptor. An artist and his creation.
Rafi at the grave of his brother Reuven.
Rafi, David Ben-Gurion and the Prime Minister's son, Amos, Burma, 1961.
Rafi and Fidel Castro at a business meeting in Havana.
Handshake with Fidel Castro.
Rafi attending a Passover *seder*, Havana, April 2001.
A Knesset session addressed by French President Nicolas Sarkozy. Rafi with Ehud Barak, Tzipi Livni, Ehud Olmert and others. (*Amos Ben Gershom for Itim*)
Rafi with Chancellor Angela Merkel of Germany, 2008. (*Avi Ochion for Itim*)
President George W. Bush enjoys meeting Rafi. (*White House*)
Koteret Rashit newspaper comments on the Pollard scandal.
Rafi with President Shimon Peres. (*Avi Ochion for Itim*)
Pensioners' Party members of the 17th Knesset: Yaakov Ben-Yizri, Rafi Eitan and Moshe Sharoni. (*Rafi Ochion for Itim*)
Rafi addresses the Knesset as Minister for Pensioner Affairs. (*Amos Ben Gershom for Itim*)
Rafi at a Cabinet meeting, with former Prime Minister Ehud Barak. (*Amos Ben Gershom for Itim*)
Siblings Ami, Oded, Rafi and Rina at Rafi's seventieth birthday celebration, 1996.
Rafi's wife Miriam, who did much to ensure the publication of her husband's memoirs.

Introduction

Rafi Eitan spent the first day of the state of Israel's independence crawling down a hill in the Galilee. He had been wounded by a mortar shell fired by the Lebanese Army and was nearly abandoned by his retreating comrades. Had he died there in the Battle of Malkiya at the age of 21, he would have never known that the Jewish state had been founded by David Ben-Gurion in Tel Aviv the previous afternoon.

He survived and for the next four decades was one of the central figures laying the foundations for Israel's secret state, first as an agent of the Shin Bet internal security service, then as an operations chief in the Mossad spy agency and finally as the last head of the small, rather obscure intelligence service, that ended up causing the biggest crisis in the history of Israel's relations with its main ally the United States.

Eitan throughout his life was never one for hiding his thoughts and opinions from his superiors, and he doesn't spare his readers either, though he left it until shortly before his death to prepare these memoirs. He died in March 2019, at the age of 92, and the memoirs were published posthumously. One of the first secret missions he was sent on, as a 19-year-old junior commander in the Palmach pre-state militia, was to deter German 'Templer' farmers who were seeking to return to the farms they had been forced to abandon in British Mandatory Palestine at the start of the Second World War. Without hesitation, he shot two of them dead in front of their families.

Once he began his career as a secret policeman, he was clear that his mission included not only uncovering Soviet moles, who had been sent to Israel under the guise of Jewish immigrants, but also making sure that Ben-Gurion's Mapai party remained in power by keeping tabs on its political rivals. In Israel's early days a quarter of the parties in the Knesset, Israel's parliament, were under his surveillance as were other targets not usually considered the business of intelligence services such as tax-evaders. In 1955, he even proposed to Prime Minister Ben-Gurion to carry out a ballot-stuffing mission which would guarantee his victory in the upcoming election.

The most famous of the missions he commanded will always be Operation Finale, the kidnapping to Israel of Adolf Eichmann, mastermind of the Third Reich's 'Final Solution', the plan to exterminate European Jewry. But the detailed and inventive stratagems he devised for capturing and then spiriting Eichmann out of Argentina, which have since become the subject for numerous books and films were just one of countless creative operations Eitan planned and led. Many of these remain secret to this day.

Eitan claims that he didn't consider heavy-handed assassinations as always the best way of achieving results, but he had no problem resorting to them when he believed they were in the interests of Israel's survival. He was very clear that ensuring survival was always his foremost and overall mission, but he could sometimes be very pragmatic when going about it. Over the years his tactics would include the most unorthodox methods, such as enlisting even former Nazi officers, including SS Colonel Otto Skorzeny, as collaborators in the campaign to deny Egypt weapons of mass destruction.

Eitan was of the school that saw Israel's spy services not only as agencies for carrying out intelligence-gathering and clandestine operations, but also as tools of diplomacy. As a senior Mossad officer he undertook secret overtures to regimes around the world which had no diplomatic relations with Israel, from Morocco to China. He was years, often decades, ahead of his time in trying to open secret channels of dialogue with Israel's enemies, such as Egypt and even Yasser Arafat's Palestine Liberation Organisation. He was no dove, and he makes it clear he believed that Israel would have to continue fighting for its survival for generations to come, but he believed in doing everything possible to try and remove enemies out of the equation. By every means possible means, even peace.

But while Eitan played a major part in building up Mossad to the status of one of the world's most respected, and feared spy agencies, he was also involved in some of Israeli intelligence's greatest failures, that demonstrated the limitations of a government's reliance on its spies. In the late 1970s and early 1980s he was one of the architects of Israel's alliance with the Lebanese Phalanges which led to two decades of tragic Israeli involvement in Lebanon and the foundation of Israel's mortal enemy Hezbollah. But while he was only a supporting actor in that tragedy, in the spy scandal that would rock Israel's relations with the United States in 1985 he was the man left holding the pieces when a Jewish-American Naval Intelligence analyst was arrested for spying for Israel.

Perhaps the cruellest irony of Rafi Eitan's long life was that the man who commanded the mission to bring Eichmann to justice in Israel, the one event that emphasised more than any other Israel's historic role as the guarantor of the Jewish people's fate, was also responsible for the traumatic event that inflamed the tension and conflicts of the 'dual loyalty' of Diaspora Jews, to their own homelands and to Israel.

Eitan was in charge of Jonathan Pollard's recruitment, his handling and ultimately his abandonment, when the spy and his wife were forced to leave Israel's embassy in Washington and promptly arrested outside by the waiting FBI agents.

It's no coincidence that in these memoirs, Eichmann's capture receives two detailed chapters and Pollard's only a few cursory pages. Whether Eitan withheld the full details of his association with Pollard due to his own personal shame or the sensitivities of the Israeli government, which linger nearly four decades after the events, is left to the reader's imagination.

In the aftermath of the Pollard debacle, Lekem, or the Bureau for Scientific Relations, was disbanded and Eitan, its last chief, was retired in disgrace. Eitan was never to realise his dream of becoming Mossad chief and was supposed to have faded away into private life, making a fortune from a farming business in Fidel Castro's Cuba. But such was his irrepressible nature that he never really went away, keeping up close relationships with Israel's leaders to whom he was a friendly supplier of fine Cuban cigars and, after a lifetime in the shadows, making a comeback in 2006, at the age of eighty, as the unlikely leader of the short-lived Pensioners' Party, which he represented in the Knesset and as a minister in Ehud Olmert's Cabinet. He simply couldn't keep away. But his brief political adventure was also a failure, highlighting his lack of suitability to a more open and democratic era in Israel's history.

Those who had the fortune to meet Eitan in his later years knew him as a fascinating raconteur, though his many stories, in his telling at least, tended to cast him as the main hero, while many of his counterparts were subjected to withering almost merciless criticism. I interviewed him three times over the years on Eichmann's capture, and no matter how many hundreds of times he had told the story, each time he managed to be spellbinding. By the time I first met him, he was in his late seventies, then in his eighties, but nothing about his appearance, his short stature or thick glasses and hearing aids, belied his sharpness, or the underlying air of menace he still carried with him as an octogenarian. He would also always dredge up new details on how another member of the team, or one of his superiors, had nearly foiled the mission. There are many of them in this book as well.

Many of his criticisms are self-serving, but Eitan's personal history of Israel's intelligence and security community also provides valuable analyses of historic failures in which he was just an observer – such as the hubris and lack of foresight that allowed Egypt and Syria to surprise Israel with a massive coordinated attack on Yom Kippur in 1973, or the cold-blooded assassination of two Palestinian hijackers in 1984, that led to the resignation of Shin Bet chief Avraham Shalom, another member of that celebrated team that two decades earlier had captured Eichmann. Eitan wants us to believe that had he been in charge then, things would have come out differently, but fails entirely to convince. After all, he was also one of the creators of the myth of Israel's infallible spies.

Both sides of Eitan's character come through in these memoirs: the ruthless foe to Israel's enemies and to his own rivals at home, and the convivial, often hilarious conversationalist, to those he sought to charm. It is clear that Eitan was not just consumed by his objective of ensuring Israel's security, he also loved both the human intrigue and secrecy of the spymaster's life. Only very occasionally, mainly in the snippets written by his wife Miriam, do we catch a glimpse of the personal price paid in a life spent on the dark side but, perhaps without meaning to, Eitan has left us in his memoirs not just one of the most vivid insider's accounts of Israel's secret state, but the story of its tragic excesses and limitations as well.

Anshel Pfeffer

Translator's Note

It is the privilege of translators to get into the head of an author and render his or her world to readers in another language. In the case of this book, I was asked by the British publisher not only to translate Rafi Eitan's book but also to reduce it to half the length of the original Hebrew version, excluding parts that might be of less interest to readers outside Israel.

I thought initially that this would be relatively easy. After all, how interesting could it be to the foreign reader to learn of Eitan's business affairs after he left the Israeli intelligence community or of his foray into Israeli politics? But I found these chapters sufficiently insightful in showing Eitan's versatility and character as well as providing a rare view into the upper echelons of Israeli society to give these topics somewhat more space than originally envisioned. In the end, I included material from every chapter of the original text, though some chapters have been merged during the translation.

I have translated with minimal edits the chapters that deal with the capture of Adolf Eichmann, intelligence contacts with Egypt, Iran and Turkey, and with Eitan's vision on the prospects of Israeli–Arab peace, assuming these likely to be of high interest to readers.

Regarding the Jonathan Pollard Affair, it was my intention before reading the complete book to give a lot of attention to this, considering that Eitan was intimately involved in running Pollard. In the Hebrew version of this book, however, the chapter entitled Pollard has only six pages. Five of them deal with the history of Zionism from 1917, so I reduced that part of the chapter radically, as readers have other sources for learning Zionist history. The paragraphs which directly address the Pollard affair, I included in their entirety – all three of them.

To keep the book a suitable length, there were chapters where I compressed long sections into what amount to summaries of what Eitan wrote, while trying to remain true to his voice.

One cannot read the book in Hebrew without being struck by the depth of detail with which Eitan writes – whether talking about an intelligence operation, his salary, his business profits, or any word of praise (oral or written) that he received from his superiors. He is also careful in giving credit to others by name. To shorten the book, I have in many cases condensed the words of praise, reduced full correspondence to summaries, provided fewer details about his finances, and left out some of the many names he mentions (whether this be his schoolteachers or operatives with whom he worked). Nonetheless, I believe I have kept enough examples of his punctiliousness for the reader to appreciate how intrinsic it was to his character, as well as to his success in carrying out the various operations he describes.

I have also excluded some of the descriptions of infighting among intelligence organisations and condensed descriptions of the extensive network of contacts that Eitan used to advance both the operations he headed and his own economic interests. However, I strove to leave enough to give the reader a flavour of these.

It should be noted that Eitan refers to almost everyone in his book by their first name or their nickname – from Ariel Sharon to Fidel Castro. However, for the English-language reader, I have chosen to prefer last names, except when a first name or nickname is used in direct quotes. I assumed that readers are less aware of the nicknames of many of Israel's leaders and less used to referring to superiors and colleagues so informally, particularly in prose.

I also choose greatly to abbreviate various diary entries from his wife, Miriam, which although highly eloquent in showing the emotional impact of Eitan's work on his family, are somewhat tangential to the main interests of the students of history or military affairs I presumed are most likely to read this book.

Ultimately, I hope the translation is to true to Eitan's way of expressing himself and retains the vibrancy of the original Hebrew in his descriptions of the various milieus in which he lived and worked.

Galina Vromen

Preface

Rafi was taken from us on Saturday 23 March 2019. He was ninety-two years four months old, almost completely blind, and deaf without a hearing aid. For some weeks, he had been having a hard time walking on his own. But he continued to participate in managing his business, which our son Yuval was gradually taking over, and did not miss a single news broadcast. Despite his objective condition, he never lost interest in what was happening, in Israel and in the wider world.

We shared a lot of quiet time during this period. Sometimes, after a long mutual silence, I would ask him, 'What are you thinking about?' His answer always involved some future initiative, while I was consistently analysing the past. You could say that throughout our lives, Rafi was busy in the future, while I was immersed in the past. To his last hour, he never stopped initiating and planning. He had an answer for every situation. He was convinced that there was always an out from any difficult situation.

He was hopelessly optimistic.

However, this book is not the result of some rose-tinted assumption that everything will be fine. It is the fruit of systematic work and continuous effort. For more than four years, Rafi met regularly with journalist Yeshayahu Ben-Porat and talked to him in great detail about his work, while Ben-Porat wrote his words down. Despite his excellent recall, Rafi took the trouble to prepare, and came to each meeting only after refreshing his memory, re-examining the historical events he referred to, verifying names and dates, and providing as much documentary backup as possible.

Ben-Porat's writing was intended more for documentation than for publication. The result was an abundance of material, rich in details, in which many secrets were revealed. It goes without saying that, in such a format, it was not suitable for general publication, but was transferred for safekeeping to Mossad's library, where it remains.

Making redactions to create an autobiographical book that could receive permission for publication was a complicated and difficult process, resulting in many delays. Three writers were involved, investing time and effort. But Rafi was not willing to sign off on the book until he felt that his own voice emanated from the text. His concerns were eased only after the excellent editing of Rami Tal. I can testify that despite immense difficulties at the end of his life, Rafi read the text in full, and was very, very pleased. However, he did not live to see the book published.

The book was, of course, submitted for review by security officials. I would like to express gratitude to Brigadier General (Res.) Dr Ephraim Lapid, Rafi's close friend, who helped overcome various obstacles and facilitated approval by all the competent authorities.

Now a few words about the nature of this book. The people whose activities are depicted in this book are special people, completely dedicated to their roles, near geniuses in some cases, who live their lives without publicity or recognition, while their actions give the state and its citizens security. They deserve recognition. Rafi lived to a ripe old age, and thus, at the end of his life, enjoyed recognition and gratitude, particularly for his role in the capture of Eichmann, that many members of his team did not live to receive. Therefore, in every operation described in his book, he made sure to give full credit to every participant. But when he thought people hid their responsibility for failures, he did not shy away from saying so. This is a book written with courage and intellectual honesty, two qualities that always characterised Rafi.

Last but not least, a few words on the Pollard affair. I have no doubt that many readers will leaf first to the section about Pollard. They will be disappointed. On Pollard, Rafi is all but silent.

For the last thirty-odd years of his life, the Pollard affair stuck like a bone in Rafi's throat. It was an affair that did not let him rest and that he did not let rest. I have reason to believe that some of the delays in dealing with this book stem from it. A number of books have already been written on the subject, and much already published, so why should Rafi not have his say too?

All those who helped write and edit this book attempted to find an acceptable version of this story, including Rami Tal, who, in coordination with Rafi, tried to compile a new account, one that Rafi and the censors would both approve. Just a few days before his death, Rafi sat very alert, read every word in the new version and then raged, 'It won't work.' He rose and tried to grab his walker and lost his balance. 'I have never lied to my government,' he told me, 'I will not do it now.'

In hospital he continued to ponder this matter, and then, on 14 March 2019, nine days before his death, he called me. There was tremendous relief in his voice. 'I have decided. I will explain why it is sometimes permissible to spy on a friendly country.' He began to describe relations between Jewish settlements in the land of Israel and the British Empire from the time of the Balfour Declaration on. Yaeli, our daughter, transcribed what he said, including details he asked Rami Tal to check and integrate. Once this was done, I think that he found peace of mind.

Both Rafi and I have always been totally secular but it seems to me that the biblical phrase: 'And thou shalt love . . . with all thy heart, and with all thy soul, and with all thy mind' is most befitting to describe Rafi.

May his memory be blessed.

Miriam Eitan
12 May 2019

Chapter 1

My Roots

I was born on 23 November 1926, on Kibbutz Ein Harod, but when I was two my parents left for Ir Shalom, a community that later became the town of Ramat Hasharon. My parents never told us in an orderly way about their families or childhood. We learned about their past during gatherings or chance conversations with relatives or friends, and even then only abbreviated episodes. Eventually, I decided to make an effort to collect and trace our family history.

My father, Noah Hantman, was born on 28 December 1896, in the *shtetl* of Ritzitza, near Gomel, in the south-east of modern Belarus, to Bilha (née Kagnovitz) and Reuven, a tailor who specialised in sewing hats. The Hantmans were religious, but not strictly observant. I never knew my grandparents, who remained in Europe and died in the late 1920s, when my parents were already in Mandatory Palestine. At least half of the 20,000 residents of Ritzitza were Jews. The shtetl had synagogues, *yeshivas*, *cheders* and other schools where Hebrew was taught. From childhood, my father, Noah, and his two brothers, Moshe and Benjamin, learned Hebrew, but daily life was conducted in Yiddish. My father recalled that his father made a good living and they were relatively well off.

In the 1990s, my brother visited Ritzitza and wrote the following in his travel diary:

> I am very moved. After all, this is where father's family started, here is where his Zionist-Socialist world view was formed; from here he set forth with his friends and with mother to the Land of Israel. Here Jewish life thrived, and the love of

> the Land of Israel flourished . . . Today (December 1990), there are only about 3,000 Jews left. Most if not all have registered to immigrate to Israel and are due to do so soon . . . Father's street remains as it was in his stories, as if nearly a hundred years have not gone by . . . Two old elderly sisters, who still live across the street from father's house and are due to immigrate, remember well Uncle Moshe, father's brother, who was the head of the Jewish community of Ritzitza and was chosen to lead it. When the Nazis crossed the border from Poland in June 1941 and headed east, to the Ukraine and Belarus, the community waited to hear what Uncle Moshe would direct them to do. If Moshe decides to leave, we will all leave, was what they said. Moshe decided to go east. The Jewish community packed what they needed and left. They locked their houses and abandoned their property; their animals were given for safekeeping to their Christian neighbours. All those who stayed behind were killed, to the very last one. Moshe himself did not survive the trek and died somewhere in the east, burial place unknown.
>
> I asked to see father's house. We drove on unpaved roads. The houses are one storey, with white shingle roofs. The yards are well-tended with flowers and fruit trees. Father's house is marked with the number 21. I remember his descriptions and it is all there: the vaulted entryway, the gate and the wooden fence. The wood table and the bench in the yard. Everything is there, as if time stood still . . . From here, he joined the revolutionary army, fought and returned, wounded. Here he packed his bags and here is where he left to wander to the Land of Israel. Now everything is sad here.

When I visited Ritzitza in 2002, my brother's predictions had been realised. Only a few dozen Jews remained. The rest had immigrated to Israel. My uncle Moshe, as mentioned, had been the head of the community, and his resourcefulness saved most its members. My father had another brother Benjamin, who was not a Zionist, but rather a member of the Communist Party, and not just a regular member, but one who rose to be the party secretary in White Russia. As happened to much of the old Communist leadership, particularly to those who were Jews, all trace of him vanished during one of Stalin's purges in the mid-1930s. Apparently, he was banished to a gulag in Siberia and died there, his burial place unknown.

Like the Hantman family, my grandmother's family, too, was divided by ideology, with some Zionists like my father, and others Communists, like his brothers. Yehudah, the brother of Bilha Kagnovitz, was one of the leading members of the Halutz (Pioneer) [Zionist] Movement of the 1920s and an immigration activist.

The history of the Hantman and Kagnovitz families reflects the deep ideological rifts that emerged in the early twentieth century in the Jewish communities in Russia, especially among the youth. As happened in our families, many joined the social revolutionaries and communists, while others embraced Zionism.

During the First World War, my father was drafted into the tsarist army and served until the Communist October Revolution in 1917. At that time, entire units of the Tsarist army defected to the revolutionary forces established by Trotsky. Thus, in 1917–18, my father fought on the Western Front, on the Polish border. During the fighting, Jewish associations were formed within the revolutionary army, including Zionist associations such as the Halutz and the Tikva ('Hope').

In 1919, my father's toes froze, and he was discharged. Luckily, there was no need to amputate, but for the rest of his life they remained numb. He returned to Ritzitza and joined the Halutz group in the town. They applied to the authorities for land for agricultural work. The request was granted and they received an abandoned estate, established a training programme and cultivated its lands for about two years. But in 1921, under pressure from the Communist Party, which took a sharp anti-Zionist line, these kinds of training grounds were closed throughout the USSR. The atmosphere only worsened over time, spurring Zionists to leave for *Eretz Israel.*

My mother, Yehudit née Wolowelski, was born on 1 February 1905 in Brisk (Yiddish for the city of Brest-Litovsk, now in Belarus). Her father, Aharon, was a lumber merchant, and her mother, Hannah née Halperin, came from a family of prominent rabbis. In 1912, Tsarist Russia revoked a decree which had severely restricted where Jews were allowed to live, and the Wolowelski family settled in Saratov on the banks of the Volga. Education and Zionism were considered essential in the Wolowelski home, and my mother received a Hebrew and Zionist education from childhood.

My mother was the first of her family to come to Israel. Even as a girl, she had a strong and dynamic personality. She excelled academically, graduated from high school at a very young age and immediately began studying at the University of Saratov. However, in 1922, at the age of seventeen, she joined the Halutz training farm near Saratov, and a year later its members moved to the town of Yartsevo, north-east of Smolensk.

In 1922, my father's training group, in small contingents of three to five young people, began to make their way to the Crimean Peninsula, and from there to Constantinople (Istanbul) in Turkey, en route to Palestine. Around the same time, my mother's training group also began to move south, through the Caucasus. In Tbilisi, the capital of Georgia, on the way to the Turkish border, my father, Noah, and my mother, Yehudit, met for the first time, and never parted.

Both were equipped with forged passports or travel permits. Arriving at the Black Sea coast, they boarded a Turkish ship. They were already a couple, and my father, who had previously written songs in Yiddish, filled an entire notebook of love songs in Hebrew, dedicated to 'My Love for Yehudit', which I published in his name in 2003.

They waited for a year for passports to allow them to enter Mandate Palestine, and in 1923 arrived by ship in Jaffa. They joined a labour brigade and were taken to the village of Malal in the Sharon, where they worked for a few months, paving the road that still crosses the village. From there, they were transferred to Jerusalem. My father worked in a quarry and built roads, my mother worked in the battalion's kitchen. But they soon joined a small group of friends who left for Kibbutz Ein Harod, which had been established about three years earlier.

My parents had already lived as a couple in Turkey, and they only got married in 1924, a year after they immigrated to Israel, in Tiberias. The reason for the wedding seems to have been the birth of my older brother, who died as a baby. I was born in 1926.

In my opinion, the main reason my parents left the kibbutz was my mother's individualistic character. Although she wholeheartedly identified with the goals of Zionism and the principles of pioneering, she found it difficult to adapt to the collective life of the kibbutz.

It is possible that this alone would not have been sufficient reason to leave, but my parents were given the financial opportunity, rare at the time, and made possible by my mother's father, Aharon. He was a talented businessman, who managed to maintain his fortune and even increase it during the First World War, the Russian Civil War, and even in the early years of the Communist regime. Furthermore, he had the foresight to obtain immigration certificates for himself and others in his family to Mandate Palestine. They arrived in 1925.

According to what I was told, Aharon Wolowelski, converted all his fortune into Napoleons, gold coins, and sent them to Palestine hidden inside furniture. When he arrived, he dismantled the furniture, converted the gold coins into mandatory money, and began to purchase land, which was ridiculously inexpensive at the time. He bought hundreds of dunams (an Ottoman unit of area) on the Jaffa–Tel Aviv border, in Binyamina, Karkur, Rishon Lezion and Ir Shalom (now Ramat Hasharon).

As early as 1927, my grandfather gathered his children and gave them these lands. My mother wanted to get the smallest plot – twenty-five dunams (six acres) in Ir Shalom, then considered remote. At that time, it was worth much less than the plots received by her brothers and sisters, but in time the price of land in Ramat Hasharon rose sharply.

This gift probably played a crucial role in my parents' decision to leave Ein Harod and move to Ir Shalom, but the five years they spent at Ein Harod left a strong mark on them for the rest of their lives. They were deeply satisfied, however, with their lives in Ir Shalom.

Slowly, with hard work, they established a home and farm: a plot of fruit trees, a vegetable garden, a vineyard, an orchard and a packing house, a cowshed for eight cows, a poultry coop that pioneered modern breeding and management methods, and a hive for honey. Both were very hardworking people all their lives. They were involved in public life, in local and national politics, both committed members of the Mapai party. My mother, Yehudit, passed away on 1 September 1966. My father, Noah, died on 9 November 1978.

My mother gave birth six times during her life. Her eldest son died as a baby, in Ein Harod. The second was me. The third, Reuven, died in 1929 from pneumonia. The next, Oded, became vice-president of Tefahot Bank. My sister Rina worked, like me, in the security service. Our youngest brother, Yehiam (known as Ami), was born during the War of Independence in 1948, and is twenty-two years (!) younger than me. He is the only one in the family who kept our original name, Hantman, and worked in manufacturing and marketing dental equipment.

During 1928–30, my father built the stone house where we lived with his own hands. At first there were two rooms. My mother did not pay much attention to order and cleanliness. I apparently inherited my external messiness from her. This trait probably later determined the course of my life. Because of my sloppy appearance, I was not accepted to an Israel Defense Forces (IDF) battalion course in 1949, and as a result I decided to leave the IDF and join the security service.

I inherited my Zionism, love of country, loyalty to the homeland, and the sense of duty to protect and fight for it, from my parents. Both were imbued with an unshakable faith in the importance of Zionism. There was a lot of debate at home about politics, and how to achieve the goal of a Jewish state in Israel. My father was considered the unofficial head of the Mapai party in the community, and more than once leaders including Levi Shkolnik (later Eshkol) visited us.

Our farm supported the family well, although we also had some difficult years. Food was always plentiful at home – chickens, eggs, milk, vegetables and fruits – nothing was missing.

Although World War II brought the Jewish people the greatest disaster in their long history, the small Jewish community in Israel enjoyed an economic bonanza. Hundreds of thousands of British troops arrived in the Middle East to stop the Nazis' attempt to occupy the area. They needed supplies, and the Jewish community, which was far more developed than neighbouring Arab countries, was able to meet a significant portion of that demand. As a result, in the early 1940s our farm underwent a revolution. My father leased an additional 25 acres, and all the produce was sold to the British Army. But despite the expansion of the economy, my parents adhered to their ideological commitment to 'Hebrew labour', and no Arab was employed on our farm.

I started first grade at the Ramat Hasharon Elementary School (the new official name of Ir Shalom, from 1930) in 1932. I was not a good pupil at first, perhaps because, unlike other children whose parents had taught them the alphabet and the basics of literacy, I had no idea, because my parents had no time to teach me. From the age of five, when I came home from kindergarten, I took care of my little brother and baby sister while my parents worked on the farm.

However, by the age of seven, I already knew how to read well, and became a bookworm, reading all the books in the small Ramat Hasharon library, which my parents helped found. Our house was also full of books, mostly in Hebrew. At home, they only spoke Hebrew, but from time to time, 'so that the children would not understand', they would exchange a word or two in Russian.

When I was in second grade, a new principal, Yosef Kalman, became the head of the school. He made many changes: introduced culture to it, organised reading classes, and established a drama class in which I was active. Every year I performed in the school show. I really liked acting, and even thought I might be an actor when I grew up.

From the age of ten, I was known as a mischief-maker and was game for any prank. I learned to breathe fire from my mouth with oil, I could catch snakes and differentiate between the species in Ramat

Hasharon. One day I put a (non-venomous) snake in the drawer of a teacher we did not like. The initiator and leader of the pranks was Moshe Kalman, the principal's son, who was one class above me. Despite his mischief, he was a bright and talented guy. At fifteen, he joined the Zionist paramilitary Haganah, and in 1941 was one of the first to enlist in the Palmach, the elite fighting force of the Haganah. Later, he became a consultant in planning and construction of industrial plants as well as a general in the Civil Guard.

One day, our gang, led by Moshe Kalman, discovered a tunnel dug in Roman times under the hills along the coast. The tunnel became our hiding place and on Saturdays, we would use it to reach a wadi that led to the seashore and the bathing beach, where today the Dan Acadia and Hasharon hotels are located.

I also liked to play soccer, and to watch games in the fields of Ramat Hasharon or Raanana. I loved sports of all kinds, and excelled in athletics, winning first place in the 100-metre sprint and the high jump in the Sharon region youth competitions. I didn't excel in school subjects, except in natural sciences – biology, botany, chemistry, zoology. To this day, I am attracted to these professions and proud of my knowledge. I did not invest much energy in religious studies or history. Two or three days before exams, I would start memorising the material. But I always got high grades in essays.

By the time I was about nine years old, I was part of the labour force on my parents' farm. I had my own cow to milk every morning and evening. I did not like the work, particularly, on Saturday afternoons, when instead of playing with my friends, I had to help prepare our produce for delivery to Tel Aviv for market early on Sunday morning.

One memory I will always hold dear is the gift my mother granted me on my tenth birthday, taking me to my first movie. Until then, I had only seen what was then called a 'magic flashlight', with a primitive slide projector. My first film was shown at a cinema in Herzliya, and we walked about three kilometres on a dirt road to get there. The name of the film was *Fräulein Doktor* ('Lady Doctor'), and it was dedicated to the life and exploits of the spy Elsbeth Schragmüller, born in 1887, who in 1913 became one of the first women in Germany (and the whole world) to achieve a PhD (at Freiburg University). She began teaching at the University of Berlin, but when World War I broke out, she travelled to German-occupied Belgium and persuaded the military commander to attach her to an intelligence unit there. At first, she worked as a censor, opening and reading mail, but soon her commanders realised she was highly skilled and she was sent on an expedited course in intelligence-gathering. At the end of it, she was transferred to an intelligence post in the occupied part of France and was later appointed commander of the Combat Intelligence Unit in Antwerp. Apparently, her contribution to German intelligence was far more significant than that of the famous spy Mata Hari. But Mata Hari was also a stripper, and she was caught and executed, and therefore gained greater fame than Fräulein Doktor. I was very impressed with the film. Oddly enough, what impressed me the most were not her adventures or the dangers, but rather the routine of her life, and the goals for which she worked and took risks. On our way home, again on foot, I said to my mother: 'When I grow up, I want to be a spy for the good of the Land of Israel.'

My mother smiled and started a conversation about spies and traitors. She took the trouble to explain to me the difference between a patriot and a traitor, and she told me about Josephus, historian and participant in the Romano-Jewish War, who in her eyes was an example of a traitor. When we got back to Ramat Hasharon, we bumped into the school principal, Yosef Kalman, who remarked to my mother, 'It is not educational to take children of this age to the cinema at such a late hour.'

The experience of seeing *Fräulein Doktor* contributed to my sense that I was always destined to dedicate my life to intelligence, and that it is no coincidence that I ended up in this field. My strong impression from the film probably stemmed from the fact that from a young age I was a very curious child with a wild imagination. I befriended other children and even led small bands of them, but at the same time I was able to shut myself off for hours, reading and imagining, two traits that have stayed with me all my life. Even today, I can leave the office and shut off my mind from daily concerns to plunge into a book.

My curiosity, along with an imagination that has a practical bent, are basic to the way my mind works. This also explains my ambition to be in charge of my time and actions in most of the positions I have held. There were times in my life when I got up and left a job because I was not given such control. I will jump ahead here, and reveal that this was the main reason for my decision to retire from Mossad following the appointment of Zvi Zamir as its head.

Tomato Salad with Paula and David

When I was fourteen, my parents sent me to agricultural high school in Kibbutz Givat Hashlosha. I believe my parents were influenced by the fact that it was a Histadrut (Labour Federation) school where the sons of the Mapai leaders studied, including Yitzhak Rabin and Meir Amit.

I was a skinny boy, much shorter than average for my age, but muscular and athletic. Very quickly in high school, I developed friendships that lasted a lifetime with Nimrod Eshel, Yossi Lieberman, David Ben-Yehuda, Shimshon Lotan, Rehavam (later Gandhi) Zeevi, Inon Ezroni, later Commander of the Ordnance Corps, and later Pinhas (Siko) Sussman, later Professor of Economics and Director-General of the Ministry of Defense.

Givat Hashlosha High School was a boarding school. We got to go home one Saturday a month and during the holidays. To get home, I would get a horse from the school stables and ride for about an hour to Ramat Hasharon, a distance of about seven kilometres.

At the end of my first year there, it became clear to my mother that matriculation exams were not part of the study programme at the school, so she pressured me to enrol in Tichon Hadash (New High School) in Tel Aviv. I missed the lively and active life of Givat Hashlosha and at the end of the term, I informed my parents unequivocally: either I go back to Givat Hashlosha or I would quit school and go to work. They had to accept my decision and I returned to Givat Hashlosha and my friends.

Among the 400-odd students in Givat Hashlosha were members of many *kibbutzim*. Members of the Hashomer Hatzair Zionist movement dominated and under their influence, I debated whether the way of communism was right, but also already knew at the age of fifteen that I was not suited to living on a kibbutz.

From tenth grade, all the students in the school were recruited to the Gadna (pre-military units), where we were given weapons and field training. My first commander there was Benjamin Gibli, later head of military intelligence. The activity in Gadna was intense, and as early as the summer of 1942, during the summer holidays, Nimrod Eshel, Yossi Lieberman and I took a Gadna officer's field course. Our commander was Mishael Schechter, later Colonel Mishael Shaham, who established Unit 101 under the command of Ariel Sharon.

The Palmach was established in 1941, with the aim of stopping a Nazi attack, a realistic concern at the time. Every evening, during dinner at the boarding school, a student would read aloud a summary of the news – first and foremost what was happening on the war fronts in Europe. In the meantime, the Tehran children (a group of Jewish Polish children who had escaped the Nazis via Iran) arrived in Israel, as did General Anders' Polish army, which had quite a few Jews. The intense exposure to events made us feel that we were partners in historical processes. It is no wonder that almost every student who graduated in those years enlisted in the Palmach or the British Army, and later in the Jewish Brigade established within the British Army.

As early as 1941, at the latest in 1942, news of the killing of European Jews by the Germans seeped into the country. But only much later, in 1943 or 1944, did we begin to realise that this was mass extermination on an unprecedented scale. We talked about it both at school and at home. After all, my father's two brothers remained in the Soviet Union, and we knew nothing about their fate.

In 1941, the German Afrika Korps, led by General Rommel, landed in Libya and began advancing toward Egypt. We feared that the

Germans would invade us. My wife Miriam remembers how kibbutz members in Afikim where she lived sewed backpacks, in case they received an order to evacuate the kibbutz.

In those years, a Palmach platoon was stationed in Givat Hashlosha for training. Zeevi and I discovered their hidden weapons cache and used to open it at night to practise with weapons. At one point, Zeevi took a gun and did not return it. I was very angry with him, but he kept the gun and I did not report him.

Even in those days, everyone spoke with complete confidence about the 'country on the way'. We were all aware that our institutions and organisations – the Jewish Agency, the Histadrut, the Haganah – would serve as the basis of the institutions of the Jewish state, and we had no doubt that this state would be established in the foreseeable future.

During the summer holidays, along with two friends who like me wanted to make some money, we worked at all kinds of jobs, including gardening for Paula and David Ben-Gurion, on what is today Ben-Gurion Boulevard in Tel Aviv. Every week, on Friday afternoon, we would work a few hours, and Paula would pay us a few pennies. Sometimes she would also invite us to eat with them in the kitchen: tomato salad with lots of onions and oil, a generous omelette and white cheese. Ben-Gurion was then chairman of the Jewish Agency, but from time to time, Paula would say to us, 'Do you think it is easy to be prime minister?' sharing with us the common attitude that Ben-Gurion was already the prime minister of the 'country on the way'.

Later, at the end of July 1954, I had the opportunity to be Ben-Gurion's driver when he was retired on Kibbutz Sde Boker. During a memorial rally at Kibbutz Maagan for paratroopers who fought in Europe during World War II, a plane crashed and fell on the invitees, seventeen of whom were killed. Among the dead was Eliyahu Shomroni, founder of the Nahal army corps and Ben-Gurion's close friend. At the time, I was head of operations for the Tel Aviv section of the Shin Bet security service and was asked to drive Ben-Gurion to Shomroni's funeral at Kibbutz Afikim. I picked him up in my newly assigned Dodge, expecting him to sit in the back. But he insisted on sitting in the front, and we drove together from Tel Aviv to Afikim and back. On the way, we talked, and I reminded him that I had worked in his garden. At the time, there was no division of personal security to safeguard important figures, a division which I was assigned to create two or three years later.

In the early 1940s, we did not think much about the borders of the Jewish state that would be established. It was clear to us that we would be the legal heirs of the British, after mandate rule ended, so that our state borders would be identical to the borders of Palestine–Israel, the official name of the mandate. Only the Revisionists, who were a minority, and with whom I had almost no contact in those years, continued to claim as ours the territory of Jordan, which was officially separated from the mandate in 1927.

And what would happen to Arabs living within the borders of the Jewish state? Surprisingly, this question did not concern us at all. Of course, we knew Arabs existed, and I remember Arab peddlers who would come to Ramat Hasharon to sell their wares to Jews. Some, by the way, were not locals but immigrants from neighbouring Arab countries, Egypt, Jordan or Syria. As a nine- or ten-year-old, I often accompanied my father on trips to the town of Qalqilya or the village of Safriya to buy cheaper onion seeds and fertilisers than we could get from Jewish dealers.

There was talk of a bi-national state in the Hashomer Hatzair (Young Guard) youth movement, but we, members of the Noar Haoved (Working Youth) or Machaneh Haolim (Immigrant Camp) youth movements, sons of parents who were mostly loyal Mapai members, rejected this possibility outright.

In the summer of 1944, I completed my studies at Givat Hashlosha. I received grades of 'very good' on my graduation certificate in the sciences and history, but in literature and the Bible I received only 'good'. About a week after graduating, at age seventeen and a half, I enlisted with all my classmates in the Palmach.

Chapter 2

We're in the Palmach Now

To me, enlisting in the Palmach was a natural, obvious act. Only a few Givat Hashlosha graduates enlisted in the British Army, which I considered to be out of the question.

There were young people who debated whether to join the undergrounds of the right-wing Irgun or the Lehi. To the best of my recollection, no one from my class did. But I felt a certain sympathy for the Lehi, stemming mainly from conversations I had with Nehemiah and Naftali Burstein (later Brosh). Nehemiah held senior positions in the Haganah, and later in the IDF and the Ministry of Defense. The two brothers were Mapai supporters, but their sister, Roni, was the wife of Avraham Stern (alias Yair), the organisation's founder and first commander, assassinated by the British in 1942. I emerged from these discussions convinced that Lehi adherents were idealists guided by a love and loyalty to Zionism. On the other hand, I considered Irgun members possible fascists. I had heard about Yair Stern when I was a teenager, but first heard the name Menachem Begin only in 1946.

Even before I enlisted, I knew quite a bit about the Palmach, its structure and that its commanders were Yitzhak Sadeh and Yigal Allon.

On the eve of our enlistment, a commander of the Palmach spoke to our class, boys and girls. He described the Palmach as 'the only army of the Haganah' to distinguish it from the renegade Lehi and Etzel groups. My parents knew, of course, that I was enlisting in the Palmach, and they unreservedly supported my decision.

We're in the Palmach Now

My class joined the Palmach's Company A in Kibbutz Yagur. All previous classes from Givat Hashlosha had also joined Company A. No ceremony was held for us. We simply got on a truck and went to Yagur. There were about twenty of us, and at the kibbutz we were assigned, boys and girls together, to rooms in tin barracks behind a wadi. The next day we went to work in the fields for the summer. I worked in the vegetable garden where I was soon appointed manager.

After six weeks, we got a break, then returned and started military training. This included lectures on the situation in Israel and around the world and for the first time my attention was drawn to the problematic position of Arabs in the country.

I want to pause here to dwell on a distinguishing aspect of the Palmach: the division between military training and agricultural work. Earlier in the war, there was a palpable fear that the German forces under Rommel operating in Libya, would move into Egypt and from there to Israel. Lebanon was under the Vichy French government, which cooperated with Nazi Germany, and small German forces were already stationed in Syria. The Palmach was established in coordination with the British authorities. Its original mission was to strengthen the northern border to prevent any incursion by German and Vichy forces, and to prepare a refuge for Jewish settlement on Mount Carmel if the Germans invaded Egypt. But by the end of 1942, Rommel's Afrika Korps had been repulsed and the danger of German invasion passed. The British demanded the return of the weapons they had made available to the Haganah and the Palmach, and some were returned. The United Kibbutz Council put forward a proposal: to adopt the Palmach so that its members worked part-time on the *kibbutzim* and trained the rest of the time. This became the arrangement.

Our training included day and night field training, topography and field warfare. We learned to use Sten and Bren automatic weapons, rifles made in Britain and Italy, and grenades. We trained for two or three weeks, then worked on the kibbutz for a few weeks. After the vegetable garden, I volunteered to work at the Nesher quarry.

In the winter of 1944/5, I was sent on a sports course that started at Kibbutz Heftziba for six weeks and continued at Kibbutz Ginosar. We learned a range of sports, including boxing, wrestling, swimming and boating. As part of the course, we also had to cross the Sea of Galilee, a swim that lasted about four hours. I had no trouble passing this test. The purpose of the course was to train us for commando units (including use of knives).

At the end of the course, I was assigned to be physical education instructor of Company A. As a result, I hardly worked on the farm, except in the winter, when I asked to work in the Torz bakery, the nickname of the person in charge of the bakery in Yagur. To this day I know how to bake bread, thanks to those weeks at Yagur's bakery. But most of the time, until the summer of 1945, I was a sports trainer for Company A, made up of four divisions scattered in various *kibbutzim*: Yagur, Ramat Yohanan, Gvat, Sarid, and Mishmar Ha'emek.

I focused on honing my skills to take part in operations, to see action. As part of that, I took a course in sabotage and one in lock-picking, an expertise that I boast of to this day.

During my first two years in Company A, I was not aware of the tension and rivalry that existed between the Mapai establishment and Kibbutz HaMeuchad (the United Kibbutz Movement), and more precisely between Mapai and the Ahdut Ha'avodah (Unity of Labour) party. It was only much later that I realised that if you were not a member of Ahdut Ha'avodah, your chances of promotion in the Palmach were next to nil.

Throughout my life I have tended to be a non-conformist, always trying to break out of any mould. I have never been loyal to anyone without also being critical, and that includes even my good friend Ariel Sharon. This trait of mine led to my departure later in life from Mossad against the background of a dispute about principles with the head of Mossad at the time, Zvi Zamir. I have never regretted this trait.

I am convinced that had I been a member of Ahdut Ha'avodah or of Kibbutz HaMeuchad, my promotion in 1944–8 would have been completely different from what transpired. Sometimes I got angry with myself for not using my elbows, for not taking advantage of contacts with commanders.

The first operation in which I participated was freeing illegal immigrants detained in Atlit camp, in October 1945. I was already a corporal. Nachum Sarig, then commander of the 1st Battalion, planned and headed the operation. A day before we carried it out, a squad of Palmach men infiltrated the camp and melted in among the hundreds of illegal immigrants. In the second stage, some illegal immigrants were transported to Kibbutz Beit Oren in trucks waiting on the road, while the rest walked. From Beit Oren we planned to drive everyone to Yagur, via Nesher. Should British Army forces intervene, our unit was to place rock barriers on the access road to Beit Oren, as well as lay half a dozen mines on the road. The mines were nothing but discarded tin boxes once filled with jam, which we stuffed with 'fingers' of gelignite explosive, with an electric detonator inside. The mines blew up when triggered by an electric current sent via an extension cord. My group of three was also given a Sten submachine-gun and two pistols, which we were supposed to use if the British arrived while the illegal immigrants were at Beit Oren, but we were warned to open fire only if we received an explicit order.

Indeed, our commanders did not want to get embroiled in an armed conflict with the British, and devised a diversionary plan in case the British arrived before the liberated immigrants left Beit Oren – as they did. When British police arrived early in the morning at the first checkpoint, Sarig ordered all members of Beit Oren to block the road to traffic. Members of the Haganah from Nesher and the Haifa Carmel were also recruited for this task. Meanwhile, between 5.00 and 7.00 a.m., several hundred illegal immigrants were transported to Yagur. Only then did we dismantle the mines.

The operation ended successfully, but for me it had a painful sequel. The mines in the jam boxes had to be destroyed, so they would not explode on their own and wound or kill anyone. Since I had taken a sapper's course, I, along with several others, was instructed to take the gelignite sticks out of the boxes and burn them on the thin gravel floor of a basketball court. Gelignite is a relatively safe explosive to handle, and if burned carefully does not explode. But as a novice sapper, I was not aware that the sticks had to be burned slowly, one by one. If several are placed in a fire together, the heat causes them to combust rapidly. And that's exactly what happened. Not only did I throw stick after stick into the fire quickly, but I stood only a metre away and bent forward. A large flame blinded me, I instinctively backed away, which saved my vision. My glasses shattered, I suffered small wounds from head to toe from the impact of the thin gravel that flew violently in all directions. For a few seconds, I lost consciousness. When I came to, I first checked if I could still see with both eyes. I could, but I heard loud ringing in both ears. I was taken to the clinic. The doctor determined that all the wounds were superficial, except for one chest wound, which was caused by a stone that had penetrated between two ribs. The stone was removed. Both my eardrums were torn and thus began my hearing problems. One eardrum eventually recovered but the other never did and I bore a few small scars, similar to tattoo marks, for the rest of my life, but was not in pain after the first few days. Two weeks after the accident and a stay in hospital, I returned to my unit in Yagur.

In October 1945, the Haganah, the Irgun and Lehi created the Jewish Resistance Movement – a cooperation of the three organisations that lasted for almost a year. Its goal was to sabotage British Mandate attempts to continue severely restricting Jewish immigration to the Land of Israel. This was against the background of the surrender of the Nazis in May 1945, and the hundreds of thousands of Holocaust survivors in displaced persons (DP) camps in occupied Germany, a vast majority of whom wanted to immigrate to Mandate Palestine but were thwarted by the British.

The Haganah's policy was: yes to actions for 'illegal' *aliyah*; yes to operations against the British for settlement; no to an unrestricted war against the British. When the Irgun and the Lehi agreed to accept this principle, the Jewish Resistance Movement was created in a cooperation that lasted until the explosion at the King David Hotel in Jerusalem on 22 July 1946.

The first operation I took part in as part of this alliance was on 20 January 1946. The first radar operation's goal was to sabotage the radar stations that the British used to try to detect immigrant ships of Jewish refugees, known as *Aliya Bet*, coming from Europe. There was one station in Givat Olga, two on Stella Maris in the French Carmel section of Haifa, and later a fourth station in the eastern part of the Haifa Carmel range.

On 17 January British naval ships, aided by the radar stations, captured the illegal immigrant ship *Enzo Sereni*, and 908 people on board were taken into custody in Atlit. In response, the Jewish Resistance Movement decided to blow up one of the radar stations.

The task was assigned to a platoon commander in Company A, Rafi Ginzburg. He was a little older than me, but we were good friends, and when I heard about the planned action, I begged him to let me take part. When he consented, I took it as a sign that he considered me worthy.

Under Ginzburg, a force of about twenty men set out in vehicles from Yagar to Sha'ar Ha'amekim, where we trained before driving in three groups to Haifa, each group to a different house. Once there, we were equipped with weapons and explosives – about forty kilos – hidden in two backpacks. At night, each group was driven separately to the radar base, then in an uninhabited part of the Carmel, fenced in by barbed wire. We crawled about a kilometre to the fence. The two security units – I was in one of them – cut through the fences, and two saboteurs crawled inside and placed the load under the caravan, which stood on wheels about half a metre high. Everything went according to plan, and we left in an orderly manner, happy and pleased with ourselves.

The next morning back in Yagur, we learned the operation had failed, through no fault of ours. According to the plan, we had informed Haganah headquarters in Haifa that the charge had been placed. From headquarters, the British were called and warned that an explosive device had been placed at the base of the radar equipment, and that it would explode within half an hour. The British took a risk. They conducted a hasty search, discovered the charge, and dismantled it a few minutes before it was due to explode.

Following this, the Haganah changed its policy. Moshe Sneh (then head of the Haganah's general staff) sent a letter to the British warning them that as long as they continued to act against immigrant ships, the Haganah would continue its attempts to sabotage the radar stations but would no longer warn the British to avoid injury. Indeed, a month later, on 19 February 1946, the radar station was blown up.

Chapter 3

Dealing with the Templers

In the late 1800s and early 1900s, about a thousand Germans, members of the Protestant Tempelgesellschaft (Templers), came to Israel, believing that by settling and working hard in the Holy Land they would bring Christ's second coming. These Templers (not to be confused with the Templar Knights of the Crusades), established several settlements in Tel Aviv, Jerusalem, Haifa and more rural parts of the country.

From the early 1930s, pro-Nazi sentiments began to reach some of the Templers in Israel. There was open Nazi propaganda delivered to young people and children, and many of them went to summer camps in Germany, where they received political and pre-military training. They held parades behind swastika flags and set up clubs adorned with Nazi symbols. When Arabs and Jews clashed in 1936, some Templers helped the Arabs. By 1938, the number of Nazi Templer members had reached 330, about a third of their adult population. Their leader was Gotthilf Wagner, a resident of Sharona in Tel Aviv with a locksmithing business in Jaffa.

On 20 August 1939 (less than two weeks before the outbreak of the war), the Templer leaders in the Holy Land received a telegram from Berlin, ordering reservists to return to Germany and on 31 August, a ship with about 550 Templers, conscripts and their families, left from Haifa. Once Britain was at war on 3 September the 2,400 Templers remaining in Mandate Israel were defined as subjects of an enemy country. About 1,200 of them were sent to detention camps and deported to Australia a few months later. The rest remained in Israel, watched by British soldiers and Jewish guards. Their buildings were seized by the British Army, but their property and belongings were not damaged. At the end of the war, the exiles sought to return to Israel and in 1945, the British approved their return.

The *Yeshuv* (Jewish community in the Land of Israel) was shocked. While blocking hundreds of thousands of Jewish displaced persons (DPs) in Europe from coming to Israel, the British were allowing declared Nazis to enter! The Templers began to trickle back, including Wagner, who went back to his house in Sharona and reactivated his business. Moshe Shertok (later Sharett), head of the Jewish Agency's political department, which served as a kind of foreign ministry for the *Yeshuv*, sent a sharp protest to the British Foreign Office, to no effect.

The *Yeshuv's* top security officials – Ben-Gurion, Israel Galili and Sneh – decided to act to deter the Templers from returning and to motivate those who had returned to leave. The operation was assigned to the Palmach. Yigal Allon marked Wagner as a target. On 22 March 1946, Wagner was travelling on the road between Mikve Israel and Jaffa when he came under fire from another vehicle. He was shot and killed. For everyone – the Templers, the British and of course us – it was clear what had prompted his killing.

But it did not stop the Templers from returning. Mostly, they came back to their agricultural settlements: Wilhelma, Waldheim and Bethlehem-in-Galilee (not the biblical Bethlehem in the West Bank). Following Wagner's assassination, they hired armed Arab guards to protect them. The response of the *Yeshuv* leadership was to decide to kill more Templers. While Wagner's assassination was targeted, meaning a specific person was assassinated, now it was decided to eliminate Templers randomly, as the opportunity arose in the rural communities, as a warning to others. It was presumed that killings would frighten all Germans in the country, motivate them to leave, and especially deter those still in Australia from returning.

We knew by then that six million of our people had been murdered in the Holocaust. Most of us had relatives who had been murdered, so killing Germans, particularly former Nazis, was considered a *mitzvah* (a good deed). We certainly didn't want them in our midst and considered them justifiable targets.

Yigal Allon assigned the job to Zalman Marat, company commander of the Palmach's Yiftach Brigade. He assembled a squad of four men, in two pairs, each with two people. One pair was led by Yehoshua Bornstein from the Kibbutz Gvat training camp and the other pair was led by me.

After initial reconnaissance, I came up with the plan. We would ambush the Templers on their way home from Haifa, on the road between Waldheim and Bethlehem- in-Galilee. And we would kill them. Marat had reservations about my plan, but I was determined to carry it out.

We acted in broad daylight. Three of us, disguised in *kaffiyehs* as Arabs, lay in ambush in a grove, a mile from Bethlehem-in-Galilee, a few metres from a dirt path between the two villages. The fourth team member served as look-out. We had no walkie-talkies, and he signalled to us when he saw a cart approach. A cart with two horses came towards us, slowing down a little as it reached a bend in the path. When it was about ten metres from us, I came out from the thicket, wearing a *kaffiyeh*, raised a hand, shouted 'Stop!' and grabbed the horses' bridle.

The cart stopped. There were two Arab drivers in the front, two German men behind them, and two women in the back seat. One Arab jumped up and ran. The other, who believed us to be Arabs, shouted '*Ana Arabi, ana Arabi*' ('I am an Arab'). The two Germans said something to each other in German. I wanted them to think we were bandits, and I shouted in Arabic '*het masari*' ('the money') and in English, 'Give me the money.' Before they could respond, Bornstein and I approached to about a metre and a half away from them, and I fired one bullet into the forehead of each man. Both Germans were killed on the spot. One of them fell forwards, the other backwards. The women screamed. To this day I can hear their screams. Bornstein approached the dead Germans and fired another bullet at each of them, to ensure they were dead. The whole process took no more than twenty seconds.

Then Bornstein and I went our separate ways. I escaped by running through the fields between Kibbutz Allonim and Bethlehem-in-Galilee. The other two team members slipped away in another direction. A shepherd, a member of the Haganah, brought out his herd as planned, in order to obscure our tracks in case there was a chase using dogs. Not far from Allonim, a member of the kibbutz was waiting for us. He took our weapons and *kaffiyehs*. We continued running and walking to Ramat Yohanan, where we got into a waiting van and changed clothes. The van drove us to bus stops, each on a different route, and we returned by bus, each to his own community. I returned to Yagur.

When my bus arrived at Check Post at the entrance to Haifa, a British policeman got on, walked up and down the aisle, already searching for suspects in the assassination of the Germans. I do not know if he was looking for Arabs, or if the British already knew that the assassins were Jews.

The next day, there was a small item about the killings on the front page of *Davar* newspaper, without the names of the victims, and without any hint of the identity of the perpetrators, but no one in the *Yeshuv* needed clues to understand who committed the act and why.

I was proud of the successful execution of the operation. My decision to undertake such a daring and dangerous action with only two years of service in the Palmach seemed natural to me. I knew I was recognised as an experienced and courageous fighter, who knew the area well, and whom one could count on to carry out successfully whatever mission he was assigned.

In the days after the operation, I had no doubts that I had fulfilled an important and justified task and felt no remorse. But in later years, I had doubts about the morality of what I had done. After all, I killed two people, not knowing who they were, what they had done. But I eventually came to the conclusion that I had done the right thing. At that time, the Germans who returned to Israel already knew what had been done to the Jewish people and were aware that their presence was opposed by the *Yeshuv.*

For many years, I did not speak of this operation to any of my associates, nor to my children or my wife, and as far as I can remember, not even my parents. It was only in 1985, thirty-nine years later, that I published the story.

Parenthetically, an entirely different kind of incident occurred in August 1948. We were fighting in the besieged Negev and decided for security reasons to dismantle and expel a number of Bedouin encampments scattered in the area. In my role as commander of a patrol company, I took on the task, and Zeevi, who was the Palmach's intelligence officer, went on one of the missions with me. Unabashedly and for no operational reason, Zeevi shot and killed several Bedouins. I stopped him and told my men not to shoot anyone unless they shot at us first. I was very angry with Zeevi then, and I held his actions against him.

Chapter 4

We Have a Country

In the summer of 1946, I was sent to a platoon commander's course in Kfar HaHoresh under the command of Yitzhak Rabin. He must have liked me because he let me use his car to learn to drive. The deputy commander of the course was Yitzhak Dubno, considered the 'military philosopher' of the Palmach, and thanks to him the course was more like a seminary. Combat theory was taught in more depth than in previous courses. Rabin and Dubno taught conceptual ideas on the principles of war, situation assessments, and thought processes. At the end of the course, when I returned to the 1st Battalion, Ginzburg, commander of Company A, appointed me as a platoon commander and, in fact, his deputy. There were about thirty people in the platoon, most were from the class below me at Givat Hashlosha or from the corresponding class in Kadouri agricultural school.

The so-called 'third radar operation' was, in fact, the third and fourth operation at the same time: two simultaneous operations to destroy radar stations, on the night of 20 July 1947. The British had by then repaired the radar station that Yosef (Yoske) Yariv's operation damaged at Stella Maris in the French Carmel area of Haifa. The British set up an additional, more sophisticated, radar station in the eastern Carmel, near Beit Oren, with a range that allowed them to locate illegal immigrant ships far out at sea, arrest them more easily on the high seas and transfer their passengers to detention camps in Cyprus.

The double operation was entrusted to the 1st Battalion, headed by Ginzburg. I was appointed commander of the platoon tasked with blowing up the sophisticated radar on the eastern Carmel. Until this operation, there had always been someone above me planning the action and commanding me. This was the first time I was entrusted with deciding what to do, and the responsibility of success or failure rested on my shoulders.

I drove to Sha'ar Ha'amakim, headquarters of the 1st Battalion, under the command of Dan Lener, who gave me a map of the eastern Carmel, marked with the radar station we were to blow up. Lener made a pickup truck available to me and told me to come up with a plan by the next day. At that time, there was a British curfew in the evenings, so I immediately set out to scout the area, together with Ezroni, a squad commander in my platoon. I appointed him as commander of one of the teams that would carry out the operation and named Sussman to head the second. Near the British Airborne Division camp where the radar station was located, we raised the bonnet of the pickup truck, as if it had a mechanical problem, so we could unobtrusively check out the field. When it got dark, we surveyed the area on foot, noting the paths leading to the camp, and the three concertina wire fences surrounding the radar station, lit with strong spotlights. No one noticed us, and I even managed to draw a diagram of the place before we returned to the truck and drove to Yagur for the night.

The next day I gave Lener a report, but I did not have a plan. A taciturn Lener informed me that the operation had to wait for approval from the top, which meant that Ben-Gurion had not yet given the nod. At the time, no operation could be carried out without his approval. Even Allon was not authorised to approve actions.

This gave me time for another reconnaissance tour with Ezroni and Sussman. We put bicycles in the pickup truck and took them out not far from the British camp, riding around as if we were biking enthusiasts. Amid vantage points we found in the brush on the Carmel, we observed the radar station for a few hours. This helped me improve my plan, which I scribbled down and submitted to Lener. It was later stored in the Palmach archives, and unfortunately lost there.

I instructed a small team to stay in the area, to observe and report any changes in the level of British activity at the station.

Five tense days passed until we received approval for the operation. A few minutes after midnight, we cut the fences, but still did not break in because we were supposed to wait until the station at Stella Maris was exploded before proceeding. But we did not hear an explosion. Only the next day did we learn that a battle had broken out there and the unit was forced to retreat before placing the explosives. One of our fighters, Eliezer Arkin, was fatally wounded.

At 2.00 a.m., after waiting two hours to hear the explosion at Stella Maris, I decided to act and we broke in. Two charges were placed under the radar unit but when the sapper tried to place the charge intended for the antenna, the British guards detected him and opened fire. We returned fire while the sapper got the charge into position near the antenna. All of us, myself last, managed to retreat and crawl away. I counted, and a second before the explosion I shouted, 'Lie on the ground,' and then there was a huge boom. The radar station flew into the air. Only pieces of charred metal remained. One of our men was wounded in the hand, and on the British side the radar operator and a guard were killed.

We crawled to the assembly point. I ascertained we were all there and checked that we had all our weapons. A machine gun and a rifle were missing, and all the way back to base, I was preoccupied with having lost those weapons. In the morning we got back to Yagur, the team dispersed to surrounding *kibbutzim* and I went to sleep. In the morning, Lener woke me up, told me what had happened on French Carmel, patted me on the shoulder and congratulated me on the success of the operation.

During this period, I participated three times in providing security when illegal immigrants disembarked on the shores of the country. In December 1945, as a platoon commander, I secured the beach between Nahariya and Shavei Zion when the illegal immigrant ship *Hannah Senesh* got stuck on rocks near the beach. Since we couldn't evacuate the 200 illegal immigrants by boat, we made a rope bridge.

In addition to being responsible for securing the coast, I was called on to strengthen the rope bridge, using anchors secured on the shore. I helped the immigrants gather their belongings and directed them to the trucks that dispersed them in nearby settlements. Later, in November 1947, already a platoon commander, I was given the responsibility of securing the village of Kfar Vitkin when the illegal immigrant ship *Aliya* arrived, and a month later, the ship *Haportzim*. Both operations succeeded, and all the immigrants were brought ashore without incident.

In the summer of 1947, I was appointed Ginzburg's successor as commander of Company A when he went off to a course. I was in charge of about 150 people and got the use of a Triumph Sapphire Twin motorcycle.

At the end of September 1947, Lener called me and instructed me to join Haim Brotzlewsky, later Bar-Lev, commander of the 8th Regiment, who was tasked with leading a series of several courses for division departments. I knew him from the physical education course I took at the beginning of my career in the Palmach. Haim suggested I be a trainer in the courses. I was with him and Arye Shahar in Kibbutz Dalia when the historic decision in the United Nation establishing the State of Israel was announced, and we were all very moved when we heard it on the radio. After the vote, Bar-Lev gave us all a short break. I went to celebrate in Ramat Hasharon and Tel Aviv, and I vividly remember dancing with my friends near the Red House, the Palmach headquarters on Hayarkon Street, and on Dizengoff Street – a whole night of celebration and dancing. At home, my mother radiated joy. None of us had had any doubt that the state would be established, but we knew that it would involve war, and that we would be at the leading edge of the army fighting it.

From end-November 1947 through March 1948, I conducted two sixty-day courses in Dalia, interspersed with occasional calls from Ginzburg to join company actions – about twenty of them in the Haifa and western Galilee region. These were basically limited hit-and-run operations, designed to force the Arabs to defend themselves, as long as the British were in the country. Immediately after the UN decision, the Arabs launched attacks on the *Yeshuv*. Our company was given the task of pushing the Arabs participating in these attacks back into their villages and preventing them from blocking roads. We would create a trap at night, with one unit opening fire until the Arabs came out of hiding. Once the Arabs responded with fire, one or two other units would crawl forward and attack the target.

One of the more complex operations was conducted in February 1948 in Acre, a city with fortifications on a cliff that dominates the road from Haifa to Rosh Hanikra, on the Lebanese border. We attacked from the east, seized a 200–300-metre section, emptied houses of residents who fled, and after ascertaining they were empty, set the houses on fire and moved on. The battle lasted five or six hours. No British force arrived. The result was that from then on, the Arabs of Acre hesitated to set up ambushes and block the road to the north.

Other actions I participated in while an instructor at Dalia included arranging security for transport to communities in western Galilee. We also destroyed Arab sniper positions in Haifa, always after midnight, blowing up dozens of houses mostly in the port area and Wadi Nisnas from where snipers shot at transport and Jewish neighbourhoods. Other actions included blowing up Arab garages in Salah a-Din Plaza in Haifa, setting ambushes to attack Arab gangs in the Tarshiha area, a raid at the edge of the western slopes of Mount Carmel (known as the Little Triangle area), blowing up bridges and roads, and attacking villages of Zar'in and Sandala in the southern Jezreel Valley.

We also operated against Druze villages in western Galilee; the Druze fought alongside the Arabs at the time. The Druze numbered several thousand, and they were well equipped. Only on the eve of the establishment of the state, when most of western Galilee was already under our control, and the Druze realised that the Jews would probably win the war, did they shift their support to the Jewish side.

Battles around Kibbutz Mishmar Ha'emek, during 4–17 April 1948, played a decisive role in the outcome of the war. The only Jewish settlements in the area then were Yokne'am and Kibbutz Hazorea. West of Mishmar Ha'emek lay the Arab village of Abu-Shosha, and to the east lay Ghubayya al-Fauqa on a hill, and Ghubayya al-Tahta, downhill. From Mishmar Ha'emek there was a road to Juwara, a large and well-known training base of the Haganah and the Palmach, and above Juwara were Dalia and Ein Hashofet.

Mishmar Ha'emek was threatened by forces under the command of Fawzi al-Kawkaji, a Lebanese who had served in the Turkish Army and was a senior commander in the riots organised by Arabs in Palestine against the *Yeshuv* and British authorities in 1936–8. During World War II, he stayed in Nazi Germany. There was a bitter rivalry between him and Haj Amin al-Husseini, although both shared Nazi views of the Jews. At the end of the war, Kawkaji returned to Syria, to organise a force intent on destroying the Zionist enterprise in Israel. In July 1947 he said, 'The battle between the Arabs and the Jews is a total battle, and the only possibility is the extermination of every Jew, both in Palestine and in all Arab countries.'

Following the UN partition decision in November 1947, the Arab League appointed Kawkaji as commander of the 'Salvation Army' – a force of volunteers, mostly from Syria and Iraq, a minority from Jordan and Druze living in Israel and Lebanon. He managed to assemble some 3,000 men based near Jenin, with their supplies coming mainly from Lebanon.

The Haganah and its later iteration, the Israel Defense Forces (IDF), had accurate information about Kawkaji's plans. In Afula, there was a relatively sophisticated telephone exchange – automatic and not manual – set up by the British and all the telephone lines of Jenin and the surrounding area were connected to this exchange. The Haganah eavesdropped on Jenin's lines and even recorded some of the calls between Arab headquarters in Haifa and Kawkaji in Jenin. During these calls, Kawkaji detailed his battle plan: to occupy the Jewish settlements along the Haifa–Afula road to Mansura (the Arabic name of Yokne'am). He predicted that British soldiers stationed in Mansura would stand by and not interfere with his forces. After conquering

Yokne'am, he planned to enter Wadi Milch and capture the Haifa–Jaffa Road. His first target was Mishmar Ha'emek. Indeed, on 4 April, the Salvation Army forces attacked the kibbutz, using artillery for the first time in the War of Independence. Some Salvation Army armoured personnel carriers managed to get close to the fences of the kibbutz, but were repulsed. We had casualties, and the kibbutz was severely damaged.

Based on the information from eavesdropping, Allon and Sadeh coordinated a general strategy, and Allon instructed our battalion commander, Lener, to plan the defensive battle for Mishmar Ha'emek. Bar-Lev ordered me to go to Juwara, along with about fifteen fighters he chose. We went on foot, armed with our personal weapons, from Dalia to Juwara, where the battalion's headquarters were located. Lener gave me the battle plan.

My mission was to join our squad with the squad under the command of Shaike Gavish and to storm the village of Ghubayya al-Fauqa at dawn. The squad of Meir Amit was tasked with conquering Abu-Shosha. It was later alleged that Amit's force carried out a massacre in this village after capturing it, killing about sixty unarmed Arabs. I was not there. All I knew was that this village was occupied and its inhabitants fled. The allegations about the massacre became known to me only many years later.

Kawkaji had one company in Ghubayya al-Fauqa, about half a kilometre from Mishmar Ha'emek, and a second company at Khirbet Ras, in the southern Mansi Valley. Lener wanted to encircle the Mansi Valley and hit Kawkaji's forces with four squads. My force included fighters with training but who had never fought together as well as Gahalniks, new immigrants who had just arrived. Our equipment included locally made Sten submachine-guns, one walkie-talkie which weighed ten kilograms, and later also a 2-inch mortar. I surveyed the area at night, and before dawn we began crawling toward Ghubayya al-Fauqa, first through a grove, then through a field of bushes. When we were about 250 metres from the centre of the village, 70 metres of which were uphill, I arranged my force, and we came under fire almost immediately. Two of our squad were wounded, one of whom later died of his wounds.

I asked for reinforcements, who arrived about three-quarters of an hour later and I ordered our men to advance. We stormed with about sixty men, and Kawkaji's forces simply fled. We had two dead and two wounded. They had at least ten dead. We did not take prisoners. The whole attack lasted about five hours. At noon the village was in our hands, and meanwhile Abu-Shosha and Khirbet Ras were also captured.

We returned to the Mishmar Ha'emek forest to recover. I was given a new task: to attack Kawkaji's men in an ambush between Megiddo and Mansi, and between Megiddo and Umm al-Fahm. For three or four days, under Lener and Gavish, we conducted a guerrilla war against Kawkaji's men, ambushing roads, blowing up houses and expelling Arabs. We reached Wadi Ara Road, about a mile from Megiddo. On the third or fourth day, all Kawkaji's forces retreated to Jenin. That ended the Battle over Migdal Ha'emek. Kawkaji disappeared from the area, retreated north, fought no more and eventually fled from Israel.

After Mishmar Ha'emek, we battled in the Sandala area between Jenin and Afula, and in Zar'in, today Kibbutz Jezreel. After this battle, which required two assaults until it was captured, I was sent to Haifa to organise trucks as part of an operation devised by Allon in order to demonstrate that the whole of Galilee was in our hands. On the Haifa–Tel Aviv Road, we stopped lorries and pickup trucks and commandeered them. To the best of my recollection, we encountered no resistance from the drivers. Within two days we collected a huge convoy of about a hundred trucks and cars, and drove a whole battalion of about 300 men, from Mishmar Ha'emek to Rosh Pina. The convoy was intended to signal that the Palmach had conquered Galilee, and to encourage the Arabs to flee from the villages they still had left.

The journey through Afula, Yavneel and Tiberias, without any battles on the way, lasted about two days. Some fighters and I rode in pickup trucks ahead of the convoy, to grab positions and secure the road. In Rosh Pina, we bunkered down in Pilon Camp, a former British Army camp that the British had intended to hand over to the Arabs, but Moshe Kalman (my former elementary school classmate, now a Palmach commander) took it over before the British had time to carry out their intention.

In Pilon camp, on 20 April, I was transferred from Gavish to Asaf Simhoni, who had taken over command of Company A from Ginzburg. Simhoni appointed me his deputy.

On 14 May 1948, David Ben-Gurion announced the establishment of the State of Israel. I, like most Palmach fighters, was far from the Tel Aviv Museum where the historic ceremony was held. I did not even know about it in real time. The previous evening, as Simhoni's deputy, I was at the staging point, with a battalion consisting of four companies, for an attack near Malkiya, a small village on the Lebanese border, with hills that overlooked the Hula Valley. Two of the other companies were commanded by Gavish and Eli Zeira. We had intelligence information, including aerial photographs taken from the Piper available to Allon, that on 15 May a Lebanese Army brigade planned to invade Israel, seize the Malkiya–Neve Yehoshua–Hula Valley road, and attack Tiberias from the north. Simultaneously, the Syrians planned to capture Degania, Tzemach and Afikim, and attack Tiberias from the south. The significance was clear: the Syrians and Lebanese were planning a pincer movement to occupy eastern Galilee. One company was delegated to handle the Syrians, while our force was tasked with stopping the Lebanese attack by seizing the section of road from Malkiya to Neve Yehoshua and Hula.

For me, the Battle of Malkiya began on 15 May at 5.00 a.m. and ended with me being injured five hours later. Under darkness, we ambushed the road descending to Malkiya, and in the morning I moved from platoon to platoon to coordinate the assault. At 10.00 a.m., a 50-mm mortar shell fired by the Lebanese landed a metre and a half from me. I flung myself down on the ground before the shell exploded, and this saved me. I was hit by shrapnel, some twenty bits, on the right side of my body, from my ankle to a bone in the leg, which broke the leg, to the middle of my body. I didn't lose much blood and I didn't lose consciousness. I immediately bandaged the ankle and leg with two dressings from my pocket. The rest of the wounds were superficial, and I tore off strips from my shirt to bandage them. People approached me within minutes, and I asked to be taken to a collection station, where I was treated and my wounds properly dressed by a paramedic. After about five hours, I began to feel intense pain in my ankle and leg, and sensed that I was in a state of shock, a routine phenomenon hours after this type of injury.

Simhoni decided to evacuate me, along with other wounded, to Moshav Ramot Naftali. Two Gahalniks carried me on a stretcher, but as they proceeded along the road to the *moshav*, we were fired on by snipers from a local gang that had joined the Lebanese attack. The Gahalniks, who barely spoke Hebrew, abandoned me and the stretcher and fled. Under the sniper fire, I decided to go back to the base of the hill and I crawled on my hands and with my left leg for about 200 metres, and then I either lost consciousness, or fell asleep out of exhaustion.

When I woke up it was already dark. I saw our forces retreating a few metres away. I called out and Simhoni approached me, looked at me, did not say a word and walked on, strange behaviour that he later deeply regretted. Immediately after him came Ezroni, who loaded me onto his back and started carrying me to Ramot Naftali, three kilometres away. When he got tired, Sussman carried me. I was only laid on a stretcher when we neared the *moshav*, where there were some fifty wounded and ten dead. I was dressed properly and set down next to Gavish, who was also wounded. It was there that I heard the news of the declaration of the State of Israel. We were elated and joyful all night. Despite our injuries, despite the retreat from Malkiya, even though we had not been successful in our mission, we knew one thing: we had a country!

The next morning, we were bundled off to hospital in Safed. The chief surgeon there was the late Dr Tulchinsky, a relative of mine who told me he would operate on the broken leg but not on the broken ankle, a complicated operation that might not be necessary if I could walk on it.

Two days later, on 18 May, still without a cast, I was taken with the other wounded, again in trucks, to hospital in Afula. On the way, we found ourselves under heavy Syrian shelling, and for several hours at night we were forced to wait on the road. This was one of the most critical days in the 1948 war: the Syrians took over Tzemah, bombed the Poriya–Yavneel area and were eventually repulsed by Palmach forces under the command of Moshe Dayan.

At Ha'emek Hospital in Afula, my foot was put in a cast. The rest of my wounds healed quickly and after three or four days, I was transferred to Kibbutz Gvat to recover. To my surprise, my mother came to visit me. To this day, I do not know how or from whom she learned that I was wounded. I certainly hadn't called to tell my parents.

After the week at Kibbutz Gvat, I rode my motorcycle, still with a cast on my leg, first to my parents in Ramat Hasharon, and from there to Sarafand where my company had relocated. This was now the brigade's staging area under Yigal Allon for forces setting out to occupy Arab areas left in the centre of the country after our successful conquest, under Moshe Carmel, of western Galilee and of Nazareth.

In June 1948, I was transferred to the brigade headquarters after Allon had been appointed to lead the IDF Southern Command. Mula Cohen was appointed commander of the Yiftach Brigade in his place and I was to serve as a liaison officer at Cohen's headquarters. My leg was still in a cast, but I used my motorcycle and I also had the occasional use of a Jeep for special missions. My most important task was to act as liaison to the 8th Battalion under Dayan, who had set out from Beit Nabala to capture Lod and Ramla. At this point, the brigade, like other Palmach units, had already been integrated into the IDF.

I waited for the battalion at Beit Nabala, and gave Dayan the incursion plan that Cohen wanted carried out in Lod. After relaying the information, I asked to join the action and thus found myself in the last vehicle of the column preparing to break into Lod.

This was my first encounter with Dayan. He struck me as an energetic man, who barely listened to Cohen's instructions when I conveyed them to him. He seemed indifferent to what I had said and I was not highly impressed by him. Furthermore, personality aside, I was disappointed when I saw his convoy, which was supposed to be an armoured convoy but had no tanks, only about thirty Jeeps, equipped with light or medium machine guns, and a few heavier vehicles. My Jeep driver and I had only our personal weapons.

On the morning of 12 July, the forces readying to go to Lod were organised on the main road of Ben Shemen youth village. The girls and boys, who until recently had been under siege, joyously gathered around as the convoy set out for Lod, a small village at the time, about three kilometres away. Midway to Lod, Dayan issued an order to fire, and all vehicles opened fire in all directions simultaneously. The effect was enormous. No one got out, we just fired, and the whole incursion did not take more than twenty minutes. At that point, Cohen told us over our communication system that the 3rd Battalion had entered Lod, and so Dayan's force continued to Ramla. I joined the 3rd Battalion in Lod.

When Operation Danny ended in July, I returned to Afula to have my cast removed. From there I went back to Sarafand where it was agreed with Simhoni that I would be an intelligence officer and go south to the Negev to set up an intelligence unit. I chose about ten men for the unit, among them Avrum Shalom, later head of Shin Bet, whom I named as my deputy, knowing from our training in Maoz that he was a man able to make decisions, with a strong sense of orientation in the field, and most importantly – a man with courage like me.

When we got to the Negev, I reconnoitred the area for a week by Jeep to learn the terrain. I visited all our outposts in the besieged Negev. I was given a Piper plane to collect information about enemy positions – and was in a crash landing. The pilot was a Machalnik (our term for foreign volunteers, mostly Jews, mostly with combat experience, mostly from Western countries, who volunteered to help Israel in its war). Above the Khan Yunis-Rafah area the engine started to sputter. Fortunately, the pilot managed to steer the plane towards Kibbutz Nirim, the safest point close to us, and landed in a field near the kibbutz, where the plane overturned. Luckily, we were not hurt and were able to get out. We were picked up and taken to the kibbutz. Two hours later, my patrol company arrived in Nirim by Jeep.

My first task was to secure the water pipeline serving half a dozen of our communities in the area, including *kibbutzim* such as Saad, Be'eri and Nirim. Their inhabitants depended on a regular supply of water that came by pipe through the wadis, from wells somewhere between Niram and Saad. Not far from the pipeline there were Egyptian Army positions in the Gaza Strip. They controlled the coastal road leading to Ashkelon, and the Ashkelon–Hebron and Beer-Sheva–Hebron roads. The Egyptians also moved freely on the Gaza–Be'er Sheva road, although we also used it at night.

When I arrived in the Negev, the water pipeline was not in use because the Egyptian forces and Muslim Brotherhood gangs had sabotaged it and cut it off. From the hills, snipers and irregulars also rained fire towards the dirt road beside the pipeline. When my patrol company first arrived at the Ruhama base in the Negev, we drove in Jeeps to the pipeline. The distance was not great, but we had to cross open expanses, since there were few roads and we feared that those that did exist were mined by Bedouins who received explosives from the Egyptians and buried them in the dirt roads. The water security mission lasted about ten days and included three intense clashes with Arab gangs. Also, our truck was severely damaged by a mine.

In my time in the Negev, although I received general instructions, I was mostly left to do what seemed right to me, responding to conditions and circumstances in the field as I saw fit. I had complete confidence in what I was doing, and the patrol company, including Shalom, trusted me fully. I am by nature attentive to the opinions of others, and of course I used to listen to the opinions of my comrades and consult with them, but the decisions were mine, and mine alone.

This period in the Negev shaped me as a decisive commander who knows what he wants, knows how to assess a situation, and knows how to make decisions. My personality as an intelligence officer was formed in the Negev. I realised that a small unit (my unit initially numbered ten people, and never grew above thirty) specialising in tactical operations could create a strategic advantage, and this insight guided and served me well in the years that followed, when I worked in intelligence organisations.

My company also took care of the regular supply of food and fuel to localities in the besieged Negev. Every night two or three Dakota planes landed in Ruhama with supplies. At least twice, we organised penetrations through Egyptian lines with supply convoys of about thirty trucks. My job was to locate the best place to do this. In this way we also transferred a field hospital to Ruhama.

After securing the water line, I told Simhoni and Cohen that in my opinion the Negev should be cleansed of all Bedouins who cooperated with the Egyptians, serving as their scouts, eyes and ears. Zeevi, who heard me when I spoke to them commented: 'Everyone except the Azma tribe' (who lived in the area where Rahat is today). Simhoni and Cohen agreed to my suggestion.

Except for Simhoni and Cohen, I don't think anyone in command, including Allon, knew about my initiative and the deportation of the Bedouin. Those who knew saw it as a vital need and did not even examine my plans. Only Zeevi was in the picture and checked the deportation plan with the help of a map. By this time, the Palmach no longer took care of anything, except personal contact with Palmach members and assistance with social problems. As of 31 May 1948, the day the Israel Defense Forces was founded, command of the military campaign throughout the country was in the hands of the IDF General Staff and the Palmach became an integral part of the IDF.

For about two weeks my company acted against the Bedouin in the Negev who helped Egypt.

In September 1948, I was assigned to maintain contact with Nevatim and Beit Eshel, two settlements east of Be'er Sheva (on the road that today connects Be'er Sheva and Dimona). The Egyptians still controlled Be'er Sheva, and Egyptian units were located along the Be'er Sheva–Hebron road. The two small settlements received reinforcements from the Negev Brigade, and supplies from Pipers or Jeeps that had to pass through the Egyptian lines. Our mission was to conduct reconnaissance and surveillance under cover of darkness and find safe routes that crossed the Be'er Sheva–Hebron road to ensure supplies to the two communities.

I believed we should conquer Be'er Sheva and I wanted to deploy look-outs who would remain in the field for thirty-six hours to report on Egyptian movements and map the area prior to launching an attack to conquer the city. I didn't know if there was a general staff plan to capture the city. But as an intelligence officer, I considered it my duty to gather intelligence that would facilitate such an eventuality.

At that time, the reconnaissance unit under my command numbered more than thirty people. All of them volunteered to act as look-outs. Among those I chose was my deputy, Shalom, who remained as a look-out in the field, a few hundred metres from Be'er Sheva, for a whole night, a whole day and about half the second night. Based on the intelligence I obtained from the observers, I sat with Simhoni over the maps and we thought about what should be done and how. We were in general agreement but had plenty of arguments with Cohen, some on principle and some on tactical points.

Before the conquest of Be'er Sheva, we managed to take over two strategic hills, Tel al-Safi and Tel Quneitra. I captured Tel Quneitra, which was deserted, on 18 September, together with forces under the command of Dov Gottesman, later one of the richest people in Israel, a well-known art collector and president of the Israel Museum. The next day, an Egyptian armoured battalion attacked the mound, and a battle ensued in which I participated alongside Gottesman. Fortunately, the Egyptians fought a static battle – standing and firing. We, on the other hand, were trained in fire and movement. I called in reinforcements who came and surrounded the Egyptians, and soon our fighters let me know the Egyptians were retreating.

Hirbat Ma'achaz, located not far from the Be'er Sheva-Hebron road and about three kilometres east of the Be'er Sheva–Tel Aviv road, was a temporary settlement of Bedouin from the Hebron area who came to the Negev in winter, took up residence in a few dozen buildings in the settlement, and planted fields of crops. We did not act against them, even though we saw them roaming around, until one day when a patrol I was riding in barely avoided being blown up by a mine planted in an open field. It was only because I noticed an unusually flat bit of terrain and ordered the ground searched that we did not drive on the mine, which would have certainly exploded. After this incident, I suggested to Simhoni that we should destroy Hirbat Ma'achaz in order to free the road to Hebron and to Falluja, where a large Egyptian force was stationed. Simhoni sent me to Cohen, at the Negev headquarters in Ruhama.

Cohen was looking for an operation that would bring glory to his Yiftach Brigade.

I explained that the presence of an Arab settlement at Hirbat Ma'achaz, whose residents no doubt cooperated with the Egyptians, threatened the airfield in Ruhama, only 15 kilometres away, which served all the fighting forces in the Negev. He enthusiastically approved the operation I proposed.

With my patrol company – five Jeeps and two half-tracks – we reconnoitred the area and, on 29 September, without firing a single shot, we took over Hirbat Ma'achaz, whose residents fled towards Mount Hebron. Simhoni then sent a platoon to hold the place, and I returned to headquarters at Mishmar Hanegev. But the next day, Egyptian armoured vehicles from the Fallujah Pocket descended on the area. The Egyptian command understood that capturing Hirbat Ma'achaz allowed us to insert a wedge between Fallujah and Beit Jubrin, thus creating a real threat to them.

The Hirbat Ma'achaz battles, which lasted five days, are considered decisive in our victory over the Egyptian Army. At first the Egyptians came, as mentioned, with an armoured battalion, then in two battalions. We conducted the battle with tricks and cunning. I was not on the front line and did not take part in the battle, but I provided intelligence and services to the fighters, and kept in touch with headquarters and the brigade's intelligence officer.

In the course of the Hirbat Ma'achaz battles, between 30 September and 4 October 1948, Israeli forces retreated twice, due to the heavy pressure from the Egyptians. But the Egyptians attacked only during the day, and finally, in a night battle we captured the settlement.

After the first battle we discovered that five of the platoon fighters were missing. At night I returned with the platoon to Hirbat Ma'achaz and we found the bodies of the five, all beheaded. We collected the bodies, brought them to Mishmar Hanegev, and efforts were made to identify them. The sight was awful, and I will never forget it.

Israeli author Yizhar Smilansky, better known as S. Yizhar, was an intelligence officer of the Givati Brigade who visited the settlement a few days after the fighting and immortalised the battle for Hirbat Ma'achaz in his novel, *Days of Ziklag*, which was published in 1959 and earned its author the Israel Prize for Literature, although the settlement is never mentioned by name and it is a fictionalised account. The battle also inspired S. Yizhar's story *Khirbet Hiza*, published in 1949, at the end of the War of Independence. Both include descriptions of battles remarkably similar to the five days of battles over Hirbat Ma'achaz. By his own account, the author did not take part in the battle for Hirbat Ma'achaz and did not strive for accuracy in the details. He first visited the site two or three weeks after the battles there and listened to the stories of soldiers who were there. At a gathering in 1998 to memorialise the battle fifty years on, S. Yizhar told the gathering that his book was 'a mixture of imagination, of fiction, and of truth in all its details, the physical truth, the truth of the environment, the truth of the people is there as they have told it to me. But this is not the truth of reality and not the truth of history, but the truth of the myth.'

Chapter 5

Switching to the Security Service

The End of the Palmach

During October 1948, our forces waged battles with the Egyptians in various places in Operation Yoav, named for Yitzhak (Yoav) Dubno, the Palmach's chief training officer, who was killed during the defence of Kibbutz Negba.

Ahead of the operation, I and my reconnaissance unit were ordered to provide intelligence about the entire Negev, including the Be'er Sheva–Hebron road and the Gaza–el-Arish road, assisted by three patrol planes seconded to us to help us gather intelligence on Egyptian movements.

Three brigades were assigned to Operation Yoav: the Negev Brigade under the command of Nahum Sarig, the Yiftach Brigade under the command of Cohen, and the Givati Brigade under the command of Shimon Avidan. They received artillery assistance – between four and eight guns per brigade, plus 120-mm mortars and armoured half-track personnel carriers. Each brigade numbered 700–800 men, of whom 100–200 were in support units.

The plan was for the Yiftach Brigade to establish a bridgehead on the Ashkelon–Gaza road to block Egyptian reinforcements coming from Gaza. The brigade was also to attack from the south the Hulikat outposts (now Moshav Heletz), which dominated the Ashkelon–Hebron road. The brigade's 1st Battalion attacked the outposts at night, but failed in its mission due to a shortage of fighters and the inferiority of our weapons. Among other things, Egypt had an artillery battery, which we had no ability to neutralise. We suffered casualties, both dead and wounded. I assisted in evacuating some of our wounded to the hospital in Ruhama.

Following this failure, I had no choice but to cross Egyptian lines in a Jeep equipped with heavy machine guns to contact the Givati Brigade and coordinate the conquest of the outposts with the brigade commander's deputy, Tzvi Tzur (then Tsertenko), later the sixth IDF chief of staff. Indeed, the next night, Givati Brigade forces attacked from the north and occupied the Hulikat outposts. After this, the Givati Brigade was tasked with attacking the Fallujah Pocket (not far from present-day Kiryat Gat), where thousands of Egyptian soldiers were massed.

The conquest of Be'er Sheva and Auja al-Hafir was assigned to the Negev Brigade. Auja, atop the ruins of the ancient Nabataean city of Nitzana about eighty kilometres south-west from Be'er Sheva, was located on the international border between Israel and Egypt, marked as early as 1906 by the Ottomans. But it was controlled by Egypt at the time and our intention was to capture and occupy the territory up to this border.

As the commander of Yiftach's patrol company, I was assigned, among other things, to lead saboteurs to blow up all the bridges on the road from Beit Hanoun in the northern Gaza Strip to Yad Mordechai.

On the eve of the attack on Be'er Sheva on 20/21 October 1948, I was instructed to place my observers in Beit Eshel to report everything happening south of Be'er Sheva. The battle for Be'er Sheva lasted about two days, and on the second day the Egyptians retreated to Auja and I stationed an intelligence unit in the area. I toured the area, but did not engage the enemy. In fact, the battle for Be'er Sheva was my last military battle, and I served there not as a fighter but as an intelligence officer. From that point until my release from the IDF, I was not involved in combat any more.

On 7 November 1948, the prime minister and defense minister announced their decision to dismantle Palmach headquarters and integrate all Palmach units into the IDF. We fighters in the Palmach were shocked and hurt by the decision. We saw ourselves as an elite both in terms of our skill as fighters but also for our special esprit de corps. I had an earnest, heart-felt conversations about this with Simhoni, who, in addition to being my commander, was a very close friend. He fully supported Ben-Gurion and believed that there was no place for a separate Palmach command within the IDF. Ben-Gurion was worried about enemies within no less than enemies without, and although he knew that the Palmach was disciplined, he feared that in a moment of crisis, loyalties would be tested.

Commanders other than Simhoni, including personal friends of mine such as Cohen, Yosefle Tabenkin and Kalman, revolted against the dissolution of the Palmach. They left the IDF and no one tried to stop them. Others, like Rabin, Allon's deputy, debated whether to leave and in the end stayed.

I agreed with Simhoni, although in retrospect, it is possible that the dismantling of the Palmach could have been carried out in a less drastic way. The Palmach created and developed unique values and patterns in training, with a strong willingness to sacrifice and high degree of group solidarity . At its peak, it numbered a little fewer than 6,000 fighters. Of these, 1,168 (almost 20 per cent!) were killed in the battles that preceded the establishment of the state and in the War of Independence. No other organisation paid such a price.

It is difficult to describe concisely the essence and nature of the life training provided by the Palmach. Alongside military training in the strict sense of the word, there was a decision-making process, from individual to general, and from general to individual. The way decisions became operational orders was very special and influenced us for the rest of our lives. We also received very solid grounding in Zionism, the geography of Israel, and many lectures on the Middle East and Jewish communities in the rest of the world.

Together with the environment in my parents' home, the Palmach gave me a sense of national responsibility and the courage to make decisions. In all the positions I was privileged to fill – from the Palmach and the IDF, through Shin Bet and Mossad, to Lekem (acronym in

Hebrew for Bureau of Scientific Relations) and the Pollard affair, to my political career as a founder of the Pensioners' Party, and my time as a minister in the Israeli government – the combination of intellectual independence and operational experience which began in the Palmach strengthened my tendency, apparently rooted in my genes, not to adapt to coercive environments, and to choose ones that gave me maximum independence. I made decisions myself, sometimes weighty and fateful ones that my superiors did not concur with. Abundant examples will be evident in subsequent chapters.

Leaving the IDF

After the conquest of Be'er Sheva, our brigade was replaced by the Negev Brigade in the area and we returned to the base in Mansura, near Yokne'am, where we were under the command of Simhoni, who in April 1949 took over the position from Cohen, who moved up to Allon's headquarters. At that point, I had already been promoted to be intelligence officer of the brigade and became involved primarily in the brigade's preparations for Operation Tooth for Tooth, known by its Hebrew acronym as Operation Shatash, which aimed to conquer Jenin, Nablus and a large part of Samaria. The intention was to conquer the entire ridge to Jerusalem and Hebron to the Nablus–Damiya Bridge road.

I was a planning partner for Operation Shatash. I gathered the necessary intelligence in February and March 1949, sending scouts to survey the area, and doing so myself in the Dotan Valley. Most IDF forces were to take part in this operation, and began moving into position on the night of 12/13 March. But the operation was abruptly cancelled that evening, which initially disappointed us. We later learned that when the Jordanians realised what our plans were, they made significant concessions in our favour in talks in Rhodes on a ceasefire (among other things, they agreed to give up the Wadi Ara area, which they had received from the Iraqi Expeditionary Force who controlled the area from May 1948).

In retrospect, the scrapping of Operation Shatash had significant long-term consequences. Some 300,000 Arabs lived in the area designated for capture under the operation. It is almost certain that had it taken place, most of them would have fled to Jordan and become refugees. The IDF would have occupied the entire ridge of the mountain, from Jenin to Hebron, and the territory would have become part of the State of Israel, and we would not have had to deal with more than two million Arabs today under our control in Judea and Samaria.

Simhoni told me he wanted to send me to a training course for company and battalion commanders. I was not at all sure I wanted to go because I realised that doing so meant committing to a future in the IDF. But I decided to give it a chance and went to the required interview with course commander General Haim Laskov, later Israel's fifth chief of staff.

I dressed sloppily for the interview, in typical Palmach style, which went over badly with Laskov, and from the disdainful look he gave me, I knew I was disqualified. I left feeling that I had been judged unfairly without having a chance to show my mettle. I returned to my brigade and told Simhoni, 'That's it. I'm done with the army.'

However, General Laskov, who was also operations officer of the Southern Command, asked me to postpone my retirement for a few months, because he had a job that he thought was just right for me: to head the planning team for the city of Eilat and its surroundings. I was 23 years old, without a high school matriculation certificate, totally lacking in any experience in urban and environmental planning. But in those days, and in the culture we absorbed in Palmach, such an appeal seemed completely natural. I agreed to stay, and with a team of engineers and experts in urban and environmental planning, I went down to Eilat. For several weeks we worked on determining the defences of Eilat against Egypt and Jordan, and planning the airport and naval port. The team at my disposal was excellent, and Eilat was built, and for many years developed exactly according to our plans and drawings.

When I finished the job in Eilat, I returned to brigade headquarters, which in the meantime had become the 11th Brigade in the IDF (instead of the Yiftach Brigade) and became an active reserve intelligence officer there. As was often done, I registered for evening classes in order to prepare for matriculation exams and decided to study chemistry at the Hebrew University in Jerusalem. It was a field in which I excelled, and I hoped to work in the chemical industry, which in those days was considered the spearhead of Israeli technology.

At the same time, I followed the advice of Simhoni, who suggested I go speak to Gibli, head of the intelligence branch of the general staff. He had been my commander during my pre-military training in the Gadna when I was sixteen. He received me warmly, gave me an overview of what was happening in the various intelligence organisations, and explained the division of powers between the IDF's military intelligence under the command of Lieutenant Colonel Chaim Herzog, the Security Service headed by Isser Harel, and Mossad, headed by Reuven Shiloah. He ended by suggested that I join military intelligence and offered me a job as deputy to Zerubavel Vermel-Arbel, the intelligence officer of Southern Command, with a view to replacing him eventually.

I turned him down, telling him: 'The army does not suit me. The structure is too rigid. I am leaving the army.' So, he suggested that I speak to Harel and called him on the spot to arrange a meeting. I knew very well who Harel was. In fact, I did not need Gibli to arrange a meeting because I had an open door to Harel. He was my mother's second cousin. I remember him from the age of ten. Before he became 'Mr Security', he was our plumber, who came by foot from his house in Herzliya to fix any problem we had at home and then have a cup of tea and a chat with my parents in the kitchen.

My fateful interview, in late September or early October 1949, was held in his home over dinner. He and his wife Rivka lived in an apartment in a three-storey building in Jaffa, on Sderot Yerushalayim Street, a few metres from the Green House (today 91 Yefet Street), where the intelligence headquarters was then.

When I entered his home, I still saw them as Uncle Isser and Aunt Rebecca. But from the moment we sat down at the table, the atmosphere changed, and he became head of the Security Service even though no word had yet been said. During dinner, I did much of the talking, elaborating on my service in the Palmach and the IDF. At the end of the meal, Harel walked me out of the house, raised his head, looked up, and asked me, 'Do you see the apartment on the third floor? There, where there's a flowerpot? Let's say you have to infiltrate into it.'

'So, I'd infiltrate it,' I replied.

'How?'

'Go into the stairwell, up to the third floor, get to the door, pick the lock, enter the apartment.'

'Without entering the stairwell. Without touching the lock,' he said.

'I'd climb up,' I replied.

'Climb from where?'

'From here, from the drainpipe,' I pointed.

'Show me.'

'Now?'

'Now.'

Within two minutes I was upstairs, inside the apartment on the third floor, waving at him, and a minute later I went back downstairs and stood next to him. 'You've just been accepted,' he said.

First Tasks in the Security Service

After accepting me to the Security Service, Harel asked me what I wanted to do there. 'I don't know,' I replied.

He then described the structure of the Security Service and the tasks of its divisions. The first one, headed by Benjamin Hochstein, dealt with internal issues, mainly underground organisations of Etzel and Lehi veterans; the second, headed by Yaakov Kruz dealt with counter-espionage, mainly against spies from Eastern European countries, but also from Western European countries; the third department, headed by Moshe Harmati, handled counter-espionage against Arabs; the fifth, headed by Benjamin Bloomberg handled security for the security forces themselves. Division 4 was still in the process of being formed, with a view to its taking over some of the activities of Division 2. Alongside all these was Division 10, the operations department which did not have agents, but was entrusted with gathering information and carrying out operations to assist the various other divisions or as instructed by the head of the service. Harel said I could join whichever department I wanted.

Truth be told, I was not sure that I wanted to work full time in the Security Service or in any other job because I was preparing to go to Hebrew University. I started by working in Division 2, headed by Kruz. Although most of its activities involved thwarting Eastern European espionage against us, I started by focusing on counter-espionage against Western countries and spent two weeks in the section that dealt with this. But it was not for me. I told Harel I wanted operational work and wasn't cut out for sitting at a desk.

'I knew that's what you would conclude,' Harel replied. 'But I wanted you to get to know the service up close, especially a division you won't be regularly involved with. I have a suitable position for you: the Operations Unit for Arab Affairs which will operate within Division 10 Tel Aviv. It hasn't been set up – you will set it up and head it.'

Division 10 Tel Aviv was one of the four operations units in the Security Service. The other three were Division 10 Jerusalem, Division 10 Haifa and Division 10 Rehovot, but the Tel Aviv division was the largest and most central.

Simultaneously with the beginning of my work in the service, I got into business for the first time in my life, leasing about 225 acres on a 49-year lease from the Lands Administration together with my friend Uri Lubrani and a new immigrant from the USA, Hananiah Bergstein. We ploughed it and sowed sorghum. We hired labourers, but also worked the land ourselves, and I remember in the autumn of 1949 ploughing the field with a tractor, which we rented for pennies.

We made a modest profit, but I turned over my share to Hananiah who needed the money more than I did.

Five years later, the Lands Administration asked us to relinquish the lease to allow some Jewish investors from Australia to set up a ranch to raise Merino sheep, known for their fine wool. We agreed, and with the compensation money we received, I bought my first apartment, in the Maoz Aviv neighbourhood (outside Tel Aviv), just then under construction.

A few months later, I accepted Harel's offer to work full time for the Security Service and I was formally discharged from the IDF on 2 February 1950. Until then, although I worked in the Security Service, my salary had been paid by the IDF.

The Security Service headquarters was then at 2 Bustros Street (now Raziel) in Jaffa, in an abandoned, large Arab building. Division 10 Tel Aviv was also in the building, one floor below Harel's office, and was headed by Gershon Rabinowitz. Division 10 carried out surveillance, covert intrusions, phone wiretaps, setting up listening devices and similar tasks. It also had a sub-unit that dealt with the arrest and interrogation of suspects. In addition Division 10 was occasionally asked to carry out cross-border infiltrations to maintain contact with agents active in enemy countries.

Our equipment included cameras, equipment to pick locks and enter premises, listening devices, and cars for surveillance. We did not yet have radios. I later equipped my unit with walkie-talkies, preceding other units in their use. I always thought that the Security Service must have the latest and best technology and equipment, and throughout my career always put an emphasis on innovating, improving and refining the technology we used.

Harel was anxious about spies and traitors, whom he believed endangered the very existence of the state. Today his anxiety may seem excessive, but in those days it was realistic and justified, and his concerns infused our unit.

My first act, as head of the new Operations Unit of Division 10 Tel Aviv was to be briefed by Harmati, from Division 3, who stressed that our counter-espionage activities should concentrate on four centres – the four branches of the Communist Party that operated in the Arab areas Nazareth, Ramla, Jaffa and Umm al-Fahm. If there were spies, they would likely be there.

I needed a team to work with and the first person I recruited was Avrum Shalom, even though he didn't know any Arabic. But I knew he was courageous and resourceful. I needed Arabic speakers, too, so I recruited to our team Elyashiv, an Arabic-speaking Yemeni whom I met walking down the hall. I borrowed two technicians from the service's technology department, and it was agreed that I could use the services of the IDF technology unit (later Unit 432) and told I would be supported by being able to use Security Service personnel, as needed.

Chapter 6

A Small Man with Big Suspicions

In the 1950s, the Soviet Union was considered the great victor of World War II and was seen as spreading its doctrine of Communism around the world, including in Israel. Cells of five or six people would convene from time to time for ideological lectures, or to pass on information, and sometimes members were sent to the USSR secretly to undergo indoctrination, including in military matters.

We kept close surveillance on the four Arab branches of the Communist Party, listening in on every phone conversation, every discussion. We soon had detailed lists of all the members and we clandestinely searched their homes, rummaged in their drawers and left everything in order so that they did not know we had been there.

I knew how to pick normal locks, so Shalom and I systematically broke into the meeting places of the cells, usually at night. We photographed what we found, especially lists of members. We did this once a month in their main headquarters in Nazareth as well as frequently in other cell centres. In addition, I set up listening posts that continuously eavesdropped on the centres, using wireless microphones.

Most of this activity, carried out by me, Shalom and two or three other people, took place from spring 1950 to mid-1951. It ceased because we came to the conclusion that the activity of the Arab Communists was so limited, it did not merit investing the effort and resources these covert operations required.

Did I have any qualms about our activities? The answer is no. Of course, I was aware that under normal circumstances, our actions were illegal. But having just emerged from a war which cost us 6,000 casualties (in today's terms, it would be comparable to casualties of 68,000 as a percentage of the Jewish population in Israel), compounded by the sense that our fledgling democracy was threatened by various underground bodies, both Arab and Jewish, I believed the actions were justified. Ben-Gurion, both prime minister and defense minister, who was elected legally and democratically, tasked the Security Service with eliminating these underground bodies and my unit was part of the effort.

In early 1951, Rabinowitz resigned as head of Division 10 Tel Aviv, and returned to his kibbutz, awaiting a new job. His temporary replacement was Dov Shenkar, a member of Kibbutz Neot Mordechai.

One day a man whose nickname in the service was Elijah asked to speak to Harel privately. He told Harel that his conscience was bothering him and said that he, along with both Rabinowitz and Shenkar, were members of a Mapam underground, Trojan horses within the security system. He named ten or eleven others, all in key positions, as spying for the leftist Mapam movement which was sympathetic to the Soviet Union. Among those Elijah named was Sarah Hefer, secretary of the operations unit I headed. These internal spies copied and photographed confidential material and sent them to an archive in a kibbutz.

Why were they doing this? To prepare for World War III. This was no joke. They were convinced another world war was coming – this time between the United States and the Soviet Union – and they wanted to prepare to help the Soviets. This included stockpiling weapons in *kibbutzim*.

In one case, a light aircraft of the Israeli Air Force with weapons aboard was forced to land in a field near Kibbutz Beit Alfa due to a malfunction. The pilot was unscathed. But before IDF forces arrived at the scene, kibbutzniks took over the plane and confiscated and hid the weapons. Initially they refused to return the weapons to the IDF until Ben-Gurion summoned the head of Mapam, Meir Yaari, and threated him with mass arrests.

Harel was not entirely surprised by the existence of a Mapam underground within the service, but was taken aback at how far and how high it had infiltrated. An investigation revealed that all Elijah had reported was true. Consequently, Harel fired about a dozen people, including Rabinowitz and Shenkar. The only two among those implicated who were not fired were Elijah and Hefer, who expressed remorse. Harel reported all this to Ben-Gurion, receiving his retrospective approval. Thus the affair ended without legal action being taken against the offenders and without any reports in the media.

In my opinion, Harel acted wisely in this matter. He acted similarly against other Jewish underground cells, especially the remains of Etzel and Lehi veterans: no criminal proceedings, an opportunity to repent, no revelations to the public. Harel was, above all, a great Jewish patriot and, in his eyes, members of Mapam, Etzel or Lehi were first and foremost Jews, who should be treated with forgiveness and an effort extended to convince them to correct their ways.

Moreover, he maintained the principle that Israel was a state of law, and therefore no one should be eliminated by the Secret Service or Mossad within the borders of Israel. In one instance, we learned that an Israeli-Arab agent was actually a double agent and his true loyalty was to his Jordanian controllers. The head of the Arab department offered to eliminate him, but Harel objected and ordered that the agent be prosecuted. More than once I heard him say, 'Israel is a state of law, and even the prime minister has no authority to execute anyone in the country without trial.' The emphasis is on 'in the country'. Abroad was a different matter.

Issar Harel was a short man and a suspicious one. There was widespread agreement on this. Regarding his other traits, opinions were divided. The fact that both he and I are short meant we always looked at each other at eye level, in every sense of the term. As for his tendency to be suspicious, I will expand on this.

People involved in intelligence, security and counter-espionage must be suspicious. For some of them – for example for me – suspicion is not an innate trait but an acquired one. The positions I have held and the environment in which I worked forced me to be a suspicious person, but when my environment changes, I have no trouble letting go of my suspicion. Yitzhak Shamir was similar to me in that. Not so Harel. He seemed to have emerged from his mother's womb as a person who suspects others.

In this, he was like Ariel Sharon. Both always seemed to ask themselves, 'Where am I being deceived and by whom?' In my opinion, both Sharon and Harel managed to harness this tendency in ways that fuelled their creativity. Suspicion served them as a doctrine of warfare.

When you sat in front of Harel, you could not avoid the thought that you were sitting with someone who had little formal education. Although his family was wealthy (his grandfather had a vinegar factory and his father was a well-known lawyer), when Harel was five years old, in 1917, civil war broke out in Russia and his family fled and lost everything, suffering at times from hunger. In 1922, they settled in Lithuania, where Harel attended elementary school and high school. It is also where he became a Zionist. His expertise in intelligence and security was acquired the same way he learned to become a plumber – learning on his own. He was a classic self-made man. I remember him at an advanced age, struggling to teach himself English. He was a paragon of self-discipline, commitment and determination. It is possible that the lack of formal education strengthened his incredible intuition and the sharp senses he was born with, reminiscent sometimes of animal senses.

His Hebrew was limited and he expressed himself in short sentences. He spoke only as much as was required, his explanations were concise, his language matter of fact, devoid of rhetoric. Whether listening or speaking, he knew how to reach the important issues in seconds. When you told him something, within seconds he got to the essence of the matter.

Unlike me, Harel rarely read books, but I learned quickly, as did others who worked with him or under him, that he was a very energetic, dominant, monastic man, with superb decision-making power, a brave man willing to participate in dangerous actions on the ground, and willing to send others into action, and to take responsibility for his decisions and their results.

His suspicious nature was welcome, perhaps even essential for a person heading an intelligence agency responsible for counter-espionage and for capturing foreign agents, spies and traitors of all kinds. Although he did not have expert training, Harel instinctively made sure to compartmentalise and even at the top of the Security Service insisted on secret cells who knew about each other's work purely on a need-to-know basis.

Over the years, I learned that while Harel unquestionably accepted Ben-Gurion's authority, he did not always seek prior approval for actions, although he always briefed the prime minister on all activities. Ben-Gurion would listen to plans and reports, but did not always give explicit permission in advance. There was complete trust between them. At that time, it was not customary to make a written record or a recording of such meetings. Harel himself did not do things illegally, but the Security Service often used illegal means. Everyone knew that in such cases – if they were done with permission – Harel would say, as he did countless times: 'The responsibility for an action approved by me rests with me even in the event of failure,' and no one doubted that he would be true to his word on this.

Harel, he and no other, built the security services of the State of Israel. The Shin Bet Security Service and Mossad are both based on the organisational structure he devised. If in the world of secret services, Israeli organisations have a good reputation, he is primarily responsible for this.

Having risen through the ranks of the intelligence unit of the pre-state Haganah, Harel was tapped by Ben-Gurion in 1948 to establish the Security Service of the State of Israel. A year later. Ben-Gurion gave him additional responsibility as director-general of the 'institution for coordination' within the Foreign Ministry, which was established by Reuven Shiloah to coordinate various Israeli security and intelligence services and eventually evolved to become Mossad (Hebrew for 'institution'). Thus Harel was head of both the Security Services, involved in operations within Israel, and for handling operations of Mossad, responsible for actions abroad. In 1952, he was named Shiloah's successor at the head of Mossad. He appointed Izzo Daphne as his deputy and made Amos Manor head of the Security Service, which became known by its acronym, Shin Bet, and later as Shabak.

Harel also received the title Commissioner of Security Services and Intelligence which he held until his retirement, ten years later. He is the only person who ever held this title. Harel claimed that Ben-Gurion invented the title and established it, but in my opinion, it was Harel who asked Ben-Gurion to give him this title and 'the old man', as Ben-Gurion was referred to, agreed to do so. Harel knew how to make sure everyone knew he was the boss.

Both Shiloah and Ben-Gurion, who read and knew quite a bit about the British administrative structure, were aware of the need to separate the body involved in gathering intelligence in foreign countries from the body dealing with internal security. Thus, they divided intelligence duties among three different bodies: the military intelligence division (known initially by its acronym Maman and then later as Aman) which was under the control of the minister of defense, the Security Service Shin Bet responsible for internal security, and Mossad, both of whom reported to the prime minister.

Ben-Gurion wanted to prevent any one body from accumulating too much power, and to be sure these bodies could not undermine the democratic essence of Israel. But when it came to Harel, he deviated from his policy and allowed him to gain tremendous power. As I mentioned, there was complete trust between Harel and Ben-Gurion. I can testify that Harel never dreamed of undermining the prime minister. Harel was eminently suitable for the job he was given. I have never seen such a great match between a person and his job.

Chapter 7

Shin Bet at Work

Harel's appointment to head Mossad led to a significant change in intelligence-gathering and operations. Shiloah was a diplomat with a liking for cocktail parties. Harel was an operations man.

Even before Harel became head of Mossad, the central operations unit of the Shin Bet Security Service, Division 10 Tel Aviv, provided operational services to Mossad, but after his appointment the nature of this division changed dramatically. Under Harel, Mossad went out into the field. Many of Mossad's special operations were handled by this unit, which I came to head.

While the Soviet Union aligned itself with Israel at its very beginning for various reasons, by 1950 Israel began to be aligned more with the Western bloc led by the United States, and began moving away from the Eastern bloc led by the Soviets. Ben-Gurion and his colleagues came predominantly from Eastern Europe, but were not communists in their political views. Although they espoused a moderate kind of economic socialism, they disliked the dictatorial regime that prevailed in the Soviet Union and its satellite nations. Furthermore, there was a growing recognition that to survive and prosper, Israel would need the assistance of the large Jewish community in the United States and about a year later it also opened negotiations with West Germany on a reparations agreement. The Soviets, disappointed that Israel did not easily fall under their influence, increased efforts to befriend Arab countries.

All this made Israel an intelligence target for the Soviets, and Mossad and Shin Bet were tasked with exposing their spies and operatives, and preventing them from gathering information that could harm Israel.

Mapam, the United Workers' Party, was established in 1948 as a union between two parties, Hashomer Hatzair and Ahdut Ha'avodah, which espoused a more distinctly socialist line than Mapai, which was headed by Ben-Gurion. Although the Soviet Union provided Israel with vital weapons assistance during the War of Independence (mainly through Czechoslovakia), this honeymoon was very short, and from 1949 onwards the Soviet bloc adopted a very hostile attitude toward Israel and Zionism. Mapam leaders were convinced that this was a temporary misunderstanding, which would disappear.

In the elections for the first Knesset, Mapam won 19 seats and in the second Knesset 15. Mapai won 46 and 47 seats in the 120-seat Knesset in these elections.

Shortly after the exposure of Mapam's internal underground within the Secret Service, and the investigation I helped conduct following the exposure, I was appointed chief of Division 10 Tel Aviv, a position I held for about four years. One of my first actions, in consultation with Harel, was to set up an operations unit to deal with internal matters. As a result, we added Mapam and Ahdut Ha'avodah to parties we were already watching: the right-wing Herut party and the communist Maki party.

The staff at Division 10 Tel Aviv consisted of forty people at the beginning of my tenure as head, and about seventy at the end. Its area of operations extended from Hadera to Eilat but did not include Jerusalem. At first, I brought in people I knew, like Shalom, and they recommended others. There were also some walk-ins. Out of every ten people we considered, we accepted two or fewer. I made sure we remained compact, recruiting only those we needed, and only the best.

In cases where people approached us and asked to join, they were required to pass a number of tests. Beyond personality, it was important to find out how close the candidate was to Mapai. We did not demand that the candidate be a party member; I myself was never an official Mapai member. We never directly asked, determining a candidate's leanings by indirect questions. Those who passed this stage were sent to the Shin Bet graphologist, where their writing was analysed. Graphology was then highly regarded in Shin Bet. At the final stage, I would interview the candidate twice, each time for an hour, and always in the presence of another person. I would ask about his worldview, his technical ability, and try to judge how he would react in various operational and technical situations. If he indicated expertise in any field, I would ask specific questions to test his degree of mastery, even though I did not always know the correct answers. It was important to test his credibility, and usually we did not make mistakes in such tests.

Our division provided operational and technological services to all the other divisions. We performed missions for the Eastern European Wing and the Western European Wing, mainly collecting relevant material on Arab countries. We also collected economic material for the government, the defence establishment and various government institutions. Although we usually acted on a specific request for a specific document, or information about a specific person, in my estimation, no more than one-tenth of the material we provided in the economic field was ever used.

During my four years as head of Division 10 Tel Aviv, I initiated, executed and managed hundreds of operations of various kinds. I was responsible, among other things, for surveillance at Lod International Airport (later Ben-Gurion Airport). I had a team of fifteen men who worked in three shifts, around the clock, including on Saturdays, to investigate anything or anyone suspicious entering or leaving the airport.

We also had an electronics department which mainly engaged in eavesdropping using the most sophisticated microphones in the world at the time, and a mechanical unit, which specialised in lock-picking. In addition, there was a technology laboratory. It developed such things as special film for our Leica cameras that could take 250 snapshots instead of the standard 36 pictures. It created tools that made it possible for us to open letters of suspects and close them again without leaving any hint that the mail had been inspected. Most of the letters we examined were to or from Eastern Europe and almost all were completely legitimate – friends and relatives writing to each other. But occasionally, we caught a 'fish' – someone who served or intended to serve an Eastern European security service. We knew that almost all emigrants from the Soviet Union and Poland were screened by security services there, and some were pressured to serve as agents. In our estimate, about a third of the immigrants to Israel from the Eastern bloc had been recruited. In some cases, they readily confessed when accused; in others, we learned about them from informers, and we were often able to thwart the tasks they had been assigned. We intercepted mail and tapped the phones of these immigrants continuously, out of necessity, to thwart the spying.

Our surveillance of the Polish embassy provided us with valuable intelligence material on the Middle East. However, it did not help us expose a spy who worked for the Poles from within Shin Bet. His name was Levi Levi, a Jew who immigrated to Israel from Poland in 1948 and was drafted into Shin Bet when it was in its infancy. His specialty was lock-picking and safe cracking. We worked together, visiting various places at night. I watched him up close. He was a first-rate professional, one of the best. Unfortunately, it later turned out that he had been recruited by the Polish Security Service before coming to Israel and sent as a spy. He was in Shin Bet for nine years. We only caught him in 1957. I was studying in Britain then. I tried to figure out why I had failed to detect him. Probably because when I came to the service, he was already there. I admit, I never suspected him. I came from Britain to testify at his trial. He was sentenced to seven years in prison, served them, and emigrated to Australia. I didn't hear from him later, but he didn't hear from me either. He died of cancer there.

The intelligence we brought was of great importance, contributing to a shift in Israeli foreign policy, and to closer ties between the Israel–Turkey–Iran triangle. The three countries felt threatened by Arab countries. Iran was mainly in conflict with Iraq, Turkey in conflict with Iraq and Syria, and all feared the ambitious policies of Egypt. Turkey, in particular, had good information on what was happening in Arab countries and by the 1950s they were passing information on to us.

Intelligence cooperation between the three countries was led by Harel. He initiated conferences of senior representatives of the intelligence services of Israel, Turkey and Iran, which took place regularly, once every few months. These conferences lasted two or three days, and various topics were discussed, including operational ones. To enable these meetings to be hosted in secret, Harel ordered the construction of a complex which became known as the Midrasha, north of Tel Aviv, where guests of Israeli intelligence organisations were provided with full hotel services.

It was the idea of Levi Eshkol, who became finance minister in 1952, to use Shin Bet to catch tax evaders. I estimate that there were several thousand tax evaders targeted for our attention. At the time, there was as yet no organised crime in Israel, and the number of people who managed to get rich was also minimal. Since such an operation required covert activity against civilians, Eshkol knew he had to enlist Ben-Gurion's support. The two then turned to Harel. He disliked dealing with this issue, but Ben-Gurion and Eshkol did not let up, and Harel was forced to set up a secret unit that collected intelligence for the income tax authorities.

Division 10 Tel Aviv provided operational services for this, using various methods we developed to track down spies. Provided with lists of names, we entered offices, shops, homes, and small-scale industrial plants. I don't know on what basis the lists were compiled, but I assume it was mostly based on gossip. Finance Ministry staff accompanied us and instructed us on what balance sheets to photograph, what documents to seize.

One of my people, Zvi Malchin (also later known as Peter Malkin) once received a list that contained a very familiar name – his brother's, a self-employed butcher, whose income was at least three times his, but who paid less than half as much in taxes. Malchin asked me what to do. I told him: 'Warn your brother that his shop will soon be visited. Then do your work. Just make sure that from now on he pays what he really owes. Take it upon yourself. The responsibility for him to pay his taxes rests fully with you.'

For three or four years I participated in hundreds of raids of this kind. Sometimes we carried out ten to fifteen raids a day, and worked also on holidays and Shabbat. We brought hundreds of boxes of documents to the tax authorities. At that point our role ended. I have no idea how much money went into the state's coffers following these raids.

For years, Harel argued that statehood and democracy in Israel were fragile, and therefore should be protected, using intelligence. Indeed, the fear of domestic subversion and violent secret activities with ideological–political roots was not unfounded in those years. In addition to threats from the left discussed above, there was reason for concern about extremist activity by the far right Etzel and Lehi underground, by religious undergrounds and from violent protests against a reparations agreement with Germany.

After a Mapam underground was discovered within Shin Bet itself in 1951, Mapam was put under surveillance, which turned up spying activity. On 30 January 1953, the Mapam newspaper *Al Hamishmar* reported that two young men had been caught in the act of entering the Tel Aviv office of Mapam's secretary-general and Knesset member Meir Yaari, to change the batteries of listening devices in his desk.

In his book *Security and Democracy*, which was published many years later, Harel confirmed that the two people caught there were indeed from Shin Bet and lamented that the government had not taken the opportunity to own up to this and reveal all the illegal activity that had necessitated such surveillance of Mapam.

Fresh Meat

During the War of Independence, the 1st Battalion of the Palmach absorbed about a hundred new immigrants. Several dozen came to our company and had to be turned into soldiers. 'You have two weeks,' Simhoni said. 'It's not long, but that's what we have.'

Until then, the immigrants I knew were my parents' generation. These new immigrants were my age, all of them Holocaust survivors, who had got off boats more or less the day before, fresh cannon fodder. They survived the camps only to come and be killed in Israel. Malkiya was their first battle, and many of them died there. I sent them into battle, fought alongside them until I was wounded and evacuated. They continued until they fell. They died without knowing a word of Hebrew. Their last cries were in Polish, Russian, Yiddish, Hungarian.

These new immigrants changed the face of the country. They had amazing survival abilities. Along with others, I quickly understood that they could be a huge asset in the kind of intelligence we conducted in those years. By absorbing and employing them, we could make use of the special skills they had developed to survive.

Among them were Shalom Weiss and Yosef Bau who were recruited to the technical department of military intelligence. They were expert forgers. Give them paper, glue, some paint – and they would provide any certificate requested, including an identity card of an officer of any Arab state.

Right-Wing Threats

In addition to internal threats from domestic left-wing activity, we had to deal also with underground right-wing activity from the nuclei of the Etzel and Lehi. Much of the activity was nothing more than debate clubs, vehemently opposed to Ben-Gurion and to a reparations agreement with Germany. But some posed a more serious risk. Among them was Yosef Menkes, who later initiated the assassination of Rudolf Israel Kastner (after an Israeli court in 1957 accused him of having collaborated with the Nazis while helping Jews escape from occupied Europe during the Holocaust).

Then there was the case of Dov Shilansky, whose name I first heard at the end of 1952. We received information that an underground cell, ideologically close to the Herut party headed by Shilansky, intended to plant a bomb in the Foreign Ministry building in Tel Aviv. I found him cross-referenced in my files as a member of the Revisionist movement in his youth, a Holocaust survivor, an underground activist in the ghetto in Lithuania, who had served in the IDF and worked as a government official. But we had information that he had continued his subversive activities.

We planted an agent in Shilansky's cell and he was arrested on 5 October 1952, in the basement of the Foreign Ministry building in Tel Aviv with a time bomb in his bag. His intention was to protest the reparations agreement reached between Israel and West Germany. He had prepared a protest proclamation which he planned to put in the basement, together with the small bomb.

When he entered the basement, I was already waiting for him. Two or three policemen hid in the stairwell, headed by Chief Superintendent Aharon Shlush, the police liaison with Shin Bet, and two other Shin Bet personnel. Shilansky did not notice them as he entered the building and went downstairs. He placed his bag on the floor and leaned over to open it. Shlush came up behind him, put a hand on his shoulder and said, 'Mr. Shilansky, hands back, please, like this, thank you very much.' He was handcuffed and taken into custody. He was sentenced to 21 months in prison and was released after serving two-thirds of his sentence. Eventually he became Speaker of the 12th Knesset. Our paths crossed several times, and he always wanted to know who had squealed on him. I lied to him and said I had no idea. I would tell him: 'In Shin Bet, we compartmentalise. One collects information, another activates, a third carries out the operation.' As far as I could tell, he believed me.

Other threats included one from Brit Hakanaim (Covenant of the Zealots), an organisation of young people with extreme nationalist–religious views, most prominent among them Mordechai Eliyahu, later the Sephardic chief rabbi. They planted bombs and threw Molotov cocktails at taxis that carried passengers on Saturday, butchers that sold non-kosher meat, and to protest the recruitment of women to the IDF. After their failed attempt in 1951 to bomb the building used at the time by the Knesset, Harel ordered their arrest, which led also to uncovering their warehouses of weapons, ammunition and explosives.

In another case, in February 1953, a underground group, Malchut Israel (Kingdom of Israel), headed by Lehi veterans Shimon Bachar and Yaakov Heruti, bombed the Soviet representative office, at 46 Rothschild Boulevard in Tel Aviv, to protest the persecution of Jews in the USSR and other communist countries. Shin Bet considered this not only an act of terrorism, but also a danger to the stability of Israel. Every effort was made to capture the perpetrators. We were aided by the fact that some members of Malchut Israel had previously been active in Brit Hakanaim and were known. Three months later, sixteen members of Malchut Israel were arrested and prosecuted for membership of a terrorist organisation (this was the first and only time so far in the history of Israel that Jews were prosecuted for this offense). Bachar and Heruti were sentenced to heavy prison terms but were pardoned two years later. In later years, I had contact with Heruti that began as a business relationship but developed into a close friendship.

Most dealings with underground organisations were entrusted to Division 1 of Shin Bet. Division 10, under my leadership, sometimes provided operational services such as surveillance, eavesdropping, vehicles, and so on as requested.

In late 1953, Harel received shocking news: an IDF officer named Alexander Israel had offered his services to the Egyptian embassy in Rome. He left them some documents, examples of what he could bring, to let them see and decide if they wanted to work with him. The Egyptians told him: 'Leave the material with us and if we are interested, we will get back to you.'

Harel summoned me, briefed me, and told me 'Go and get him. We'll put him on trial in Israel. Get the file on him from the operations unit.' He glanced at his watch. 'You have a flight in three hours.' Other than a few days in Cyprus, I had never been abroad and I knew no foreign language.

The file was a thin binder, with only a faded photograph from the air force and very basic information. Even his address and marital status were not indicated and I only learned later that he had abandoned his pregnant wife and disappeared.

I took along Emanuel Talmor, Nehemiah Meiri, and two other guys from operations on the flight to Rome, where Benjamin Rotem, the Mossad representative in Europe, was waiting for us. He told us that our 'client' had bought a ticket on the Rome–Vienna train, but that his destination was actually Zurich, one of the stations on the line.

We inquired and learned that two trains left Rome every day for Vienna. Both passed through Zurich. We went to the Rome train station and kept an eye out. We did not have to wait long. Alexander Israel arrived and boarded the train, and we followed him. More of our people were already on the platform in Zurich – Rotem took care of that.

Israel disembarked in Zurich. Our people there followed him and saw him buy two Swissair plane tickets, one from Zurich to Vienna, and after a two-day stay in Vienna, a ticket from Vienna to Paris. I immediately decided that Paris was the right place to trap him and passed this on to Harel, then left for Vienna, to follow him there.

Harel came back to me with an idea: he had located a woman who knew Israel, and recruited her. She would meet him, supposedly by chance, in Vienna, and then 'by chance' they would discover they were both flying from Vienna to Paris. Not only that: at Paris's Orly Airport, a 'relative' would be waiting to pick her up, and would offer to take Israel to his destination. I flew to Paris to prepare the operation there, and met Talmor, who was to pose as the relative.

Israel and the woman got off the plane and into the car with Talmor. I was sitting in a vehicle which followed the car, with a driver who was one of my operations people. Talmor proceeded as planned to the new wholesale market area that was then under construction, which I had set up as our meeting point. Talmor stopped the car. We stopped a few feet behind him. The operations man driving the vehicle I was in got out, and with Talmor, they blindfolded Israel, bound him and laid him on the back seat. He did not make a sound. They proceeded to drive to a safehouse and I joined them there. We interrogated him for a few days. He admitted everything.

At that point I left the scene, continuing to London, where I was scheduled to get a state-of-the-art hearing aid, something experimental, in hopes of solving my hearing problem. Talmor acted as my replacement and our people continued the operation in my absence, but under my responsibility.

The air force sent a Dakota plane to Paris to pick up the 'cargo'. It was a transport plane and did not have a heating system. At maximum altitude, the temperature could drop to -10° Centigrade. An anaesthetist from Tel Hashomer Hospital, also came from Israel.

The Dakota with Israel aboard was flown from Paris to Rome, where it refuelled, then to Athens on a flight that lasted four hours. It refuelled again, and flew to Lod Airport in Israel. The whole process lasted close to a day. Alexander Israel was put to sleep three times: before being boarded in Paris, a second time prior to landing in Rome, and a third time prior to landing in Athens. He did not wake up. He may have received an overdose of the anaesthetic, and the cold may have affected him while he was anaesthetised. In any case, we landed with a corpse.

Harel ordered that the body be stripped, any identifying marks obscured, and had it loaded onto a plane and thrown into the sea, 200 kilometres from shore. And so it was.

Afterwards, Harel briefed Ben-Gurion, who did not report to anyone. Nor did he write a single word about it in his diary. In the years immediately following the death of Israel, no one – to the best of my knowledge – tried to locate him. But a few years ago, the affair resurfaced when his son, born after the father's death, filed a claim for compensation from Mossad. Eventually the lawsuit ended in a settlement.

The Alexander Israel affair highlighted the need to establish an operational branch in Paris. Under Harel, Mossad developed and grew. Its Paris office dealt not only with contacts with the French intelligence services, but also other tasks, including photography and surveillance. When we set up an operational branch in Paris, I assigned Shalom, who spoke French, to head it. He travelled to Paris with his wife Rachel (incidentally, I introduced them to each other) where they were stationed for a year and a half, from end-1953 to mid-1955.

Chapter 8

Working with Ben-Gurion

In late 1955, before I left for London, I formulated a warfare doctrine for Israel's security services and a training curriculum with the help, among others, of Yitzhak Rabin, then head of the IDF Training Department, and his deputy, David Elazar, who passed on to me their IDF training manuals. We wrote thirty training manuals that dealt with subjects such as eavesdropping, surveillance, reconnaissance, observation, burglary, covert break-ins, recruiting and operating agents, drafting operational orders and writing reports, decision-making processes, and chain of command.

The instructions include clear guidelines that the operational echelon should assume responsibility in the event of operational complications. In such cases, responsibility ought to stop at the operational level and should not flow up to the political level, regardless of whether the political level knew about the operation or not. That's the way it should be, and that's exactly what I did in the Pollard affair. I formulated these rules, and when it came to the test, I proved my commitment to them.

While compiling the training manuals, I gave lectures to training courses, mostly to members of Shin Bet and Mossad, and sometimes also to members of military intelligence. Shimon Peres, then director-general of the Defense Ministry, who wanted to learn about the work of the secret services, received a condensed private course from me. I paid special attention, too, to the research and development units of the secret service. From my first days in the service, I considered staying on the leading edge of technology to be critical to success.

In December 1953, Ben-Gurion resigned as prime minister and defense minister and settled in Kibbutz Sde Boker in the Negev, but he still pulled the strings in Israeli politics and would come to the centre of the country from time to time. He had no car and no driver. Harel asked me to take care of this, using Shin Bet vehicles available to me. Ben-Gurion's wife, Paula, or an aide, would call me, and I would send a car with a driver. But occasionally, I went myself. I drove and he sat next to me on the road. No security. We talked quite a bit on those trips, including about politics and his concerns about left-wing parties.

Moshe Sharett replaced Ben-Gurion as prime minister, while also continuing to serve as foreign minister. Pinhas Lavon was appointed defense minister. On 8 December 1954, the Egyptian government announced that it had uncovered an Israeli spy and sabotage network operating in Egypt. The affair, which was referred to as 'That Bad Business' (*Ha'esek Habish* in Hebrew) or as the Lavon Affair, shook Israel to the core.

Neither Mossad nor Shin Bet were involved. Despite denials, the network was indeed operated by Israel, but it was operated by military intelligence, through its Unit 131, which conducted espionage operations in Arab countries. Military censorship in Israel has cast a heavy shadow over the affair. Most of the public knew nothing about it other than what was reported from Egypt, where members of the network were put on trial and two were sentenced to death, with the rest receiving long prison terms.

Immediately after the network was uncovered, a sharp conflict erupted between the head of military intelligence, Colonel Benjamin Gibli, and Pinhas Lavon, over who had given the order to operate the network in Egypt – a matter that brewed up a storm that did not settle for years and has not been resolved to this day.

I am convinced that if Harel or Manor had been called on to investigate the affair early on, the matter of who gave the order would have been determined quickly. Ben-Gurion, who replaced Lavon as defense minister soon after the network was uncovered, apparently did not want Shin Bet investigators to interrogate Lavon or Gibli, and determined it was more respectable to have a state committee of inquiry look into the matter, one which did not reach an unequivocal conclusion and led to the matter being dragged out for years.

Elections to the 3rd Knesset were scheduled for July 1955. If Mapai won, Sharett would not return to the prime minister's office. Instead, Ben-Gurion would form the next government and head it, and if he also wanted to serve as defense minister, his request would be granted.

Together with my old friend Moshe Gidron, who was commander of the 7th Brigade (IDF Liaison School), we arranged a meeting with Ben-Gurion. We expressed our concern that Mapai's victory was uncertain. Ben-Gurion was silent, but we got the impression that he, too, was worried about the outcome. 'If you allow me, I can guarantee that Mapai will win the election,' I said.

He glanced at me and it was clear he understood my intentions. He didn't shout, 'How dare you,' or throw us out. He just muttered, 'It's not time for that yet.' Had he expressed interest in my proposal, I would have acted without hesitation. It was possible, for example, to open ballot boxes when they were transferred from polling stations to the Central Election Commission, take out some of the envelopes and change the ballots. I could have thought of other ways as well. I never did this, but others have, and even today such things can be done.

I do not know if Ben-Gurion shared my concern that Mapai would be defeated in the election. There were no public opinion polls at the time. If he really feared a loss, would he have considered my proposal? I have no answer to this question. Although Ben-Gurion believed in democracy, the future of the State of Israel was more important to him than democracy.

In any case, our concern turned out to be excessive. Mapai did see its forty-five seats reduced to forty, but the advance of the left-wing parties was modest. Indeed, three months later a new government was formed under Ben-Gurion, who also served as defense minister. The big winner was the opposition right-wing Herut party, which won fifteen seats, compared to eight in the previous election.

Chapter 9

Seeing the World a Different Way

During 1955–8, I lived and worked in London. It was not a desire to travel that motivated me to go there but rather a sense that I was at a disadvantage in knowing only Hebrew fluently. How far can you go in the Middle East or in the world if you only speak Hebrew?

The question was what other language was worth learning. I was torn between focusing on English or on Arabic. After a lot of thought and consultation with friends and colleagues, I concluded that if I learned Arabic, I would be committed to a career concerned with the Arab world. If I learned English, the Western world would open up to me. I chose English.

I signed up for evening classes in English, but the intensity of my job prevented me from studying in an orderly fashion. I decided, therefore, to take a leave of absence, expand my horizons and conquer English. I consulted Manor, the head of Shin Bet. He recommended that I go to London to study for a year. But I also wanted to go to university to expand my general education.

My friend and colleague Uri Lubrani convinced me that Britain is the best place to study English, and that attending the London School of Economics would allow me both to learn English and broaden my horizons. But how was I to get into such a prestigious and selective institution given my scant knowledge of English and my lack of a high school diploma?

In such situations, it is good to have Shimon Peres around. He was then the director-general of the Ministry of Defense. I had worked a bit for him and we became somewhat close. He made some phone calls and sent some letters, including to Hugh Gaitskell, the leader of the British Labour Party, with whom he had good ties. Gaitskell turned to a colleague with the right connections, who recommended me to the London School of Economics, and I was accepted. I enrolled in the departments of economics and political science, and committed to passing the British matriculation exam at the end of the first year. I knew it would not be easy. Shalom was called back to Israel from France to take my place as head of Division 10 Tel Aviv.

Manor agreed to give me a salary of £25 a month during my first year in London, enough then to keep me alive, but too little to live any sort of life. Luckily, a few months later, Lubrani arranged for me to work as a guard at the Israeli embassy in London on weekends, a job that gave me £15 a month. During the week, I also worked as a salesman in an antique bookstore, for another £10 a month. So, I got by, paid my tuition and could eat in modest restaurants.

I enrolled in a language school and studied English intensively for three hours every morning. It meant forgoing many lectures, but I had no regrets, because in the first months, I couldn't understand most of the lectures in any case. I also hired a private tutor to help me prepare for the matriculation exam. As a second foreign language, I chose – not surprisingly – classical Hebrew.

One weekend, Yitzhak Rabin, then a general whom I knew from the Palmach, arrived at the embassy. I stood guard at the door. 'What are *you* doing here?' he asked.

'I'm the security guard,' I replied. 'Identification please.'

When he returned to Israel, Rabin called Harel and said: 'Your people are guarding embassies abroad. Does that seem right to you?' Harel apparently agreed that the situation was ludicrous and arranged to appoint me as the liaison between Mossad and MI6, the British counterpart of Mossad, at a salary of £60 a month.

At the end of the first year, I took the matriculation exams in English and passed. I immediately applied and received a scholarship which covered tuition and dormitory accommodation. This spared me the need to work while studying. I undoubtedly didn't receive the scholarship because of my grades, which were mediocre (out of ten papers I had to submit, I submitted two, maybe three). I probably got it because I was considered exotic – the only Israeli student enrolled. I have no other explanation. In any case, it was not because Peres intervened.

Despite the significant salary I received from Mossad, my role as liaison with MI6 did not occupy me more than once a week. On Saturday mornings, I would receive letters or oral messages from Mossad via diplomatic channels to pass on to a representative of the British intelligence organisation, an impressive woman whom I believe was MI6's director for the Middle East. Occasionally, when senior Mossad officials, including Harel, came to London, I would arrange meetings for them. My relationship with MI6 was purely technical and not operational, but it was friendly and very pleasant, allowing me to learn from them about innovations in technology, eavesdropping or tracking. Whatever I learned, I passed on to Shalom, back in Israel.

London also taught me to look at the world and examine it from the perspective of *The Times*. Reading the British newspaper clued me in to the kind of information that decision makers seek, receive and consume. I learned to home in on the essential when faced with a lot of information.

Along with economics, which gave me a grounding that served me well later in business, I also heard lectures in political science. I was most fascinated by the history of Britain, the Soviet Union, the United States and France and the differences in their governmental structure and political outlook. The first roots of my understanding of international affairs were planted in London more than sixty years ago, and developed afterwards due to my almost compulsive reading ever after on such subjects.

In London, I began to realise that international relations had more to them than covert operations. It was not that I ceased to attach importance to intelligence gathering, but I began to understand that there were other options worth using at various times.

The London School of Economics reflected the socialist worldview of its founders both in terms of the teachers and the students, who came from all over the world, including Arab countries, particularly Egypt. When I arrived in London, I saw Arabs as one large block of *kaffiyehs.* In London, I first learned that there are nuances that differentiate the Arabs from various countries. The Egyptians, particularly educated ones, did not consider themselves Arabs but as descendants of pharaonic dynasties that were conquered by Arabs who imposed Islam on them. They took pride in their pharaonic heritage and looked down on those other Arabs.

I spoke to Egyptian students at university and told myself that they could be partners in negotiations and peace. Even then, in 1956, I thought that Egypt would be the first Arab country to reach a peace agreement with Israel.

When I returned to Israel and got back into intelligence work, I made efforts to contact the Egyptians, but the Sinai Campaign in 1956, when Israel collaborated with Western powers, struck a deep wedge between us and the Egyptians.

Studying and living in London, talking with people from other countries and cultures was highly beneficial, but also caused a certain disconnect between me and Israel. In October 1956, a year after my arrival, the IDF attacked the Egyptian forces in Sinai, and soon after the British and French entered the fighting. The war caught me totally by surprise. Despite my role as Mossad's liaison with MI6, I knew nothing about the pact forged between Israel and France and Britain. Just a day before the start of the Sinai Campaign, I was called to deliver an envelope with a secret message to MI6 and ordered to be on alert for further instructions.

When the campaign began, I telegraphed home, asking if I should return. The answer was no. I was told to stay in London and be prepared to receive instructions and carry them out at all hours. During the campaign I repeatedly considered going back to Israel and returning to the IDF as my good friend Simhoni advised. Two days after the campaign, he died in a plane accident which has never been fully explained. With his death, ended any consideration of my returning to Israel to re-enlist in the IDF.

The Sinai Campaign aligned Israel with imperialist, exploitative states, on the side of the old order. With the perspective of years, it is now clear that the campaign was also the first time Israel waged a war of choice, not for its existence, but for its interests. It was not a war that had to happen. The *fedayeen* incursions and Nasser's arrogant remarks about a 'second round' in which Israel would be defeated were not sufficient reason for war.

However, I have no doubt that Ben-Gurion considered Egypt a serious threat. Tensions between Israel and Egypt had increased greatly following the 'the bad business' of the Israeli spy ring. Ben-Gurion rightly feared the consequences of the 1955 arms deal between Czechoslovakia and Egypt to supply Egypt with 150 MiG-15 fighter jets, as well as other aircraft, tanks and artillery – all equipment that far surpassed IDF weapons. Israel is not Switzerland, and it could not take a neutral position.

Israel's decision to launch the campaign in cooperation with France and Britain had a considerable political cost. On the other hand, it closely aligned France with Israel at a time when Israel needed the support of a larger power. Although France was already something of a second-rate power, it was still a significant player, with strong industry and modern technology. It was a member of the UN Security Council and Israel's closest ally until the United States took its place.

It was Peres who made France an ally. That alliance made it possible for him to realise his grandiose idea of building a nuclear reactor in Dimona, after convincing Ben-Gurion. I tend to assume that he believed my going to the London School of Economics would broaden my horizon and lead me to see eye-to-eye with his word view. This would lead me to help him when needed, admire his work and give him the credit he deserves. And so it was, and I will not expand beyond that.

Beyond formal studies, London opened me up intellectually. Although I did not become a man of literature, theatre and cinema, the cultural environment of London influenced me, although not enough in the opinion of my wife Miriam. Cultural refinement, according to Miriam, did not continue beyond British borders. Maybe, they were instructive and enriching years. Did I come back from London a different person? Emphatically no. Inside, I remained the same.

Chapter 10

Heading the Operations Division

After my third year at the London School of Economics, I decided to return to Israel. I would have liked to stay and get a degree, but it was not to be. Manor, head of Shin Bet, had allowed me to extend my study leave from one to three years, but on the condition that I would return to Israel when necessary.

Even before I left, we agreed that my next position in Shin Bet would be to head Division 10 for the whole country and at the end of 1958 the right circumstances arose when Ephraim Rosen-Ronel, head of Division 10, was moved to a senior position in Europe. Manor told me: 'If you want to head Division 10, the job is yours – now. Tomorrow, it's not certain.'

I became head of Division 10 at the start of 1959, a position I held until April 1964. It effectively meant that I was in charge of all operations for both Shin Bet and Mossad, with a staff of about 200 people, including Division 10 Tel Aviv, Haifa and Jerusalem.

I got my assignments from Manor and Harel, for Shin Bet and Mossad respectively. I manoeuvred between the two. They were not always coordinated. I gave priority to Harel's needs, as he was the Commissioner of Security Services and therefore senior to Manor.

The first structural change I instituted in my new position was to unite Division 10 for the whole country with its Tel Aviv section. I moved all personnel to one office, in Jaffa. Previously staff of Division 10 nationally and in Tel Aviv were spread out in three different places.

Around this time, we received a valuable gift from the FBI: Motorola-made radios. Consequently, we upgraded our communications system, and installed them in all our cars, nationwide. We developed new technologies that led to significant improvements in various areas. We had a small operational unit, code-named Colossus, to carry out tasks for Mossad. I appointed Haim Lerman Eilam, who had been involved in training in the Palmach, to head its office in Europe, which he did until 1963.

I renovated our detention and interrogation facilities in Abu Kabir on the outskirts of Tel Aviv. In consultation with psychologists and other experts, we created stress conditions in the cells: these were opaque cells without windows, some with a very low ceiling and others with a very high ceiling, and slots for observing prisoners without their noticing us. It should be emphasised that torture of any kind was absolutely taboo, even what is today defined as 'moderate physical pressure'. The difficulty of dealing with those who have left ticking bombs was not yet commonly encountered.

I do not remember what the division budget was at the time I headed it, but I think it was between a million and a million and a half dollars, a considerable sum in those days.

As mentioned before, during the 1950s, Shin Bet focused on internal issues, particularly on Jewish political parties and movements on the far left, the far right or religious zealots. When the leftist Mapam bloc joined the government after the Knesset elections in 1955, the unit that dealt with such affairs was phased out and became defunct in 1957. Given Israel's military achievements, its quick economic development and the confidence voters continued to express in Mapai, Ben-Gurion's concerns receded and he loosened the reins on monitoring internal dissent.

During my time in London, Harel also began recruiting prominent former commanders of the Lehi and the Irgun, including Yitzhak Shamir and David Shomron, and appointed them to senior positions, thus reducing the likelihood they would operate underground groups.

Shamir was drafted into Mossad in 1956 and headed a unit whose mission was to plant agents in Arab countries, primarily to provide early warning of any plans to attack Israel. The intelligence information these agents gathered was passed on to Unit 188 (formerly 131) of military intelligence. This led to some competition and conflict between the comparable units in Mossad and the IDF, but no one interfered in Harel's decision. After his departure, the two units merged in 1964 and became the Caesarea operations department.

During 1959–64, I focused on two issues. The first was battling Soviet and Eastern European espionage. The spies were Russians, Poles, Romanians, Czechs, Bulgarians, some under diplomatic cover, some, as previously mentioned, who were recruited before immigrating to Israel. The second focus was operations abroad which I will describe in coming chapters.

Other areas of activity included assuring the personal security of Ben-Gurion and other Israeli leaders. In the early 1960s, we began receiving information from our agents in Arab countries and from wire-tapping of Arab communication networks of plans to attack Israeli targets and assassinate Israeli personalities, first and foremost Ben-Gurion. The personal security unit headed by the late Yosef Shiner started as a small unit attached to Ben-Gurion on all his trips abroad and later also to the president. At our request, the FBI provided us with instruction manuals in this area, which we used to train the security personnel and drivers assigned to leading Israeli politicians.

In the early 1960s, we began taking steps to enhance the security of El Al planes, following warnings of possible hijackings or sabotage attempts. Among other measures, we appointed a security officer to El Al. It was not until 1968 that an El Al plane was hijacked for the first time and landed in Algeria. Had security been carried out in accordance with procedures, the hijacking would have been thwarted.

Harel was extremely careful about who he chose to join the secret services. The human core of the services in those days excelled in loyalty, reliability and integrity. He opposed taking anyone with a criminal record into Mossad or Shin Bet. This was less true of military intelligence, which recruited Motke Kedar, suspected in the early 1950s of a robbery in Afula and the murder of a taxi driver in Hadera.

While I was in Britain, in early 1957, Kedar was sent to London for six months to improve his English ahead of a placement in Argentina. I was asked to take care of him and met him in London several times, until he moved to Argentina. Later, he was accused of murdering his Jewish contact in Buenos Aires and stealing $15,000 in cash from him, a huge fortune at the time. He was eventually arrested, tried in military court, convicted, and served seventeen years in solitary confinement in Ramla Prison until his release in 1974.

As a result of such incidents, a committee was established in Israel, still during my stay in London, to discuss the issue of recruiting those with a criminal record. Its conclusion was unequivocal: the recruitment of criminals into intelligence and security organisations should be banned.

In the context of the Kedar affair, it is also worth noting that the Security Service has always had a legal department to deal with the mishaps which inevitably occur. In addition, we had a liaison with the Israel Police which, when necessary, would send police officers to make arrests at our request. Only in 2002, was the Shin Bet Law passed, which gives members of Shin Bet the power to act like police in some cases, including making arrests.

There were some secret arrests and imprisonments in those days. Prominent among them were Aharon Cohen, a Mapam activist who had contacts with a senior Soviet spy, and Professor Kurt Sita and Israel Bar (discussed below) as well as Kedar, who was known as Prisoner X.

In addition, we had at least ten other cases of new immigrants from Poland or the Soviet Union recruited there by the local intelligence services. We estimated that about 80 per cent of the recruits voluntarily confessed as soon as they arrived in Israel. Some also pointed out to us other recruits who did not voluntarily come forward. Work in this area required surveillance of suspects, reconnaissance, wire-tapping and covert intrusion. When we reached the unequivocal conclusion that we had identified a foreign agent, the police – not the service – arrested the suspect, who was interrogated by Shin Bet, usually at its Abu Kabir detention centre.

While I was in London, there was a significant increase in the number of Arab citizens of Israel who were recruited to spy for Arab countries. Division 10 worked in conjunction with the relevant department in Shin Bet in charge of counter-espionage in the Arab sector. At the same time, several spies sent to Israel from the 'periphery' nations – Turkey, Iran and Ethiopia – also infiltrated the country. We handled them too.

Aharon Cohen, a Mapam activist, was arrested in October 1958, less than a month after I returned to Shin Bet, so I had no part in exposing him. Suspicion about him first arose after an observant policeman noticed a car with diplomatic plates parked in the evening hours near the entrance of Kibbutz Sha'ar Ha'amakim a few times in relatively short succession. Cohen was put under surveillance, and it emerged that he regularly met a Soviet diplomat in his room on the kibbutz, a KGB agent who worked in Israel as the science attaché at the Soviet embassy. No one in the kibbutz knew or had noticed.

By that time, Mapam membership no longer rendered people automatically suspect. So Harel invited Cohen for questioning in his office. I was already in Israel in my new position by that time, and, with Manor, I listened in from the next room. Cohen lied blatantly and stupidly, insisting that he had only met the diplomat at cocktail parties. When he repeated this lie, Harel had him arrested and he was eventually sentenced to two and a half years in prison. In our estimate, he did not severely harm national security because he did not have access to secret or sensitive information, but his sentence was justified not only because meeting with a purported diplomat is *a priori* forbidden but also because he lied about the contact.

The Israel Bar Affair

As soon as I became head of Division 10, Harel summoned me alone to a meeting, without the knowledge of Manor. The subject was Israel Bar, a native of Vienna, who immigrated to Israel in 1938, joined the Haganah and was a long-time activist in the leftist Mapam and Mapai movements. He retired from the IDF in 1950 as a major general, disillusioned because his political affiliation with the left had stymied his advancing to a top position in the army.

Bar and I were part of the same social set around 1950, and we would meet at the home of mutual friends. He was affable, a good storyteller and knowledgeable. Harel, however, suspected that Bar was a security risk as early as 1953 and summoned him to a conversation, as was his habit. He asked Bar, who had switched between the Mapam and Mapai parties, for an explanation for his tendency to change his political affiliation. I do not know what Bar replied, but this sort of conversation with Harel was supposed to signal to a suspect that he was under surveillance and to watch his step, but it did not seem to have that intended effect on Bar.

I personally took on the task of monitoring Bar and made it my business to get close to him, which was not difficult, since we spent many Friday evenings with mutual friends, singing. Furthermore, he dealt with security matters in his job at the Ministry of Defense, as I did, so we had common topics of conversation.

One evening, our group of singing friends were invited to gather at Bar's home in north Tel Aviv. I gladly accepting, planning to combine business with pleasure. How? Bar had a dog. If I ever wanted to search his house, I would have to neutralise her so she wouldn't bark. I was a graduate of a dog training course and knew how to win over dogs. That evening, while everyone was singing, I petted her and fed her all sorts of treats under the table, so she would remember me favourably in a future meeting. Needless to say, when I left, I also had a copy of the apartment door key in my pocket.

Shortly afterwards, when Bar was at work, I entered the apartment. The dog welcomed me happily. I searched the apartment thoroughly and found nothing suspicious. I reported this to Harel.

In the following years, Bar flourished and prospered. He became an internationally renowned military commentator; doors were opened to him all over Europe. He published books in Germany, gave lectures in Sweden, Norway, France, came and went from foreign embassies in Israel. In 1955, Ben-Gurion, then defense minister, appointed Bar as the official historian of the War of Independence. Bar was given a room at the ministry, right across from the ministry's director-general, Shimon Peres. Everything was open to Bar, his network of contacts kept growing, among them Soviet diplomats. Harel's suspicion of him only grew and he summoned Bar, warned him against contacting foreign intelligence, mentioning Bar's visits to the Russian embassy in Tel Aviv and his frequent trips to Germany. But Bar was not deterred. No one had ever snubbed Harel so blatantly.

When Harel again raised the name of Israel Bar to me in 1958, I reminded myself that for some years, since the early 1950s, Harel had suspected Bar, but had failed to prove anything against him. This time, it seemed Harel had a more concrete reason to suspect Bar. He told me that, during two trips to West Germany, Bar met the head of the secret services there, Reinhard Gehlen. I was tasked with bringing evidence that he was indeed actually spying.

I went into Bar's apartment twice – at the same address on Brandeis Street in Tel Aviv, same lock, same dog. I did not find anything to prove that he was a spy. Nothing even slightly suspicious.

By the 1960s, we had already introduced the 'comb' method of surveillance in Tel Aviv, tracking the activities of suspects by posting agents on city streets and having them relay the movements of the suspect to each other by walkie talkie. It was a method we had imitated from observing the Soviets doing it to us. One of our agents, Moshe Tavor, noticed how he was being followed in Moscow without being followed – by seeing men mumbling into walkie talkies at road junctions. We had improved the method so that the mumbling was not discernible.

In any case, we regularly operated comb surveillance on Vladimir Sokolov, who was the chief case officer at the Soviet embassy in Tel Aviv. When I returned from a business trip to London on Passover Eve in March 1961, people from my staff met me at the airport. 'An hour ago, near his home in north Tel Aviv, Israel Bar met Sokolov and handed him a closed bag,' they told me. We drove right to the office. Manor was already on his way to Kibbutz Ma'agan for the *seder*, but his deputy, Eli Gabrieli was still at the office. It was clear to both of us that Sokolov would look over the material he got from Bar and then return the bag and material to him. We called Harel who told us: 'Get the cops from Shlush and detain Bar right away,' referring to our liaison at the police whom we contacted whenever it was necessary to arrest someone.

I urged Harel to wait and let a few more transfers occur to strengthen the evidence. 'Absolutely not, immediately, today,' Harel insisted, not even attempting to hide his eagerness.

Two hours after receiving the bag, Sokolov returned it to Bar on a street near Bar's apartment in north Tel Aviv. Bar went home and three police officers knocked on the door and arrested him. As soon as he was taken from the apartment, we entered it. The bag was lying on the table. I flipped through it: There were handwritten pages of Ben-Gurion's diary that Bar had received for his research on the War of Independence as well as confidential documents, passed on to him for his research but not intended for publication.

Bar's interrogation took weeks. It emerged that he had fabricated much if not most of the life history on which he had built his reputation in Israel, including his claims to have a doctorate in literature from the University of Vienna, to have fought in the Schutzbund social-democratic militia in Austria, to have taken part in the Spanish Civil War. He insisted he had acted for the good of the State of Israel because he was convinced that the Communist bloc would win the Cold War and he wanted Israel to be closer to the victorious side. All indications were that he began spying for the Soviets in 1957 or 1958.

Bar was arrested on 31 March 1961, but this was made public only on 16 April, five days after the trial of Adolf Eichmann began. The state leadership wanted to separate the two events. Given Bar's prominence in Israeli society, his exposure as a spy caused a sensation. The editorial in *Maariv*, then the most popular newspaper in the country, opened with the words, 'Like thunder on a clear day, the news fell on us . . .' Maybe on us, but not on Harel, I thought at the time.

Bar was initially sentenced by a district court to ten years in prison. He appealed. This was a mistake on his part: the Supreme Court increased his sentence to fifteen years. He was imprisoned in Shata Prison, and died on 1 May 1966, of a heart attack.

I did not have a part in exposing the spy Professor Kurt Sita, a non-Jewish Czech physicist with left-wing tendencies who had been imprisoned by the Nazis in Buchenwald concentration camp until the end of the World War II. He taught afterwards in Britain, the USA and Brazil. Along the way, he was recruited into the ranks of Czech intelligence, apparently around 1950. He agreed to come to the Technion Israel Institute of Technology in Haifa to head its physics department in 1954. He became a member of the Israeli Atomic Energy Commission and also worked in the areas of aeronautics and rockets.

Beginning in 1955, Sita provided his operators with information that reached him in the course of his work and received a handsome monetary reward. In March 1960, quite by accident, his meetings with his handler, a diplomat at the Czech embassy, were detected.

In June 1960, Sita became deputy director of research at the Technion, and immediately asked his colleagues for detailed reports on their research. Following this, he was arrested, interrogated and sentenced to five years in prison, His colleagues lobbied on his behalf and he was pardoned after two years and 10 months by then President Yitzhak Ben-Zvi. He moved to West Germany, where he became professor of physics at the universities of Freiburg and Heidelberg.

Our conclusion, from Sita's investigation, and from many others, was that he did not have access to substantial sources of classified information, but through his work at the Technion he learned about Israel's first moves in the field of nuclear energy, as well as in other fields. However, in our estimation, it did not cause any real security damage.

Cooperation with Iran and Turkey

Not long after I returned from London in late 1958, Shin Bet sent me to Tehran to meet representatives from Iran's security service. This was part of the Periphery Alliance, a strategy conceived and initiated by Ben-Gurion, and motivated to a great extent by the meteoric rise in Egypt of Gamal Abdel Nasser.

During Israel's War of Independence, Nasser served as the intelligence officer of a brigade which was besieged in the Fallujah pocket in the Negev desert for several months after which its soldiers returned to Egypt as part of the armistice agreement. On his return to Egypt, he was the driving force behind the Free Officers Movement, an underground organisation which aspired to put an end to the reign of the corrupt King Farouk. In 1952, they led a military coup, Farouk went into exile, the monarchy was abolished, and General Mohamed Naguib, one of the Free Officers, became President of Egypt. Naguib was nothing but a figurehead, with Nasser the real ruler until April 1954, when Nasser ousted Naguib and became Egypt's ruler both in practice and in law. His fortunes rose even more after the 1956 Suez Crisis, in which Israel fought along with the British and French and won militarily but which, in the aftermath of American and soviet intervention, achieved for Egypt the political goal of recognition of Nasser's nationalisation of the Suez Canal. He became not only the undisputed leader of Egypt, but of the entire Arab world, and was among the initiators of the Non-Aligned Movement, which included Asian and African countries, among them major ones such as India, Indonesia, Iran and Ethiopia with which Israel wished to establish official diplomatic and economic relations. Israel also wanted close ties with Turkey, which had diplomatic relations with Israel but refused to expand beyond that, for fear of a strong Muslim response.

In the same year as the Suez Crisis, Nasser published *The Philosophy of the Revolution*, a book in which he explained his doctrine that Egypt should operate within three circles – the Arab circle, the Muslim circle and the African circle, in a position of influence in each.

Even before Nasser's rise, under Ben-Gurion's guidance Israel sought out potential regional allies and intensified efforts to tighten relations with two peripheral Muslim countries beyond the belt of neighbouring Arab countries: Iran and Turkey. These efforts were successful and led to an informal alliance between the three countries, which Israel termed the Northern Triangle (at the same time Israel built ties with Ethiopia and Sudan, and these were known as the Southern Triangle).

Most of the ties between the three countries were conducted not through government or foreign ministry channels, but rather through their security services. A permanent tripartite committee of the security service heads of each country was established, convening regularly on a rotating basis in each of the three countries. The committee was codenamed Trident (for the three-pronged spear of Poseidon in Greek mythology). From 1958 to 1968, this committee met once or twice a month, in Tel Aviv, Tehran or Ankara.

In order to host this committee, Harel established a complex known as the Midrasha (Hebrew for seminary), where various security forces courses were initially held. Located at the Glilot Junction, on the municipal border between Tel Aviv and Herzliya, it became the permanent home of Mossad under Harel's successor, Meir Amit and to this day the name Midrasha has stuck and is still used by those in Mossad to refer to their headquarters.

In addition to the three secret service heads mentioned above, various experts or department heads of various security services attended deliberations of the Trident Committee. As head of Division 10, the operational division of Shin Bet, I too was summoned several times to the committee's deliberations. At the end of 1958, Harel dispatched me for the first time – and not the last – to Tehran.

My main mission was to stay in touch with my counterparts in Turkey and Iran. Ties with the Iranians were usually warm and ongoing. In contrast, relations with the Turks were chillier, and generally more formal. My visits to Ankara were also less frequent than to Tehran.

The second mission was training. Among other things, we created modern telephone tapping systems for our colleagues, and provided them with advanced equipment we produced ourselves or obtained from various Western countries, all the while making sure to keep specifications secret to maintain a qualitative edge. Our 'clients' were mostly the Iranians. We provided the training for free, but charged them for the equipment.

We also trained the Iranian security service in personal security, first and foremost the security of the Shah, and took an operational part in this. We also participated in a number of their black bag operations (covert penetration of private homes and offices). We trained their surveillance units in tailing by foot and by car, and maintaining contact between trackers.

It is no secret that the Iranian government was deeply corrupt at the time. It was impossible to get any service there without paying off the official in charge. I must note, however, that in my dozens of visits to Tehran, I never personally encountered this and never needed to pay off anyone I came in contact with. I guess the main reason was that their intelligence chief was in charge of the security systems of the oil wells, so that any bribe he might receive from an Israeli wouldn't have amounted even to loose change for him. But there were some Israelis who diligently learned the art of bribery from their hosts during their service in Iran. Without mentioning names, there were some who learned the art so well that they adopted their ways.

Our efforts in Iran and Turkey reaped important, sometimes even vital, information about their Arab neighbours, especially Iraq and Syria. One area that Israel considered very important was aid to the Kurdish uprising in Iraq. This assistance was provided by Mossad and the IDF, but Israel could not have done anything in this respect without the assistance of Iran.

The intelligence cooperation was continuous but let me make it clear that I did not manage our intelligence relations with Iran and Turkey. This was under the responsibility of Mossad, and I took part in certain tasks in my capacity as head of the operational division of

Shin Bet, reporting to Harel, who was in charge of both Mossad and the Security Service. Manor, head of Shin Bet, was always informed and of course agreed to my participation.

In 1958, it seemed that Nasser was moving towards fulfilling his dream of establishing a large and united Arab power, led by Egypt, stretching from Morocco and Algeria in the west to Iraq and Saudi Arabia in the east. On 1 February 1958, a union was announced between Egypt and Syria, the United Arab Republic (UAR). This development increased the importance Israel attached to the tripartite alliance of Iran, Turkey and Israel. Ben-Gurion considered this alliance a high-value political and security asset, equivalent to the Arab alliance formed under Nasser.

Cooperation with Iran, especially in the economic, agricultural and medical fields, left a nucleus of support for Israel – even after the fall of the Shah and the Khomeini revolution – which continued to exist for many years. A special department in the Ministry of Defense continued contact for a long time.

In my opinion, shared by others in Israel, in the USA and in Iran itself, the Carter administration's decision in 1979 to stand by and let Khomeini take over Iran was one of the most serious and tragic American foreign policy mistakes since World War II. American aid to the Shah could have prevented Iran from falling into the hands of fundamentalist zealots. Israeli officials at the time warned the Americans about their policy in Iran, but they did not heed our warnings. Iran was lost and became a dangerous enemy of Israel and the USA, and the biggest destabilising factor in the Middle East.

Our ties with Turkey – which began with intelligence ties – have not ceased since the 1950s but have seen steep fluctuations. At times they became very close and included extensive military and intelligence cooperation. As of this writing (mid-2018), relations are at a standstill, after Turkey expelled the Israeli ambassador following the IDF firing on protesters in Gaza, but Turkey still allows Israeli planes to land in its territory and economic ties between the two countries have not been harmed.

Apart from Iran and Turkey, I also had intelligence ties with the security services of Burma (today Myanmar). In 1955, the Prime Minister of Burma, U Nu, was the first head of state to pay an official visit to Israel. The relationship with Burma, managed by Mossad's international unit, grew stronger. The then chief of staff of the Burmese Army was General Ne Win (in 1962 he led a military coup, following which he ruled as dictator in the country for the next twenty-six years), and the head of intelligence was his cousin, Lee Win. In the late 1950s, Lee Win visited Israel, along with senior members of the Burmese Intelligence Service, and I met them as part of my position.

I first visited Burma in December 1961 before an official visit there by Ben-Gurion, landing in Rangoon a few days ahead of him to handle security and logistics for the visit. The truth is, I really wanted to visit Burma, and I knew who to contact and what to do to make sure I got this assignment.

Our intelligence ties with Burma were not very important, but the political connection mattered, especially to Ben-Gurion. Young Israel, twelve years old, was thirsty for recognition from foreign countries.

Chapter 11

Catching a Nazi People Have Heard Of

Hundreds of books and numerous films exist about the capture of Adolf Eichmann. I have no intention of delving into the arguments that have arisen among various writers. I will confine myself here to describing the events that preceded the capture and re-creating the operation itself – from my personal point of view only – as the head of the Security Service's operations unit, which was recruited to the effort.

In the first decade after Israel's establishment, the Holocaust did not occupy a central place in the priorities of state institutions nor in public memory. Although Menachem Begin tried to inflame the Israeli public against accepting reparations from Germany, most people understood the crucial need for reparations and supported Ben-Gurion. Occasionally, survivors discovered people who had served as *kapos* (assistant guards) in concentration and extermination camps, and some were prosecuted. But Israel had other priorities: within a few years, more than a million immigrants arrived, and it was necessary to absorb them, provide them with housing and food, and try to create jobs. Arab states did not give up their intention to destroy the 'Zionist entity' and prepared for a 'second round' of fighting.

Israel's various security forces, including Shin Bet, invested most of their efforts and resources in monitoring embassy staff from Communist countries, most of whom worked for the intelligence services of these countries, and in monitoring right-wing and left-wing elements. To the best of my knowledge, until 1957, Mossad and the Security Service did not deal with any issue related to the detection and capture of Nazi criminals.

The head of Shin Bet, Amos Manor, had a personal accounting with the Nazis. Born in 1918 as Arthur Mendelovich in the city of Siget in the Transylvania region of Austria-Hungary (later part of Hungary and then Romania), he studied engineering in France, but with the outbreak of World War II, he was forced to leave France. In 1944 he was sent with his whole family to Auschwitz and was the sole survivor. Mossad personnel identified his skills and recruited him. He managed to organise and bring several illegal immigrant ships to Israel. In 1949, he immigrated to Israel and was accepted into the Security Service. Manor was soon appointed head of the counter-espionage department, and by October 1953, Harel had appointed him head of the Security Service.

From Manor I heard that it was he who pressured Harel to set up a special unit to search for senior Nazi criminals who had managed to survive and hide in Europe and elsewhere in the world, especially in South America. Harel himself, Manor said, did not even know the names of the senior Nazis who had disappeared without a trace. It was Manor who told him who the four at the top of the wanted list were: Martin Bormann, Hitler's deputy and bureau chief; Heinrich Müller, head of the Gestapo; Adolf Eichmann, in charge of deporting European Jews to extermination camps; Josef Mengele, the devilish doctor from Auschwitz, who performed 'selections' and horrific experiments on humans.

The task of hunting Nazis was first allocated to Shin Bet but soon was moved to Mossad. It numbered about half a dozen people, and relied on operations personnel as needed. Starting in 1959, its head in Mossad, Zvi Aharoni, would occasionally ask me as the head of Division 10 for assistance in surveillance or photography.

I do not know when and to what extent Ben-Gurion was involved in the decision to establish the unit to hunt Nazis. The head of Ben-Gurion's office, Haim Israeli, read me an excerpt from Ben-Gurion's diary, in which he wrote that in one of his meetings with Harel,

Ben-Gurion ordered, 'Catch a Nazi and bring him here to trial in Israel.'

'Who do you want me to catch?' Harel asked, according to Haim. 'It doesn't matter who,' replied Ben-Gurion 'The main thing is that it be a Nazi people have heard of.' Ben-Gurion made it clear to Harel that he had no interest in 'small fry'.

Eichmann's first mention in Ben-Gurion's diaries was only after his capture, but Harel told me and others that he reported to Ben-Gurion on the establishment of a special unit within the Security Service to hunt Nazis and the nature of its activities, and there is no reason to doubt his remarks.

The first information that Eichmann had managed to escape and settled in Argentina was provided by Shimon Wiesenthal, an architect by profession, a Holocaust survivor, who dedicated his life after World War II to collecting information that would help bring Nazi criminals to justice. Dubbed the Nazi Hunter, Wiesenthal began the hunt for Eichmann in the early 1950s. With the help of the West German police, he raided Eichmann's parents' house to find photographs and other material, but the parents, who no doubt knew where the criminal had fled, destroyed any material related to their son. However, Wiesenthal was a stubborn Jew: he recruited volunteers who, under various pretexts, approached people who knew Eichmann. One of these volunteers courted a woman whom Eichmann had unsuccessfully dated before marrying his wife, and she gave the volunteer pictures of Eichmann in his youth.

Wiesenthal continued his efforts, and in 1954 he received a message from an Austrian friend, who like him was an avid stamp collector. The friend showed him envelopes with Argentinian stamps on them, and told him that the writer of the letters said that Adolf Eichmann was in Buenos Aires. Wiesenthal immediately passed this information on to Dr Nahum Goldman, president of the World Zionist Congress. The letter was later found in Goldman's archive.

It is not clear what Goldman did with the information. He may have ignored Wiesenthal's letter, or he may have relayed the information to some Israeli entity: the Foreign Ministry, Mossad or another body. If the information was relayed, it was probably archived, and forgotten. In any case, Harel stated in later years that he did not know about the information passed on by Wiesenthal, and learned of it only many years after Eichmann was tried and executed. It goes without saying that there is no reason to doubt Harel's statement.

In 1953, an Israeli delegation was set up in Cologne, West Germany, led by Dr Felix Shinar, which dealt mainly with the issue of reparations, but also with other issues related to the mostly secretive relationship between the two countries. Dr Fritz Bauer, the district attorney of the German state of Hesse, a Jew on his mother's side and himself a survivor of the camps, developed a warm and close personal relationship with Shinar.

In September 1957, Luther Herman, a half-Jew of German descent, blind in both eyes, who lived in Argentina, made contact with Bauer. Herman claimed to have verified information that Adolf Eichmann was living in Buenos Aires. (It later emerged that Herman had previously sent a similar letter to the Israeli embassy in Argentina. The embassy forwarded the letter to the Foreign Ministry in Jerusalem, and it appears that someone filed it somewhere in the archives, without dealing with it. After waiting and receiving no reply, Herman decided to contact Bauer.)

Bauer knew that the West German authorities would not be enthusiastic, to say the least, about any attempt to capture Eichmann and bring him to justice. He assumed that the State of Israel would be more interested. He therefore forwarded Herman's letter to Dr Shinar, who relayed it to Mossad. In November 1957, Mossad official Shlomo Cohen-Abarbanel, the brother of Haim Cohen, then Israel's Attorney-General (and later vice-president of its Supreme Court), arrived in Frankfurt and met Bauer.

In late 1957 and the beginning of 1958, we received news from various sources of our own and from the international media about Bormann, Müller and Eichmann. Almost all of these reports said they were in Latin America: Bormann in Guatemala or Panama,

Müller in Panama, Eichmann in Argentina or Brazil. Some of this information seemed to be nonsense (and indeed turned out to be so), but gradually it became clear that the reports on Eichmann were the hottest and most concrete.

Following Bauer's letter and his meeting with Shlomo Cohen-Abarbanel, the idea was raised that Zvi Aharoni would leave for Argentina and meet Herman in his home town, Tucumán in northern Argentina. Aharoni was the head of the Investigations Division of the Security Service, and at the same time commanded the unit that dealt with finding Nazi criminals. He was born in Germany as Hermann Aronheim, and immigrated to Israel in 1938. But Harel decided otherwise and delegated the initial contact with Herman to Emanuel Talmor (formerly Spector), who was fluent in Spanish because he had previously spent two years in Argentina as an emissary for the Jewish Agency. Aharoni was very angry and personally offended at Harel's decision, but Harel's decision was not for any personal reason but rather economic ones. The budgets of the Security Service and Mossad were still very meagre, and to save the high cost of flights to Argentina, Harel took advantage of the fact that Talmor had been invited to conduct a summer seminar in Argentina on behalf of the Zionist movement, at the expense of the movement, of course.

Summer in Argentina is winter in the Northern Hemisphere. Talmor left for Argentina in December 1957, with the help of Ephraim Ilani, a researcher on the history of Jewish settlement in Argentina. His mission did not uncover any new information.

Immediately afterwards, Harel took another opportunity to double up again on expenses on a courier who left the country for Argentina. This time it was Deputy Police Superintendent Ephraim Hofstetter (later Elrom, who was killed by a terrorist in Turkey in 1971), who left for Argentina as Israel's representative to an Interpol conference. Harel asked him to go to Tucumán and talk to Herman, Bauer's source. Hofstetter, a native of Poland who spoke German, did Harel's bidding, and we learned how Herman located Eichmann: Herman's daughter had attended high school in Buenos Aires, where she met a man named Nick Eichmann who courted her. When she moved to Tucumán, he came to visit her, and more than once expressed anti-Semitic views in her company and in the company of her father, without knowing of their Jewish origins.

The father investigated the matter, and found that the war criminal Adolf Eichmann had three sons by the end of World War II: Nicholas or Klaus, born in 1936, Horst, born in 1940, and Dieter, born in 1942 (named after war criminal Dieter Wisliceny, one of Eichmann's senior aides who was sentenced to death and executed in 1948 in Czechoslovakia). He continued his private detective initiative, discovering Nick's address: 4261 Chacabuco Street in Buenos Aires. Hofstetter immediately returned to Buenos Aires and conducted an initial observation of this house. There were no substantive results, but before returning to Israel, Hofstetter met Herman again, handed him half an Argentinian banknote, and asked that he cooperate with anyone who came and showed him the other half of the bill.

In December 1959, Dr Bauer visited Israel, and met Haim Cohen. The attorney-general, in consultation with his brother Shlomo, invited Harel to meet with him and Bauer. At that meeting Bauer provided new and critical information: Eichmann lived in Argentina under the alias Ricardo Klement. He did not provide the source of the information.

To be honest, Harel was not enthusiastic about the chances of capturing Eichmann. I assume that the main reason was budgetary: in those days, we were short of money, and capturing Eichmann would require a large team abroad, and would be costly. But Manor, Aharoni and I increased the pressure on Harel, and he finally decided to send Aharoni to Argentina. I equipped Aharoni with cameras, covert photography kit and communication equipment.

Aharoni stayed in Argentina from February until the second week of April 1960. He was assisted by the historian Ephraim Ilani, military attaché Yitzhak Elron (later treasurer of the Tel Aviv municipality) and trainers of the Argentinian Zionist youth movement about to immigrate to Israel who knew the streets of Buenos Aires and the country's local customs.

At 4261 Chacabuco Street, Aharoni discovered an empty house undergoing renovation, where a family named Klement had recently lived. Neighbours did not know the new address of the family, but one of the workmen told him a member of the Klement family was employed at a nearby garage. Aharoni discovered that it was Dieter Klement, Eichmann's third son. Equipped with this information, Aharoni decided to conduct a sophisticated exercise.

Detailed files existed on anyone who served in the Nazi SS. These files survived the war and were used, among other things, in lawsuits against war criminals. Eichmann's file included the names of all his family members – his wife Veronica (Vera) and his sons, Nicholas, Horst and Dieter, and a description of Eichmann's physical characteristics, from the shape of his skull to his shoe size to scars on his body. We received a copy of this file from Dr Bauer, and Aharoni took it to Argentina. The details of Eichmann's sons were also recorded in this file. Aharoni found that Eichmann's eldest son, Nick, had his birthday coming up. In order to photograph Dieter Klement in the garage where he worked, and to follow him home, Aharoni decided to send Dieter – supposedly in the name of Herman's daughter whom Nick had tried to date – a bouquet for Nick's birthday, along with a note asking Dieter to deliver the gift to his brother. A female staff member at our embassy in Buenos Aires bought a suitable gift of flowers and a birthday card, and handed it to an innocent courier, who took it to the garage where Eichmann's son worked, without having any idea what the real purpose of his mission was. He handed the gift to Dieter while Aharoni and his young assistants photographed them, from a safe distance, of course.

Next, Aharoni and his assistants conducted a prolonged surveillance operation on Dieter, who rode home on a motorcycle, so that they learned that the Eichmann family's new address was in a new, out-of-town suburb called San Fernando. Eichmann lived at 22 Garibaldi Street, where so far only two other houses had been built, but none had yet been connected to the municipal electricity grid; another two or three houses were under construction. An inspection revealed that the house was registered in the name of Vera Liebel. Liebel was the maiden name of Eichmann's wife Veronica.

A lengthy surveillance of the house ensued, and the observers from the first days noted that there was a man in the house, but the distant photographs obtained were blurry and insufficient for a definite identification. After a while, the man disappeared for a few days, leaving only a woman and a small child about six years old, whose presence initially confused Aharoni. Later we learned that it was Ricardo, the youngest son of Vera and Adolf, born in Argentina. But one weekend the man reappeared, and this time a successful photograph was obtained.

Aharoni sent the photographs to us via diplomatic mail, and it took a week or even longer for them to arrive. Although I had not yet been assigned a specific task, I already felt deeply involved and prepared myself for an operation.

As soon as the photos reached us, I took them to the Forensic Department of the Israel Police, which had a state-of-the-art laboratory, and asked them to compare the photos Aharoni had supplied with Eichmann's photos in his SS file. The first batch of photos was disappointing, and the lab workers' efforts to ascertain the identification were unsuccessful. But in the second batch, we hit the jackpot: a person's ear is like a fingerprint. No person has an identical ear to another person's ear. His SS file included profile photos of Eichmann showing his left ear. They were some twenty years old, but an ear does not change after a person reaches adulthood. Aharoni knew that an ear photograph of Ricardo Klement would be gold for us. One of the surveillance team managed to get a photograph of Klement's left ear from a distance. The conclusion of the forensic experts was unequivocal: the older man in the photo from Buenos Aires was the young man photographed in Germany or Austria about two decades before, documented in Adolf Eichmann's SS file. We had what we wanted.

For the time being, we knew we had to make do with this identification. When direct contact would be made with Eichmann, it would be up to us to look for further evidence that this was indeed the man we were looking for, but we were off to a good start.

Having provided important information and photos, Aharoni returned to Israel, but not before receiving detailed instructions from me to obtain everything needed to prepare for the operation, including car numbers, driving licences, various diplomatic certificates, detailed maps, exact locations, names of restaurants, hotels, coffee shops, and details on the seaport and Buenos Aires airport.

Meanwhile in Israel, we located German-speaking operatives who looked 'Aryan' as well as immigrants from South America who could be used when needed. For this, I went to Kibbutz Bror Hayil in southern Israel, whose members were immigrants from Brazil, and indeed found some who later helped us in South America, chief among them Erwin Semel, Yigal Haychuk and Benjamin Reicher.

By this time, late 1959 and early 1960, I was already thinking about the general plan for an operation with still vague objectives. Although I had no clear instructions from Harel, it was clear to me that the aim would be to abduct Nazi criminals to Israel and prosecute them.

The desire for revenge was natural and understandable, but that alone was not a reason to call into action Israel's secret services. Only an action that would lead to the trial of a living person would justify investing in the effort. Therefore, in planning, I took into account the lessons of the failed operation in which suspected spy Alexander Israel, whom we were supposed to bring to Israel alive, had instead died while being flown under sedation to Israel. It was clear to me that if we managed to kidnap a criminal, we would have to bring him to Israel by Israeli transport. We began to check possible arrangements with El Al, but also looked into the feasibility of using refrigeration rooms on ships belonging to former Mossad personnel Azriel Einav and Yossi Harel (commander of the immigration ship *Exodus*), who imported beef from Argentina to Israel. We also started working out how to instal hidden compartments, which we call *sliks*, in hired cars abroad as well as obtaining or making certificates and documents to use for operations in possible destination countries.

After thoroughly examining all the possibilities, we came to the conclusion that if we succeeded in kidnapping Ricardo Klement in Buenos Aires and confirmed that he was indeed Adolf Eichmann, it was best to bring him to Israel by air for trial. Of course, we did not want to risk smuggling him in a foreign carrier, so it was clear that we would use the national Israeli airline El Al. At the time, El Al did not operate regular flights between Tel Aviv and Buenos Aires, but we did not need a scheduled service, only one flight, and figured we would find a solution.

Aharoni landed in Israel on 7 April 1960. A few days before, Harel had invited me for a face-to-face conversation at his liaison office in the Kiriya, the Defense Ministry's Tel Aviv offices, and instructed me to prepare an operation to capture Adolf Eichmann and bring him to Israel. I left Harel, went to my office, took out a new notebook, and started making lists: Everything I needed to do, who should be involved, who I needed to talk to, what to bring to Argentina, what we could acquire when we were already in Argentina. Everything. I have kept that notebook to this day.

From that moment on, I concentrated my efforts on preparing the operation in all its aspects. Every day, to obtain approvals and coordinate with relevant parties, I sat down with Harel. At the same time, I updated Manor, who was not involved in planning the operation or practical preparations, but I felt it only proper to keep him in the loop.

Although I was only thirty-three years old and had not gone through the horrors of the Holocaust, I was well aware of the weight of the responsibility on me and also of the moral and historical significance of capturing Eichmann. I visited Yad Vashem (the Holocaust Remembrance Centre) and purchased every book in which Eichmann was mentioned. From a list that Harel prepared for me, I met and talked to Holocaust survivors who had had contact with Eichmann. Of course, we did not in any way hint of our intention to go to Argentina to kidnap him. They were asked to identify him in the photos Aharoni had obtained, and we gauged their willingness to testify about his identity were he to deny that he was Eichmann.

In consultation with Harel, I determined who should be part of the operational team and who should be in on the secret. Together with Harel, I held working meetings with Ephraim Ben-Artzi, CEO of El Al, and with the head of the company's operations department, Yehuda Shimoni. Together with Shimoni, we selected the pilots who would fly the El Al plane from Israel to Argentina and back. El Al was one of the first airlines to receive the new Britannia turbojet, which had a much longer flight range than other airliners at the time. We thoroughly explored where within this kind of aircraft we could possibly conceal a human being. In the end, we came up with two options: close off a toilet cubicle (by putting a sign on the door and saying it was out of order) and hiding Eichmann there, or by opening up the gap – usually closed off – between the rear of the passenger section and the area where luggage was stored, and stowing him there.

Simultaneously, I also examined the possibilities of hiding Eichmann on one of the two refrigerated ships that regularly imported frozen meat from Argentina, behind a partition in the captain's cabin which only the captain has access to. But from the start, we considered a ship to be the less desirable option.

In any complex operation of this kind, unplanned things happen, often disruptive and sometimes frustrating ones. But there are also pleasant surprises. One happened on 18 April when Harel noticed a newspaper article which reported that Argentina would be marking 150 years of independence on 20 May with a big celebration. Israel had normal diplomatic relations with Argentina, and Harel assumed that Israel had received an invitation to participate in the celebrations – which the Foreign Ministry confirmed to be true when we inquired about this. Our ambassador to Argentina was slated to represent Israel at the celebrations, but Harel got fired up with the idea that the celebration would give him a great cover and a date for the operation.

Ben-Artzi was already in the know about our intentions to bring Eichmann to Israel – alive – to be put on trial. Now Harel asked Ben-Artzi to speak to Foreign Minister Golda Meir and make her 'an offer too good to refuse'. An official high-level Israeli delegation would go to Argentina for the celebrations but it wouldn't have to spend a penny of its budget, because all costs would be covered by El Al, since – Ben-Artzi was to tell Golda Meir – the airline was planning to send a plane to Argentina to check the feasibility of opening a scheduled service between Israel and South America in view of the long range of its new Britannia aircraft. The participation of a high-level delegation would be a nice diplomatic achievement for the Foreign Ministry, and surely contribute to strengthening relations between the two countries – without having to pay for the cost of flying the delegation to Argentina. (In the end, El Al did not pay for the flight either. All expenses were covered by Mossad.)

Of course, Meir accepted the offer. The delegation Ben-Artzi envisaged would be headed by Abba Eban, well-known as the former Israeli ambassador to the United States and the United Nations, president of the Weizmann Institute of Science, and at the time minister without portfolio in the prime minister's office. Another senior figure in the delegation would be the head of Northern Command, General Meir Zorea. A piquant detail, which to the best of my knowledge was coincidental, was that Zorea, who had been a captain in the Jewish Brigade, was a former leader in the Avengers, a group of Jewish soldiers who eliminated Nazi criminals in Germany at the end of World War II.

Once the Foreign Minister approved the idea, Ben-Artzi approached Eban, and without revealing the plan to capture Eichmann, told him the same cover story: El Al planned to try out the new Britannia plane and check the feasibility of opening a direct line between Israel and South America, and saw this as a golden opportunity to bring an official delegation to Argentina on behalf of Israel to participate in the celebrations there. Eban jumped at the opportunity to 'contribute to improving relations with Argentina' and enthusiastically accepted the offer. At the explicit instruction of Harel, Zorea was also not given any hint about the real purpose of the flight. For obvious reasons, Harel considered it particularly important to ensure total secrecy and compartmentalisation as far as this operation was concerned, sharing information only with those who absolutely had to know. I guess he also did not want an Israeli minister to be wittingly involved in an operation to abduct an Argentinian citizen, whether the operation succeeded or failed.

From that moment on, we stuck to a strict schedule, which revolved around 20 May. It was clear that the plane had to land in Argentina at least a few days before the festivities to allow optimal time for the operators. Preparations shifted into high gear, with frequent consultations on a daily basis with Avrum Shalom, Zvi Malchin, a master of creative tricks, and of course with Aharoni, who returned from Argentina knowing the area where the abduction would take place like the back of his hand. At that stage, although it had not yet been finally decided that Eichmann's capture would take place near his home, we tended to favour this from the start. The house, as mentioned, was in a remote suburb, about thirty kilometres from the city centre.

Aharoni explained the lie of the land to me on a map: 'Here's Route 202: this is his bus stop, line number 203, which he takes to work in the morning and takes back home in the evening. Here's the turn to Garibaldi Street. Here there are railway tracks on a small hill, 100–200 metres from the house. This is our observation post. On weekdays, Eichmann leaves the house a little before 7 in the morning and returns around 7.30 in the evening.'

Based on Aharoni's inputs, I planned three options for the abduction: the first, near Ricardo Klement's home. The second, somewhere on the way from home to work or from work to home. Third, in his workplace, although we still did not know where he worked or what he did for a living.

Based on the three options, and assuming that the abduction would likely be discovered while it was under way or shortly thereafter,

Rafi Eitan during a hike to the historical site of Masada in 1946.

Rafi Eitan's parents, Noah and Yehudit Hantman, 1922.

Rafi (*centre*) with friends at Givat Hashlosha, 1942.

Back row from right, Noah Hantman, his wife Yehudit, Elisheva; *front row, from right*, Rafi's brothers Oded and Yehiam – known as Ami (holding Aza the dog).

Rafi (*left*) and his brother Oded in the Negev during the War of Independence.

On holiday in Cyprus with Avrum Shalom, in their early days in the Security Service.

Avrum Shalom and Rafi in the early 1950s.

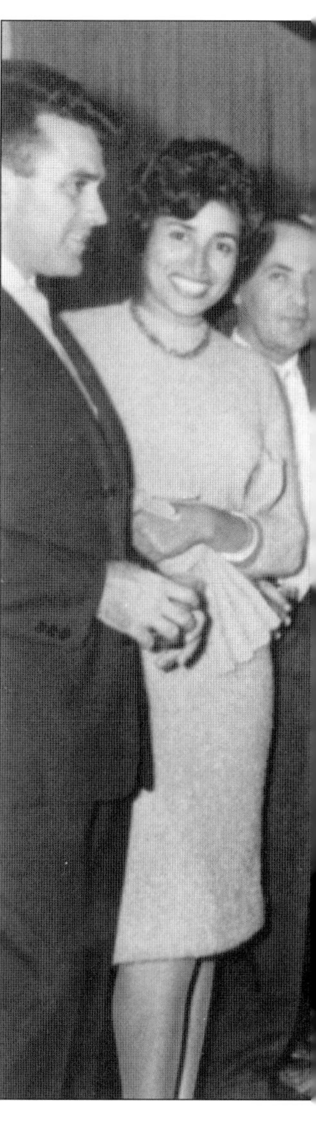

Rafi, Zvika Malchin and Avrum Shalom socialising. Miriam is to the right of Rafi.

Most of the team involved in the capture of Eichmann at a gathering with Prime Minister David Ben-Gurion to acknowledge their work. Rafi is to the right of the Prime Minister and to the left (also in glasses) is Avrum Shalom. The tall figure behind Ben-Gurion is Yaakov Gat, one of the four who actually abducted Eichmann.

(*From right*) Amos Manor, Paula Ben-Gurion, Zvika Malchin, and Rafi at the Ben-Gurion family home.

'General' Morris Cohen, who helped Rafi develop contacts with China, at his home in Manchester, 1966.

Rafi and Yehuda Segev inspecting damage after an incident at their Tropi Fish business.

Proceedings at a mock trial of the Nazi doctor Josef Mengele at Yad Vashem, 1985. The seated panel includes Rafi (*left*), Nuremberg prosecutor Telford Taylor (*4th left*) and Nazi hunter Simon Wiesenthal (*5th left*).

Amiram Nir (*right*), who replaced Rafi as counter-terrorism adviser to the prime minister, with Rafi and his deputy Gideon Mahnayimi (*left*).

Ariel Sharon (*right*) during his time as Industry Minister, and Rafi, chairman of Israel Chemicals, with potash factory director Arieh Shahar.

Rafi with Lily Sharon at the Sharon family home, March 1987.

I set up a scaled topographic model of the Eichmann home and its immediate vicinity at our 'camp' in Abu Kabir: Garibaldi Street and San Fernando, Main Road 202 simulated by a road near us. A nearby bus station served as a simulation for the bus stop on line 203, and the Tel Aviv–Jerusalem railway line passed not far from the 'camp.' In this way, we practised for the abduction. Using the detailed maps of Buenos Aires and the San Fernando neighbourhood that Aharoni provided, and a training method I developed at the time, we also learned to get around Buenos Aires city, which none of us, other than Aharoni, had ever visited. But it didn't help Malchin. His ability to navigate was dismal and he could never find his way around big cities. He used to say, 'Bring me to any door and I will break into it, but bring me to it.'

A very important exercise during the preparations was 'kidnapping' a person in the heart of Tel Aviv, at noon, to ensure our proficiency at this. We did it on Dizengoff Street, then the main street of Tel Aviv. We chose two different people, who walked a regular route (we knew this from following them). In each case, our vehicle stopped next to the man, two people got out of it, and said to him, 'Hello sir, we are from the police, come with us.' Without waiting for his answer, the two pushed him into the back seat of the car, not roughly, but in a way that prevented him from resisting. The 'kidnappers' sat on either side of him, and the car drove off. In both cases we did not encounter any opposition from the 'kidnappee'. After a short drive we explained who we were, why we had seized him ('operational training', without specifying, of course, what operation), apologised and released the man. In both cases, the 'kidnappees' were employees of Mossad or Shin Bet, whose discretion we could count on. Innocent passers-by might have called the police, and we wanted to avoid that.

We knew we would have to put Eichmann to sleep before boarding the plane. Following the bitter lesson from the case of Alexander Israel, ensuring that Eichmann would not be harmed by the anaesthetic was an issue that preoccupied me. I knew how important it was for him to arrive in Israel alive, without any physical or mental injury, fit for trial. I decided that this time, too, we would be assisted by Dr Yonah Elian, the senior anaesthetist at Tel Hashomer, who also assisted in the Israel affair. To train myself, I asked Elian if I could observe a surgery where an anaesthetic was used. He let me into a surgery, in full gear, and introduced me as Dr Flatfoot to his colleagues. For the abduction operation, he gave me detailed instructions on the equipment he would require. Among other things, he asked for more than double the amount of oxygen that might typically be needed when used on land.

At the same time, I was busy forming my team. Harel knew I would not go ahead with the operation if I could not pick the people I thought were best for it, and left choosing them to me. The first one I wanted was obvious: Shalom. He was a lieutenant in the operations unit, and I had known him from his days in the Palmach. I knew that if something went wrong he could step in for me with no difficulty. In addition, Shalom was born in Vienna, and immigrated to Israel when he was eleven years old so he spoke Austrian German like Eichmann, who was born in Germany but moved with his family when he was eight to Linz, Austria. The choice of Aharoni was also self-evident: he had pushed for the operation to locate Eichmann, advanced it and brought the essential information from Argentina. The capture of Eichmann would not have been possible without him. Like Shalom, Aharoni's mother-tongue was German. His rank was equal to mine, but in the operation to capture Eichmann, he was subordinate to me. If he had no problem with it, I certainly didn't. This was the spirit that Harel instilled in Shin Bet.

Malchin was the best field man I'd ever met, a fighter in the full sense of the word: physical, strong, penetrating, adept at disguises and able to break through any obstacle, always able to solve whatever problem presented itself. There was nothing he couldn't find a way around. Every Purim he would disguise himself differently, then go to visit his mother, and she would not recognise him. She would sit at home, waiting for him and each time he'd show up in a way that fooled her.

Yaakov Gat was the administrative director of Division 10. A man who focused on the fine details, he never forgot things, everything was always shipshape and efficient. I knew that every detail of the operation he would be charged with would be tested in every possible way and that he would help me prepare at least one contingency, if not more, in case something went wrong unexpectedly.

Moshe Tavor headed the mechanical department of Mossad. A technical expert with golden hands, he was Mossad's Number 1 lock-picker. He was a mountain of man, from whom a punch could be fatal. He had served in the Jewish Brigade and at the end of the war joined Nakam (a vigilante group that sought revenge against Nazis by seeking them out and killing them). Several SS men paid with their lives in an encounter between their skulls and Tavor's fist.

I have already explained my choice of Elian as the anaesthetist. Harel decided that as the commander in charge, he too must be present, from the beginning to the end of the operation. It was not my decision.

In addition to the seven members of the abduction team, additional team members dispersed in Buenos Aires were also chosen: Yaakov Meidad, who rented us two houses, two apartments and three cars. He was a huge asset to an operation of this kind. Not only did he speak many languages with absolute mastery, but he was also a consummate actor, who knew how to adapt his identity to each language he spoke. When he spoke French no one would suspect that he was not French by birth, when spoke German, he seemed totally German, and so on. As well as Meidad, the team included 'locals', the historian Ephraim Ilani and the military attaché Yitzhak Elron.

I put a lot of thought into the team's documentation. We had to prepare various types of documents for each person: a passport for travel to Argentina, a passport or papers for use in Argentina before the operation, ID for use at the time of the operation, and documents for their departure or escape. All team members were provided with diplomatic credentials and driving licences from foreign countries. I carefully selected the foreign countries we used: I wanted to ensure that in the event that something went wrong and our men were arrested for any reason by local police, who were very much present on the streets of Buenos Aires in the aftermath of the 1955 military coup that had overthrown President Perón, our team would have an identity that would give them a chance of extracting themselves as smoothly as possible.

All this complex and extensive documentation was perfectly prepared by Shalom Weiss, our expert for this sort of thing, codenamed 'Danny' for this operation, a codename which stuck for the rest of his life. He used, of course, the documents Aharoni brought, according to the instructions I gave him. Harel ordered us to add Weiss to our team (although he did not have a role in the capture itself) in case we needed any additional documentation while we were in Argentina.

Another addition to our team, was Yehudit Nessyahu, She was born in Holland, worked for Mossad and took part in various operations, including bringing Jews from Morocco to Israel. She knew Dutch, English, German, French and Spanish. Harel assigned her to manage the house where we were supposed to stay before and after the abduction – for about ten days. The cover story, in case neighbours became curious, was that she and Meidad were a couple who had just moved to the area and were settling in.

Eleven people came from Israel, including Harel, and there were the two 'locals'. If I am not mistaken, together with the El Al employees who helped in the operation, only twenty-six people were directly involved in capturing Eichmann and bringing him to Israel.

The Britannia plane was scheduled to land in Buenos Aires on 11 May 1960, and stay in the Argentinian capital until 20 or 21 May. Based on this schedule, I planned the operation to capture Eichmann ten days before the Britannia landing in Buenos Aires. This operational decision obliged us to keep Eichmann in hiding for ten days or more if we were successful in capturing him. Why did I think this was right?

First, because when I plan an operation, especially one in a foreign country, I consider the possibility of failure on the first attempt. In such a case, I want to leave myself an option for a second attempt. Of course, it is not possible to try a second attempt immediately after a failed first attempt, so one needs to plan for a leeway of several days between attempts.

I asked myself, and consulted with my people, how dangerous it would be to keep Eichmann in a hideout for a few days, until we smuggled him out to Israel by plane. Our conclusion was that although there was a risk involved in such choice, it was not a big one.

We figured that if the abduction itself passed quietly, without notice by police or passers-by, the chances the family would contact the police were slim. We knew that Eichmann – if it was Eichmann, and we were almost 100 per cent sure it was – was hiding under a false identity as Ricardo Klement. In contrast, his wife was going under her maiden identity, Veronica Liebel. If she turned to the police, the police would assume that she was reporting the absence of an unmarried man with whom she was having an affair, who had decided to skip out on her, perhaps because of an affair with another woman. It seemed highly unlikely that she would tell the police her husband was a wanted war criminal whom she suspected had been abducted or murdered.

We knew that there were hundreds, if not more, former Nazis living in Argentina, and that Eichmann may have been in contact with them. It later emerged that in the years immediately following World War II, there was an organisation called ODESSA (acronym for Organisation der ehemaligen SS-Angehörigen which means Organisation of Former SS Members), which helped Nazi criminals hide, disappear and flee abroad, mainly to South American countries. But suppose the Eichmann family turned to these Nazis, what could they do? The chances of them getting to us were very close to zero.

Our more serious concern was police intervention, either at the time of capture or in the days that followed. I decided that in such a case, I would bind myself to Eichmann, identify him as a wanted war criminal, and demand access to the Israeli ambassador to Argentina. In fact, our most serious concern was that Klement or those around him would feel some sign of impending danger, and if he was really Eichmann, or any other Nazi, he would immediately flee.

Fortunately, none of these concerns materialised.

From Aharoni's surveillance report, we knew that Eichmann stayed at home on weekends, but we couldn't be 100 per cent sure. We assumed that if we could not capture him on the first weekend, we would have to wait at least another week for the next opportunity. This is what led me to conclude that we needed to be all set to go at least ten days before the plane was available to bring Eichmann to Israel.

Then there was a serious issue that threw off our feverish plans. At the request of the Argentinian authorities, the date of Britannia's landing in Buenos Aires was postponed from 11 to 19 May. Eichmann's departure to Israel was scheduled for the night of 20/21 May. I was still in Israel at the time of this upset and made the necessary changes to our plan, including arranging for all of us to get to Argentina on commercial flights.

On 15 April, we began dispatching our team. The first to arrive in Buenos Aires were Shalom and Meidad. They handled logistics, rented apartments and safehouses, and large American cars. They also began surveillance to learn of the daily routine and habits of Ricardo Klement. Immediately after them came Tavor, who prepared secret compartments in apartments, houses and cars. Harel arrived in Buenos Aires on 1 May, and immediately began meeting with staff members, each time at a different café. I do not remember exactly when Aharoni, Gat and Dr Elian arrived. The last to set out were Malchin and myself. Talmor remained in Israel as temporary chief of operations in my absence, and joined us four days before the plane took off back to Israel.

My and Malchin's flight to Switzerland was scheduled to leave in the morning of 4 May. Two days earlier I had gone to Kibbutz Afikim, where Miriam lived. She was not yet my wife, but there was no doubt that we would marry. I told Miriam about the planned operation. The next day, I returned to Tel Aviv, and went to dinner at my parents' home in Ramat Hasharon, and invited Malchin along. My parents were used to hosting my friends and colleagues. Their neighbour, psychologist Dr David Rudy, happened to join us that evening for dinner, which lasted late into the night. At one point, I said to Malchin that we really should leave because we had a twenty-hour flight ahead of us the next morning. My parents did not know where and why we were flying and did not ask. When the news of Eichmann's abduction came out, Dr Rudy called me and said, 'When I heard that Eichmann was brought to Israel, I knew that you were the one who brought him, because I remembered that you talked about a twenty-hour flight.'

In the morning, Malchin and I set out for Buenos Aires, with stopovers in Zurich and Geneva. Thanks to my studies in London, I spoke fluent English, but Malchin did not. This caused an awkward moment at passport control during our transit in Zurich, when a border policeman asked Malchin something, and I, standing behind him, answered in his place. Luckily for us, the next question was in German, a language that Malchin, a native of Poland, understood. He answered in broken German, with bits of Yiddish, and that satisfied the policeman. In transit in Zurich, I also met up with Zvi Zohar who exchanged a large sum of dollars for me into pesos, the currency of Argentina.

By the time we arrived in Buenos Aires, each of us already knew the name and address of the hotel chosen for him. Malchin was sent to one hotel, I to another. There was a mistake made in this matter, and it was Harel's. I wanted us to go to large, first-class hotels, with a lot of foreigners and different languages, where we could fit in easily and unobtrusively. For some reason, Harel believed that in small hotels, there was less of a danger that someone might know or recognise us, so I ended up in a small family hotel, with only about thirty rooms. I ran into a problem regarding the foreign passport I was carrying, but managed to get out of it.

I changed hotels in Buenos Aires several times from the time of my arrival until Eichmann was captured and brought to a safe house, switching to different neighbourhoods as needed for the circumstances.

My first task in Buenos Aires was to meet up with Harel and the team, inspect the area, complete the capture plan, and check the apartments and safehouses we rented in the periphery of the city. Immediately I arrived, Harel and I disagreed over a technical matter, but one with operational implications. Harel moved from café to café throughout the day, meeting with one or two members of our team at each café. He thought that this way he would be able to exercise 'remote control' with an update from whomever he met and pass on instructions. I preferred to save time and concentrate our efforts by meeting the whole staff once a day in a safehouse. I reckoned that as long as we were not breaking any laws, we should behave as a group of tourists would, and transition to another *modus operandi* only once the operation got under way. In later operations, Harel and I had similar disagreements and conflicts. I tended to plan operations down to the smallest detail well ahead of time with a very limited number of subordinates, so that when an operation I planned was launched, each team member already knew what his role was at any given moment and in any situation. By contrast, Harel liked to deploy a large operations unit – sometimes dozens of people – and do the planning on the fly, and in real time. Only once people were deployed in the field, did he start figuring out the final execution plan. Naturally, this method required improvisation and moment-to-moment changes. Harel saw this as an advantage, because of its flexibility. I saw it as a disadvantage. I considered improvisation inferior to planning, something to fall back on when there was no other choice.

I also vehemently opposed Harel's frequent meetings in cafés, which I considered highly unnecessary, and personally refrained from attending. It also bothered me that instead of there being one field commander for the operation, as is customary and proper, there were two in Buenos Aires: the overall commander of the Security Services and the head of Mossad Harel, and myself, head of Division 10, the operational division of the Security Services and the commander of operations for Mossad. To Harel's credit it should be noted that he did not interfere in tactical issues, and that after I complained about this in one of our meetings, he proposed a division of labour between the two of us: 'The capture – on you; the transport of Eichmann to Israel – on me.' I gladly accepted this offer.

Chapter 12

The *Dybbuk* is in Our Hands!

We had ten days to prepare on the spot for the operation. Ten days is quite a bit, but also not much for such an operation, and those days were very busy. Operators are supposed to know the city in which they operate. They come for just a short time but must know the place as if they were born there. Aharoni, who had spent two months in Buenos Aires, was the only one on the team who really knew the city; the rest of us had to study it.

Buenos Aires was already a huge city. At the time, it had a population of about six million inhabitants (including the suburbs). Today (2018) the number is more than double – 13.1 million. For the operation, we had safehouses and apartments scattered throughout the city, including in the suburbs. We studied maps, marked focal points, toured around to get to know every alley and path leading to our safehouses. More than that: we needed to know the exact characteristics of every street: how wide it was, how many vehicles could pass through it, when was traffic heavy, where were there often traffic jams, what roads to use if there was a traffic jam, which roads were closed for repairs. We marked our maps with first, second, third, fourth options, then went out to the field to make sure that our drawings matched reality.

In the days before the capture, Aharoni and Shalom continued to observe the house on Garibaldi Street from a position on the embankment of the nearby railway track, overlooking the house. Several times I also participated in these observations, which were intended to verify Ricardo Klement's daily habits.

On one occasion, when Klement was on his way from the bus stop to his house, Shalom gave me the binoculars, and for the first time I saw the man clearly. Was I excited? Not at all. At such times, I have no room for emotion. My mind is totally focused on the goal, on the object, on the person as an item in the operational plan. All emotion, all sensitivity, any hint of excitement gets pushed away.

Klement had a regular route in the morning from his home to the nearest bus stop to catch the No. 203 and in the evening from the stop to home, about 150 metres. Near the bus stop was a small kiosk, and from there Klement would walk through a field to his house. Whenever we observed him, he came home from work at 7.30 p.m. exactly. German. On the weekends he stayed at home. We never saw him leave the house in the evenings.

The house on Garibaldi Street was quite small, with two or at most three rooms, and rather shabby. Unlike other Nazis, who had managed to smuggle out money and valuables looted from occupied territories, Eichmann apparently fled to Argentina without financial resources. We did not find an indication that his house was connected to the electricity grid, although the neighbourhood already had infrastructure for this. The garden was fenced, with a small vegetable plot in one corner.

Not only in the case of the capture of Eichmann, I have been asked and have also asked myself, how I neutralise my emotions during an operation. I don't know the answer. Although I understood the significance of Eichmann's capture to the history of Israel and the Jewish people, and was aware of its moral significance, the truth is that I was not excited or moved when I looked through binoculars at Eichmann for the first time. I did not see him as a mass murderer, but as an object of an operation that I had planned and was responsible for successfully executing. For half a day, I surveyed the area on foot, chose the ambush site, and drove around to check out alternative escape routes on Route 198 and Main Road 202.

Malchin and Aharoni constantly argued over the optimal observation point and I took it in my stride that this sort of argument often arises in such operations, but I knew that each one was motivated by the desire to ensure the operation succeeded. What angered me at the time was the impression, even before the capture, that Harel was setting out his stall to be the hero of this story. Aharoni shared my impression, and this was indeed Harel's account in the first edition of his book, *The House on Garibaldi Street*, in which he eliminated practically any mention of our part in the operation. Only in subsequent editions did he make some effort to redress the injustice.

To fit El Al's new schedule, the capture was supposed to take place on 10 May, but at the last minute I decided to postpone the execution to 11 May for three reasons. First, on 9 May, we conducted our tenth observation of the house, ostensibly the last observation before the operation. But on the bridge over the road to San Fernando, a policeman stopped us and asked us to take him and an injured motorcyclist lying on the road to hospital (the policeman was on foot). Of course we said yes. As a result, we missed our chance to observe Klement's return home and then I had to change the car, for fear that the policeman would recognise it. Second, the team was exhausted from the stress and strain of previous days, and I wanted to make sure they got some rest before the operation. Third, I wanted to tour the area one last time, to set the plan firmly in my mind and iron out every last detail. I told Harel and he accepted my decision; no one on the team objected either.

On the day before the capture, the team held a meeting. Malchin took the lead in making sure we were set with all the details, and most of his ideas and recommendations were accepted.

On the evening of 11 May, we left for San Fernando in two cars. Shalom drove a Chevrolet, Aharoni drove a Buick. Gat and Dr Elian were in Shalom's car. We did not plan to anaesthetise Eichmann during or immediately after the capture, but Elian was in the car in case Eichmann went berserk and had to be sedated. In the second car, next to Aharoni, sat Tavor, and behind them, Malchin and me.

We arrived at the operation site at 6.50 p.m. The two cars were parked about 100 metres apart, on opposite sides of the road. Shalom's

Chevrolet was on Route 202, close to the bus stop. He turned on the high beams, their intense light making it difficult for anyone walking towards the car to see who was inside. The Buick was parked on Garibaldi Street, a few feet from the gate to the Klement home. This was the vehicle into which we planned to put Eichmann.

Malchin stood by the Buick, on the driver's side with the bonnet raised, as if he was dealing with an engine problem. This was what we wanted Eichmann, or any passer-by who happened along, to see; the high beams from the Buick were also lit.

None of us spoke Spanish, but there were German speakers among us. We did not have radios, we did not carry weapons. We did not come to talk, nor did we come to kill. We came to capture a man, to bring him to trial.

At 7.30 p.m. the No. 203 bus arrived at the stop. We tensed up, but no one got off and then, suddenly, there was a glitch. A cyclist stopped beside Malchin, who was bent over with his head under the bonnet, fiddling with the engine. The man offered to help – in Spanish. Malchin tried to get rid of him, explaining with his hands that he didn't need help. It took a minute or two to convince the cyclist to leave us to our own devices. We breathed a sigh of relief when he did. In retrospect, it was a mistake not to bring along a Spanish speaker. Fortunately, this did not thwart the operation.

Another 203 bus passed by, without Eichmann debarking. It was already 8.00 p.m.'Rafi, it's not working out for today,' Aharoni told me. 'Let's leave and come back another time.'

'We're staying,' I replied.

At 8.05, a third 203 bus arrived. Eichmann got off and began walking home.

According to the plan, Malchin was to approach Eichmann, say '*Momentito, señor*' ('Just a moment, sir'), and attack him from the front, grabbing one shoulder towards him, pushing the other shoulder back, and then dragging him to the car. At that moment, Tavor was supposed to get out of our car, close the bonnet, grab Eichmann and help push him into the car.

The capture was executed with a slight departure from the plan. As Eichmann walked home, Aharoni, who was sitting behind the wheel, noticed that he had a hand in his pocket, indicating he might be hiding a gun. Aharoni managed to alert Malchin to this. As a result, Malchin adapted his attack strategy to first immobilise Eichmann's hands.

Malchin said '*Momentito, señor*,' Eichmann recoiled slightly. Malchin grabbed both Eichmann's hands, and they rolled together on the ground at the side of the road and fell into a shallow ditch – no more than twenty centimetres deep. I immediately got out of the car and called Tavor to get out too. He grabbed Eichmann by the legs and I grabbed him by the head. Malchin was still holding Eichmann by both hands, so we dragged him into our car, which was four or five metres away. Eichmann tried to shout out, but his voice sounded strangled, like the growl of a wounded animal. We dragged him to the back seat, his head resting on my knees and his body sprawled on the floor, and I held my hand over his mouth. Malchin sat on the other side of him in the back seat.

The capture took less than a minute. Our target was now breathing heavily. As agreed in advance, Aharoni told him in German, 'If you keep quiet, nothing bad will happen to you.'

'*Jawohl*,' was the trapped man's answer, and when I heard this, any remaining doubts dissipated. I knew he was the man we wanted. *Jawohl* is not just 'Yes' in German, but a 'Yes' said to a superior, to someone with a higher rank than yours. Even at this moment, Eichmann remained an obedient German.

In silence, we drove along the planned route. After more than a mile, we reached a rendezvous point we had arranged in case one of the cars lost the other. 'Stop. Change,' I ordered Aharoni, in English, so that Eichmann would not immediately recognise us as Israelis. Tavor got out and changed the car number plate. Shalom did the same with the other car, where Gat and Dr Elian sat.

With special biker glasses I had had adapted so that he could not see out of them, I now covered the eyes of the '*dybbuk*' – that's what we called Eichmann throughout the operation. I laid him down on the floor and covered him with a blanket, but kept it slightly above his face so he could breathe freely. He mustn't die in our hands, God forbid, like Captain Israel did.

From this position, I slipped a hand under his shirt and felt across his torso. I knew exactly what I was looking for: a scar in the lower abdomen from an appendectomy he underwent as a teenager. The scar was where it should have been. I looked at Malchin and held out my hand to shake his. He understood my intention: the first phase of the operation had been accomplished successfully. 'The *dybbuk* is in our hands.'

After changing the number plates, Shalom led the way and our car followed. We passed a police checkpoint, but were not asked to stop. Then we reached a level crossing, just as a train was passing, and had to wait long minutes in a large convoy of cars. The drive to the 'castle' safehouse took about fifty minutes and passed without incident.

At 8:55 p.m. we entered the safehouse where Meidad was ready to open the gate for us. The garage door was open, and both cars entered. Malchin pulled Eichmann by the legs, I pushed him from behind, and once he stood up, the biker glasses still over his eyes, I held him by the hand and led him up the indoor stairs from the garage to the prepared detention room, one floor up, above the garage. Adjacent to the room were a toilet and a shower. The windows were already covered with thick blankets to muffle any possible shouts. In addition, we had removed all light bulbs, except one on the ceiling, and another in the toilet. There was no furniture in the room except an iron bed with a mattress, with sheets and blankets. Handcuffs and a rope were also prepared to tie Eichmann to the bed. Shalom and I stripped him naked as the day he was born, examined the scars on his body and his blood type, which was tattooed under his armpit as was customary for all SS men. The tattoo was blurry since he had tried to make it disappear while in an American POW camp. Although I had no doubt about his identity, I insisted on using a measuring tape to check his height and head circumference – fifty-six centimetres, as written in his SS file. All the signs verified his identity as Adolf Eichmann.

Gradually, all the members of the capture team entered the room, but we still had not exchanged a single word. Only when, as agreed, I mentioned 'the man at hand' did Aharoni begin an initial interrogation of Eichmann, who was still naked and standing on his feet. The first question he asked him was, 'What is your name?' The first reply was, 'Otto Heninger', one of the two fictitious names Eichmann used after the war, when he escaped from an American POW camp. 'Your real name,' Aharoni insisted, and he replied, 'Ricardo Klement', his name in Argentina. When Aharoni persisted a third time, he finally gave his real name: Adolf Otto Eichmann, and also his SS number. Immediately afterwards, he asked for a glass of red wine. We didn't have any wine, so we couldn't oblige. I later asked myself if we would have granted it if we had it. I did not have an unequivocal answer.

Then I asked the doctor to check him out. Our main fear was that he would try to commit suicide with a poison pill – cyanide or strychnine – hidden in his mouth, as Heinrich Himmler did when he was captured a few days after the end of World War II by a British military unit (whose officers included Chaim Herzog, later Israel's sixth president). Or as Hermann Göring did the day before he was to be hanged along with other Nuremberg criminals. Dr Elian probed his mouth, found nothing, and later stated that Eichmann was in good health. When the medical check-up was completed, we allowed Eichmann to wear clothes, and I signalled to Aharoni to continue the interrogation.

Eichmann's initial interrogation lasted about an hour. The main thing we wanted to know at that point was whether he had connections with Nazi organisations in South America that might seek him out, once his absence was discovered. We also tried to find out how he thought his wife and sons would react to the fact that he had not returned home from work. It was only at this point that we learned that he worked at the Mercedes-Benz dealership in Buenos

Aires, which employed him in their spare parts warehouse. This was the life of one of the main people responsible for the extermination of six million Jews: getting up early in the morning, going to work on the bus, arranging cardboard boxes on shelves, taking out parts according to instructions, returning in the evening by bus, to a house without electricity.

We asked him about Dr Josef Mengele – prosecutor Fritz Bauer had told us he was in Argentina – and demanded that he reveal Mengele's Buenos Aires address to us. Harel had a big appetite. He hoped to capture Mengele as well and bring him to Israel on the same flight with Eichmann. Eichmann first claimed he had no idea who Mengele was, then admitted that the name 'sounded familiar', but continued to insist that he had no idea about the whereabouts of the satanic doctor from Auschwitz. In the following days, quite a few arguments arouse between Harel and myself on this matter. Harel wanted to invest most of our efforts in capturing Mengele. I argued that we should invest all resources in guarding Eichmann and preparing to smuggle him to Israel, and that diverting resources to capture Mengele could lead the entire operation to fail.

Eichmann was very tense under interrogation, but with characteristic obedience he complied with every instruction given to him.

I scheduled round-the-clock guard duty on him, as well as stringent guarding arrangements in the backyard. True, we assumed that his family members would not call the police, so as not to be forced to reveal 'Klement's' true identity to the Argentinian authorities. Although the risk was low, we could not rule it out entirely. We also did not know the neighbours near our safehouse and, as with any operation, we had to take into account the possibility that an innocent passer-by might see something that seemed suspicious and contact the police. So we stayed inside and kept a look out.

While the initial interrogation was going on, Harel sat in a downtown café waiting for updates. I had agreed with him in advance that if the capture was successful, we would first interrogate Eichmann, and only after this was completed would I send someone to inform him. However, if there were any complications, I would let him know immediately. Later, when we returned to Israel, Harel admitted that he had endured several very tense hours, and only breathed a first sigh of relief after that.

It was only at midnight, about four hours after the capture, that I sent Shalom and Aharoni to update Harel and inform him of the success of the first stage of the operation. I did not go myself, and not only because I thought it was my duty, as the commander of the operation, to stay in the most important place – in the 'castle' safehouse with Eichmann. I admit that I was reluctant to meet Harel, both because of our arguments over the best *modus operandi* in the days leading up to the capture and because our conflict over Mengele had already erupted.

As soon as he arrived in Buenos Aires, Harel contacted the Argentinian police on some pretext and asked if they had any information about Mengele. To his surprise, and to ours, the police gave him an address. It turned out that Mengele had lived in the Argentinian capital without hiding his identity. Harel did not hesitate and sent David, the Mossad's representative in Argentina, to check this out, but David found that although Mengele had lived at the address until recently, he had left. Based on this, Harel wanted Aharoni to seek out neighbours in hopes of learning Mengele's current whereabouts. I strongly opposed this, firmly convinced that conducting a second operation of this kind could jeopardise our main objective – to catch Eichmann and bring him back to Israel alive. 'Look for Mengele if you want,' I told him. 'But don't complicate our main operation which we are advancing in the best possible way. Every member of the operations team is essential and has a specific role. Only after we get Eichmann to Israel will it make sense, perhaps, to think about capturing Mengele.'

I further argued that, from a moral and historical point of view, it was sufficient for Israel to prosecute Eichmann alone. If, afterwards, we found Mengele and were able to bring him to Israel, fine. If not, perhaps we could simply kill him. But bringing Eichmann to justice in Israel was our stated objective, and nothing should threaten that.

With his usual punctiliousness, Harel was silent for a moment, then immediately moved on to another subject. Knowing him as well as I did, it was an unmistakable sign that he expected I would eventually see the light and 'come over to his side of the fence' as he used to say in other controversies between us. So I was in no hurry to meet him because I feared now, in light of the success of the capture, that he would resume the debate over Mengele. Indeed, Harel persisted in instructing Aharoni to look for ways to locate Mengele. I did not like this at all, because Aharoni was Eichmann's chief interrogator, questioning him for hours every day. But I had no choice, and released Aharoni – but only him – for this mission. Aharoni checked, observed, tried to extract information from neighbours. As is well known, his efforts did not yield the desired results.

We stayed locked up in our 'castle' for nine days. On the second day we were joined by Yehudit Nessyahu, who landed in Buenos Aires on the night of the capture. Harel had her join us with the expectation that she would keep the place clean, cook and function as a kind of housekeeper. He probably assumed that any woman would know how to do these sorts of things. Not only was she not a good cook (to say the least) but all of us were more adept in the kitchen than she was. So we men prepared the food.

Only two people, Malchin and I, sat with Eichmann most of the day. I slept very little during those days. I checked up on the guards constantly. Eichmann was tied to the bed, but enjoyed relative freedom of movement – inside the bed. We told him to let us know whenever he needed the toilet, and the door was left open, with Malchin or me watching him.

For the first three days after the capture, Eichmann suffered from severe constipation, perhaps due to the tension of his situation. Malchin or I, who accompanied him had to watch and hear his desperate efforts to defecate. The problem was finally solved when Dr Eilan gave him a laxative and instructed that he be given light meals: porridge, vegetables and chicken soup. These also ensured that, if necessary, he could be anaesthetised without risk to his life. I prepared a plan in case of an emergency – such as police suddenly appearing at the safehouse – to anaesthetise Eichmann and hide him in a special concealed compartment built for this purpose.

Malchin drew a portrait of Eichmann. He had a talent for drawing, but at the time did not dream that one day he would become an artist whose paintings would be in demand. He drew Eichmann's likeness for many years in his works. Malchin did not have any real contact with Eichmann. He spoke a bit with Eichmann in a language he might have thought was German, but was actually Yiddish. Usually, Eichmann understood him. But all serious interrogation of Eichmann was conducted solely by Aharoni, and in my presence.

Eichmann had no difficulty guessing the identity of his captors, and already during the first interrogation he uttered the words to us of '*Shema Yisrael*' (one of the most recited Jewish prayers, known by its first words, 'Hear, Oh Israel'). He said that as part of his role in the SS, he learned the words in Hebrew from Judaism lessons he took in Berlin from Rabbi Leo Baeck, the leader of the German Jewish community. We found it quite sickening to hear one of the main perpetrators of the murder of millions of Jews say the words of '*Shema Yisrael*', but it soon became clear that apart from these few words, he did not know Hebrew. On the other hand, he showed a familiarity with Jewish life and customs.

Before we left for Argentina, Attorney General Haim Cohen prepared a document with some main points which he asked us to try and persuade Eichmann to sign. It included a declaration that Eichmann was willing to come to Israel, of his own free will and without coercion, and to be prosecuted once an attorney was made available to him and he was given access to all relevant documents and materials needed for his defence. Cohen explained to us that this document might help us, if we were caught in Argentina with Eichmann. Aharoni sat down with Eichmann and together they drafted the affidavit. Eichmann asked for twenty-four hours, and the next day signed it, without any coercion on our part. (Unfortunately, Malchin claimed in a conversation with Harel that he was the one who convinced Eichmann to sign the affidavit, and later even wrote it in a book. The truth is that Aharoni, and he alone, was responsible for this achievement.)

At the time, Eichmann seemed enchanted by Aharoni, so much so that when he signed the affidavit, he told Aharoni that he was willing to come to Israel on his own volition, no need to guard him, no need to take him there. 'Tell me when to arrive, give me something to wear, some money and a plane ticket and I will report to Israel,' he said. I believed him, though of course, we had no intention of taking him up on it. He was eager to do whatever Aharoni asked. Eichmann knew how to please his master, and now Aharoni was his master. As we continued to talk to him about this, it became clear to us that he was afraid that we intended to fly him to Israel in a small plane that might fail to make it across the Atlantic. It never occurred to him that he would arrive in Israel on a regular flight, in one of the most sophisticated passenger planes in the world.

On 15 May, four days after the capture, Harel visited the safehouse and the two of us had heated arguments about two matters. First, as I've already mentioned, I strongly opposed his decision to take Aharoni from me and divert him to the task of trying to find Mengele. Now I fought his demand to release more of our team for that task. I explained that even their leaving our 'castle' was dangerous. Not only that: sniffing around for Mengele could attract attention and bring down our entire operation.

But Harel was unconvinced. One of Mengele's neighbours told Aharoni that Mengele had gone on holiday and would return in a few days. (The neighbour was wrong, or misled Aharoni. Mengele never returned to that address in Buenos Aires. It is now known that as early as 1959 he left Argentina, moved to Paraguay, and soon settled in Brazil, where he lived until his death in 1979.) Harel tried to convince me not to forgo the chance to catch another senior Nazi criminal and bring him to Israel.

To get Harel off our backs, I said to him: 'You know what? You take Eichmann to Israel on an El Al plane, and most of the crew with you. I will stay here with Zvika [Malchin] and Avrum [Shalom], and wait until Mengele returns from his holiday. We will capture him, lock him up and bring him back to Israel by ship. Of course, for that to work, we must keep secret the fact that Eichmann is in our hands. Obviously, if Mengele hears that we have Eichmann, he will flee.'

Harel looked sceptical but said nothing. Then I said something that rekindled the argument between us. 'Tell me, Isser, how will we take care of the family?'

'Which family?' he asked.

'Eichmann's family,' I replied. 'Especially the little boy [six-year-old Ricardo, born in Argentina]. The other three sons are grown and can take care of themselves. But we have to take care, arrange financial support for the wife and the little boy, because we took from them the father who supports them. It will show the world how moral we are, how different we are from the Nazis.'

I must admit that I raised this issue partly to instigate a clash with Harel, who angered me quite a lot during the operation. As I knew he would, Harel would have none of it, presented counter-arguments, and a moral–philosophical debate developed between us. But to his credit, in his book on Eichmann's capture, *The House on Garibaldi Street,* he praised me for my position and expressed admiration for 'this *sabra*, Rafi Eitan, who revealed his moral-value side'.

What happened with Harel in Buenos Aires was typical for us and exemplified my attitude towards him. I expressed great appreciation for him from the beginning of my time under his command until the end of his appointment as head of the intelligence and security services. I never defied his orders, I never denied his authority and always acknowledged that he was my superior, but I was not built to accede blindly to superiors, and I certainly was not one to admire superiors by virtue of their being my superiors. To this day, I am not one for personality worship. Nearly sixty years have passed since and, in retrospect, I tend to think that my ambivalence towards

Harel was expressed, perhaps blatantly, in our confrontations in Buenos Aires, which occurred also in operations I will recount later. There is no doubt that our being under great tension exacerbated the confrontation.

After the debates regarding Mengele and Eichmann's family ended, we moved on to discuss a primary operational issue – transport – that is, how we would get Eichmann to Israel. As I mentioned before, although Harel was to head this part of the operation, Aharoni, Malchin and I discussed it with him.

While still in Israel, El Al's operations chief Shimoni raised the possibility of bringing the plane in for maintenance at Buenos Aires Airport to avoid taking Eichmann through the passenger terminal, with its routine passport checks. At all airports in the world, pilots and technicians enter and exit through a maintenance zone gate. They need to have permits, but do not go through passport control. Considering this, it was decided during a pre-take off discussion, that before the plane's 20 May scheduled departure, El Al personnel would make appropriate arrangements to bring their plane into the maintenance area. Harel said that one of his boys, Meir, who looked a bit like Eichmann, had meanwhile been brought from Israel and taken to hospital in Buenos Aires, pretending to be sick, so that if necessary, it would be possible to use a medical certificate saying that he needed treatment in Israel, and fly Eichmann out on the plane under Meir's identity. But this was only an alternative to the original plan, which was successfully implemented. Therefore, we had two passports, both Israeli, ready for Eichmann. The first (which was actually used) was with the name of an El Al technician, and the second with Meir's name.

On the eve of our departure, I went out with Malchin to buy ties to look suitably respectable. At a clothing store we asked in English for ties. One of the sellers said to his friend in Yiddish, 'On the top shelf we have *aparakakteh binder* [crappy ties].' I don't know much Yiddish but I understood the meaning of the word '*aparakakteh*'. On the other hand, Yiddish was Malchin's mother tongue. 'Should I answer him,' he whispered to me in English. I answered in the affirmative. To the astonishment of the two sellers – Jews, needless to say – the English-speaking 'tourist' answering them in fluent Yiddish, 'You can stick your *aparakakteh* ties up your ass.'

After all the details of the operation's transport phase were in place, the topic of Mengele came up again and Harel accepted my proposal. It was agreed that I and two others would not return on the El Al plane, but would stay in South America and try to locate Mengele. I chose Malchin and Shalom, in whom I had total faith. I told Harel that as long as we were in South America, Eichmann's presence in Israel should be kept secret, so that Mengele and perhaps other Nazi criminals living in South America would not panic and flee. I could tell from Harel's expression that he did not like this, but he didn't object.

Transporting Eichmann was relatively simple. He bathed and shaved, then wore the uniform of an El Al pilot. Dr Elian gave him an injection which did not put him to sleep, but blunted his senses and made it difficult for him to walk steadily. We put Eichmann in the middle of the back seat of the car. The doctor sat to Eichmann's left, and I to his right.

The drive to the airport took about forty minutes and passed without incident. At the gate of the maintenance area, an El Al man was waiting for us, with the entry permits we needed. The guards opened the gate in front of us without checking us at all. Within seconds, the car was parked next to the plane's ramp. Behind us drove a minibus with the real crew members. As agreed in advance, an El Al man who was in the know managed to distract the local policeman who was standing by the steps of the ramp, and we boarded Eichmann. The four of us supported him, dragged him up the stairs, and seated him in a first-class seat, close to the toilet, which could be used to hide him if needed. A few minutes later the plane made its way to the passenger terminal.

We left the plane at 11.15 p.m. Our part in the operation to bring Adolf Eichmann to trial in Israel was over.

Harel was waiting for us in the cafeteria of the terminal. 'Maybe you should fly to Israel with us, after all,' he told Shalom and me. 'No,' I replied without hesitation. 'We will stick with the plan. If we don't succeed, at least we'll get a trip in South America out of this.' Furthermore, I pointed out, we needed to clean up after the operation, remove our traces from the safehouses, return the hired cars and complete other technical matters. I reiterated the need to conceal Eichmann's presence in Israel for at least a month to give us time to locate Mengele without alerting him to possible danger. Harel replied that he doubted whether Eichmann's presence in Israel could be kept secret for so long, but reluctantly agreed to try.

Equipped with Israeli passports, we left the terminal. Talmor, Shimoni, Adi Peleg, Shalom Weiss, Tavor, Gat and a few others who had been brought to Argentina by Harel boarded the plane to guard Eichmann during the flight. Harel was the last to board before the plane took off.

Shalom, Malchin and I waited outside the terminal until we saw the plane fly off. Then we returned to the 'castle' safehouse and with Meidad and Nessyahu we got rid of anything that might have revealed what we were doing there. I later learned that the Jew who rented the safehouse to us recognised the smell of the chloroform we threw down the toilet, and when Eichmann's abduction became public, he understood what the house had been used for.

Malchin, Shalom and I, using foreign passports, boarded a train to Santiago de Chile, a journey of about twenty hours. Why Chile? Because we had no clue, not a shred of information, as to where to look for Mengele. The only thing we knew was that he had disappeared, perhaps escaped, from Buenos Aires. If he fled, it was probably to another country. If by land, it could be to Brazil, Uruguay, Paraguay, Bolivia or Chile. We heard that Chile was beautiful and more developed than Paraguay or Bolivia. Besides, a woman I knew from the Palmach, Ariana Goldman, lived in Chile. So we started there.

We crossed the Andes by train – they were covered with snow – and arrived in Chile during a period of earthquakes. In Santiago, I found

Ariana Goldman's beauty salon in the phone book and called her. She took us on a tour of Valparaiso, a port city two hours from Santiago. She bought a newspaper at a bus stop. The headline across the top read 'Adolf Eichmann kidnapped in Argentina and is in Israel.'

'You did it?' Ariana asked.

The three of us smiled and denied any connection. 'We're here with you, and Eichmann is in Israel,' I said to Ariana. I don't know if she was convinced.

It was clear that either Harel or Ben-Gurion had decided not to wait until we concluded the attempt to capture Mengele. I do not know why. In any case, immediately after we took leave of Adriana, I called Manor's office. It took two hours to reach him. Manor ordered us to return to Israel, as I expected. It was clear that after Eichmann's capture became public, every Nazi criminal hiding in South America would go underground, making any additional capture impossible. Despite Manor's instructions, we stayed in Chile, and, not wanting to miss this opportunity to travel, drove on to Brazil. To enter, we needed visas, and for that we needed health certificates, signed by a doctor. We chose a doctor with a Jewish name. He peered at us and at our documents, with a suspicious twinkle in his eyes. I have no doubt he suspected our credentials were fake, but he examined us and signed the requisite certificates. We visited Rio, and flew from there back to Israel. The whole trip to Chile and Brazil lasted ten days.

As far as we know today, Mengele probably left Buenos Aires a long time (almost a year) before we arrived in Argentina. In 1959, during the trial in Freiburg, Germany, of SS men who had served in Auschwitz, Mengele's name was mentioned and the German government contacted the Argentinian government, asking for information on whether Mengele was there. Mengele apparently learned of this and immediately fled Argentina. He first stayed in Paraguay, whose then-president, General Alfredo Stroessner, had a German father and willingly provided refuge for Nazi criminals. After about a year in Paraguay, Mengele apparently moved to Brazil, where he eventually died in 1979. It's a shame we did not capture him, and it's a shame he died of natural causes, but even before I knew all this, I did not for a moment regret opposing Harel's demand to divert personnel from the mission of capturing Eichmann to finding Mengele. It could have attracted unwanted attention, led the police to us or alerted Eichmann, and we would have lost out on both counts. Better a bird in the hand than two in the bush.

On my return to Israel, I immediately reported to Harel. At his request I wrote a report, describing the operation in detail. Over a number of days, Harel gathered all the members of the team in a conference room, and each one in turn described his or her part in the operation, all of it recorded for the sake of history.

I visited my parents' house, of course. Even before I came, they had guessed where I was and what I had done. In Kibbutz Afikim, Miriam, who was not yet my wife, and her parents received me as a hero.

Two days after Eichmann was brought to Israel, Prime Minister and Defense Minister David Ben-Gurion convened a special Cabinet meeting to inform ministers of the capture of one of the main perpetrators of the Holocaust of European Jews. At the end of the session, members of the government went to the Knesset, and the Prime Minister announced the following:

> I am informing the Knesset that some time ago the Israeli security services found one of the greatest Nazi criminals, Adolf Eichmann, who along with other Nazi leaders was responsible for what was called 'the final solution to the Jewish problem', that is, the extermination of six million European Jews. Adolf Eichmann is now in detention in Israel, and will soon stand trial in Israel, under the Nazi and Nazi Collaborators Law of 1950.

There was tremendous excitement in the Knesset and the whole country, as well as in Jewish communities around the world. A diplomatic crisis arose with Argentina, but it was resolved over time.

Needless to say, admiration for Israel and the prestige of its security and intelligence services soared.

From about the time I was seventeen I had been conscious of the Holocaust and the targeted extermination of European Jewry and it was clear to me that we were establishing Israel to prevent such atrocities in the future. But the capture of Eichmann and my role in his capture deepened and strengthened my consciousness of the Holocaust. I became close to Superintendent Avner Les, who was appointed by the Israel Police as Eichmann's chief interrogator in the criminal investigation that preceded Eichmann's trial. I visited Bureau 06, which was set up specifically for this purpose, and together with Les I visited the Jalameh police detention station, between Haifa and Shar Ha'amakim, where Eichmann was held until he was transferred to Ramla Prison. I also saw Eichmann in Ramla prison twice, and through Les's mediation, I questioned Eichmann on various topics, such as the organisation and management of the SS, training methods, SS command relations with the Wehrmacht command, the German Army, and so on. I was mainly interested in the training of an SS officer: how a normal person is turned into a mass murderer. I can't say that I received a full answer to this question.

My impression from Eichmann's answers was that he was a mediocre officer, a quintessential technocrat, punctual, meticulous and obedient, talented in the field of organisation and logistics, but with a very low intellectual level compared to an IDF officer. His ability to read and understand those around him was very limited. It seems to me that it would not be an exaggeration to say that almost every lieutenant colonel (the rank equivalent to *Obersturmbannführer*, Eichmann's rank in the SS) in the IDF was at a significantly higher intellectual level than Eichmann.

On 31 May 1962, I received a call from Tuvia Dori, then Deputy Commissioner of Prisons. I knew immediately what it was about, since I had agreed in advance with him and the commissioner, Arie Nir, with whom I was friendly, that they would let me know when Eichmann was to be executed.

'Come to Ramla immediately,' Dori said. 'He will be hanged at midnight.' When I arrived at the Ramla prison, the priest had already finished his visit, which included a final confession. Eichmann had just been taken out of his cell. Our gazes met, but we did not exchange a word, and I do not know if he recognised me as one of the people who captured him. I was the only one from the team who captured him to be present at his last moments on earth.

The distance between Eichmann's cell and the hanging cell was several dozen metres. He walked upright, steady, and, as far as I could see, his legs were not shackled. I walked behind the group of people who accompanied him, and heard him mumble a few words in German, which I did not understand. I was then told that he said, 'I hope you all follow me shortly.' As we approached the cell he muttered a few more words, and I was told that he said, 'Long live Germany. Long live Argentina.'

We arrived at the hanging cell, which was the size of a small lift. They blindfolded him, and a guard put the rope around his neck. I heard the thud of his body after the hanging. A few minutes later, after a doctor confirmed his death, we went down to the courtyard, to the special furnace built by Amichai Paglin for cremation. Paglin was the Irgun's operations officer, and after the establishment of the state he set up a small factory to manufacture furnaces. The body was put in the oven and two powerful burners on each side were turned on.

Incidentally, many years later, when Menachem Begin became prime minister, he appointed Paglin as his counter-terrorism adviser. About four months after his appointment, he was seriously injured in a car accident and died about a month later. I was appointed as his successor.

The night of the execution, Dori invited me to join the boat which sailed far from the territorial waters of the State of Israel to disperse Eichmann's ashes, but I politely declined. I had had more than enough, and drove home.

Perusing the minutes of the Cabinet meeting in which Ben-Gurion informed the Cabinet of Eichmann's capture, I find that much of it was devoted to a dialogue between the prime minister and his ministers on a tribute, a show of gratitude for the guys who captured Eichmann and brought him to Israel. Six ministers – Eshkol, Sapir, Dayan, Ben Aharon, Golda Meir, M. H. Shapira – begged him to praise, in some way, those involved in the capture when he spoke to the Knesset session later that day, and he did not agree to do so. Those involved in the capture remained in the shadows, anonymous. Their names were not released.

About two years after the capture, Ben-Gurion invited the members of the capture team, along with Harel of course, to his office. He thanked us personally and posed for a souvenir photo with us. However, the anonymity of Mossad and Shin Bet operatives was maintained very strictly in those days, and it took years before the photographs could be published.

In 1975, fifteen years after Eichmann's capture, Harel published his book, *The House on Garibaldi Street.* In the book he mentions himself a lot, as well as giving the names of dear colleagues who contributed to locating Eichmann and assisted in the operation. But those who actually carried out the capture, the operatives in the field, are mentioned only with fictitious names. Even in the second edition of the book, which came out in 1990, fifteen years after the first, I am the only one mentioned by his real name.

This bothered me. I thought that the people who carried out the operation, one with such great historical significance for Israel and the Jewish people, and perhaps for the whole world, deserved that their deeds be fully told, and their identities made public. I found a way to do this in 2007, forty-seven years after the operation, when I served as a minister in Ehud Olmert's government. I initiated and promoted a special Knesset event aimed at expressing Israel's appreciation to all those who participated in the operation to capture Eichmann and bring him to Israel. After this event, no participant remained anonymous. This is the speech I gave at the Knesset event:

> Madam Speaker of the Knesset, head of the Mossad, head of the Secret Service, former heads of the Secret Service, my

most honoured guests who participated directly and those who participated indirectly in the capture and prosecution of Eichmann in Israel, dear families and distinguished guests:

Forty-seven years have passed since that day, 22 May 1960, when Prime Minister David Ben-Gurion announced from the Knesset podium that Adolf Eichmann had been captured by the security services, brought to Israel, and would stand trial under the Nazi and Nazi Collaborators Law.

The capture of Eichmann was not about revenge. It is impossible to avenge the deaths of six million people, including one and a half million children. The poet [Nachman Bialik] has already said: 'Satan has yet to devise, Revenge for the blood of a little child.' The goal was to expose the horrors of the Holocaust and bring them to the consciousness of every person in the world, so that this knowledge would be passed down from generation to generation until the end of days.

Until the operation, no major organisation was searching out Nazi criminals. Nor were we. Moreover, the subject of the Holocaust was largely taboo. The survivors did not speak. For those who were not there, it was difficult to know and even more difficult to understand. Many Holocaust survivors who lived among us felt like Michael Goldman, that child in the ghetto who was sentenced to eighty lashes and survived them against all odds, but when he told his story, after immigrating to Israel, he was not believed. People thought he was making it up. For Goldman, it was the eighty-first blow. Reality was beyond what anyone could grasp. Through the trial, the world, the Jewish world and the people of Israel heard the full story of the Holocaust for the first time.

We are gathered here today, all those who took part in the capture of Adolf Eichmann, members of the Security Service, members of Mossad, staff of El Al, and members of the defence establishment, all of us, all those who participated in the operation. Its success depended on the quality of the people involved. All of them were excellent operatives, very brave, dedicated to their job and fearless. They possessed extraordinary organisational skills and the word 'impossible' did not exist in their minds.

Dozens of people participated in the various stages that preceded the capture of Eichmann – from the search phase until his arrival in Israel. Some are no longer alive, and I will mention those who were part of the operational force on the ground:

The late Isser Harel – who was in charge of the Security Services, initiated the operation and was its top commander; the late Zvi Malchin – a commander in the operational unit of the service, a professional operative chosen because of his creative ability and phenomenal improvisation ability. Malchin was the first to seize Eichmann, and he was joined by the late Moshe Tavor, a technological whizz, a man with physical strength and impressive ability to solve problems; the late Shalom Danny – a gifted painter, who functioned as a walking documentation lab who could turn any random slip of paper into an official certificate; the late Zvi Tohar, the flight captain, who when asked by the people of the control tower at Dakar Airport, Senegal, in astonishment – how we got there on a direct flight from Buenos Aires to Dakar without refuelling, he replied: 'We pissed into the engines.' The late Yehudit Nessyahu, who stayed with us for ten days in hiding, and also did not live to be with us this day.

The Ministerial Committee on Ceremonies, headed by Minister Yaakov Edri, has decided to include all those who had any part in the operation. All of these people, or their families, are today receiving a token of thanks from the state, in whose name they participated in an operation, unparalleled in its justice. Forty-seven years after the operation, the State of Israel grants you, for the first time, a certificate of appreciation for your part in that operation. But not only the state thanks you today for carrying out the mission. In the row of those granting you this recognition here, stand many others. The missing are present, the dead victims of the Nazi oppressor who were not saved. They were the driving force of this operation, and they are the ones who gave us the fortitude and moral validity. It was the least we could do for them. Their voice was faithfully represented in prosecutor Gideon Hausner's chilling opening speech at the Eichmann trial. As he put it: 'I am not standing alone. With me are six million accusers. But they cannot rise to their feet and point an accusing finger towards him who sits in the dock and cry: "I accuse." For their ashes are piled up on the hills of Auschwitz and the fields of Treblinka, and are strewn in the forests of Poland. Their graves are scattered throughout the length and breadth of Europe. Their blood cries out, but their voice is not heard. Therefore, I will be their spokesman and in their name, I will unfold the terrible indictment.'

Alongside the dead, the living victims of the Nazi oppressor also stand with us here. Those Holocaust survivors who bravely clung to life and survived the inferno. They thank you for the fact that after years when Israelis ignored the Holocaust, unable to cope or contain the magnitude of the horror, many were first exposed to that dark chapter in the history of the Jewish people, a nightmare that is so hard to put to rest. It is something that no one can fully comprehend, something, as one of the witnesses in the Eichmann trial, the writer Ka-Tsetnik describes as 'another planet'. 'The inhabitants of this planet had no names, they had no parents, and they had no children. They were not born there and did not give birth. They did not live by the laws of the world here and did not die by them, their name was a number.'

The trial, which began in April '61 in Jerusalem, was not the trial of a single killer but of a well-oiled extermination machine. It was not just a sentence. It was a historic journey and a ground-breaking event that resounded world-wide. In its wake, those who had hitherto been accused of going like 'sheep to the slaughter' were seen as our brothers, venerable heroes, who faced torments of hell beyond all human endurance – and surmounted them!

Following the trial, Holocaust and heroism were no longer two separate words, but one complete phrase. Since then, Holocaust survivors have been cured of their silence and others of their deafness. And Michael Goldman, the little boy from the ghetto, whose story no one believed, sat in the courtroom, dressed in the uniform of a senior Israeli police officer in charge of guarding Eichmann, and knew that the eighty-first lash had been rescinded!

The capture of Eichmann by the long arm of Israel, his trial in Jerusalem and his execution were important historical steps in the resurrection of the Jewish people in Israel and the Diaspora after the Holocaust. The trial brought about a change of consciousness, with the message that there would be no more harm to the Jews, no second Wannsee Conference at which the mass extermination of the Jewish people will be decided. No one else, including an Iranian called Ahmadinejad or Hezbollah, can threaten or dare to challenge the existence of the State of Israel. As the words engraved on the concrete dome that covers the huge heap of ashes in the Majdanek extermination camp say: 'Let our disaster be a warning to you.'

After I finished my speech, Knesset Speaker Dalia Itzik read the names of the those from the capture team who were still alive: Zvi Aharoni, Avrum Shalom, Yaakov Meidad, Yaakov Gat and Dr Elian, and invited them to receive the certificates of appreciation from her. Only a short time later did anyone notice that my name had not been read. I had only myself to blame. I forgot to add my name to the list given to Dalia. But I did receive a certificate. Dalia gave it to me and asked me for a copy of my speech. I complied with her request, I do not know if she kept it or passed it on to the Knesset archives.

Operation Cosine

Although the affair described below occurred about eight years after the capture of Eichmann, it is closely related to our efforts to capture senior Nazi criminals who escaped at the end of the war, and thus it seemed appropriate to include it in this chapter.

In October 1967, while I was in Paris, Aharoni contacted me and told me that he had substantial indications that Heinrich Müller, the commander of the Gestapo, the Nazi secret police, was still alive, hiding somewhere in the world.

Müller joined the Nazi SS in 1933 and became head of the Gestapo in 1939, in charge of eliminating any internal opposition to the Nazi regime. His loyalty to Hitler was such that he was one of the few people with the Führer in the bunker in Berlin until 29 April 1945, the night before Hitler's suicide. He disappeared from the bunker several hours before Hitler and Eva Brown's suicide. Various rumours claimed that he was killed while trying to escape, that he escaped and hid in Germany, that he managed to reach South America, that he was captured by the Soviets, transferred to Moscow and subsequently served the KGB, the Soviet intelligence organisation.

In 1967, an American citizen, Francis Willard Keith, was arrested in Panama and it was claimed that he was Müller. Müller's wife, Sophie confirmed (on the basis of photographs of the arrested man) that he was her husband, and the West German government demanded his extradition, but after examination of his fingerprints, it turned out the man was not Müller and he was let go.

Meir Amit instructed me to make every possible effort to figure out conclusively if Müller was still alive, so I made this a high priority in an operation called Cosine. We knew that Sophie Müller lived in a Frankfurt suburb. One evening, when Sophie Müller was visiting her daughter, our operatives entered the house to install eavesdropping equipment. Unfortunately, neighbours noticed lights on the top floor of the house, which was usually dark, and called the police. Two of the operatives, Yair Racheli and Baruch T., were apprehended in the house and taken into custody.

Under a false identity, I visited them in jail and tried to reassure them. I hired a German lawyer, a criminal law expert, initially to present the intrusion as a standard burglary attempt to steal money and valuables. But it soon became clear that if we continued along this line, the two would end up imprisoned for at least two years. We felt we had no choice but to turn to the German secret services and admit what we had been up to. With their help, the affair ended with a fine and two months in prison for both men.

Despite this failure we persisted not only in our search for Müller but also for Josef Mengele, whom we were convinced was still alive somewhere in South America. We located a woman, registered as his wife, in fact his brother's widow, who married him for convoluted reasons to secure the family inheritance. We eavesdropped on this woman, who lived in the Italian Alps. But despite our concerted and prolonged effort, we were unable to locate Mengele himself. Regarding Müller, we came out empty-handed. In my opinion, the chance that he was alive was very slim. It seemed far more likely to me that he was killed while trying to escape from Berlin at the end of April 1945. My reason for concluding this is that in 2013, the head of the German Institute for the Commemoration of the Resistance to Hitler, disclosed that in August 1945, the body of a man between the ages of forty and fifty, wearing a uniform with the rank of a general in the SS, was discovered in the Jewish cemetery (!) in Berlin. As with Martin Bormann, Müller was apparently killed by a tank shell while trying to cross from territory held by the Soviets to territory occupied by the Americans.

I took full responsibility for the failure of the operation, both in a report to Meir in 1967 and in another one in 1968 to Aharoni, who was then a kind of internal auditor for Mossad.

What really bothered me about this unfortunate affair was that on their return to Israel, Racheli and Baruch T. suffered the humiliation of being hauled to the Shin Bet facility and interrogated for two days to make sure that the German investigators had not been told anything beyond their cover story. Both were professionals, 100 per cent trustworthy. They told me in detail everything they said. I reported everything and saw the matter as closed. Apparently, the internal security service thought differently.

Chapter 13

Where is Yossele?

The capture of Eichmann in Argentina and his prosecution in Israel turned the spotlight on Israel's intelligence and security services. We were already known and respected globally, in part for obtaining the full text of the February 1956 'secret speech' of USSR ruler Nikita Khrushchev before a closed session of the Soviet Communist Party's 20th Conference in which he denounced Stalin's crimes. Although some details about the speech were leaked to Western countries, no one managed to obtain a full version of the speech, which lasted about four hours.

A Polish-Jewish journalist named Victor Grayevsky, who visited relatives in Israel in December 1955 and then returned to Poland, managed some months later to get a copy of the speech from the safe of the secretary-general of the Polish Communist Party, Edward Ochab. Grayevsky got the copy from a friend who worked in Ochab's office and took it to the Israeli embassy in Warsaw, where the diplomat who saw it quickly understood its significance, duplicated the speech on a copier on the spot, and returned the speech to Grayevsky, who returned it to his friend to put back in Ochab's safe. It is important to note that Grayevsky was not an agent we recruited. He acted on his own initiative, out of identification with Israel and immigrated to Israel about a year later.

The copy of the speech was handed over to Manor, head of Shin Bet who was ordered by the prime minister to pass on the precious document to James Angleton, head of counter-intelligence at the CIA. The Americans asked Israel's permission to publish the document publicly and parts were subsequently printed in the *New York Times*, sending shock waves around the world, in both communist and non-communist countries. Its publication is considered one of the most important events in delegitimising and undermining the Soviet regime. Needless to say, among those in the know, regard for Israeli security and intelligence services soared, and the CIA, which until then had been reluctant to cooperate with us, began gradually to soften this policy. The capture of Eichmann further raised our prestige, and we came be viewed as among the best intelligence services in the world. Undoubtedly, this played a central role in Ben-Gurion's decision to insist that Mossad focus on an affair that preoccupied all of Israel in the early 1960s – uncovering the whereabouts of Yossele Shumacher.

Yossele, as the was called by all of Israel, was born in 1952 in the USSR and immigrated to Israel in 1957 with his parents. In their first months in Israel, they put him in the care of his paternal grandfather, who lived in Jerusalem and was a follower of the Rebbe of Satmar, a rabid anti-Zionist. When the parents' financial situation improved after a few months, they sought to get their son back, but the grandfather, Nachman Strakes, refused. He considered the parents insufficiently observant and declared that returning the child to them was equivalent to taking him to extermination! He defied a court order to do so, and through various channels in the ultra-Orthodox community, moved his grandson first around the country, and then smuggled him out of Israel via Europe to the USA to a family within the Satmar community. Yossele cooperated after his kidnappers told him that his parents intended to return to the USSR and force him to convert there.

Though the affair attracted a great deal of public and media attention, the police made no headway in finding the child. In early 1962, Ben-Gurion ordered Harel to find Yossele and bring him home to his parents.

Although this is not the kind of task that security and intelligence services usually handle, Ben-Gurion was right to ask Mossad to do so in this case. Yossele's abduction mocked the police and the state. Furthermore, failure to capture him would only encourage anti-Zionist groups like Naturi Karta who flagrantly defied the state's authority.

Division 10 was recruited to the effort. Harel summoned me and put me in the loop. I made available an entire unit of my people, who scattered to airports in Europe and near ultra-Orthodox *yeshiva* sites in Switzerland, France and England, to track the movements of about half a dozen ultra Orthodox whom Harel was convinced were partners in the kidnapping. Harel himself took operational command from the office of Kruz, then head of Mossad's foreign relations branch, Tevel, in Paris, sometimes even spending the night on a sofa there.

I provided personnel but did not take part personally in the operations. I had learned my lesson from Operation Eichmann, and I disagreed with Harel's *modus operandi*. In my opinion, in the operation to find Yossele, as before, he recruited and deployed too many people in the field, making communication unnecessarily complex. I believed in carefully planning an operation, and limiting the number of operatives in the field. Harel did the opposite: first he dispersed people, then he planned, which meant that a large number of people were activated in the field, in my opinion, too many. However, I am not claiming that my method is the only effective one. Indisputably, Harel knew how to produce results from his operational method.

I will not go into the details of the operation, which I did not participate in directly and which has been described by Harel himself, among others. After the arrest and interrogation of people within the ultra-Orthodox community, the boy was traced to the USA. Israeli Foreign Minister Golda Meir contacted then American Attorney General Bobby Kennedy, the FBI intervened and Yossele was returned to his family in Israel in July 1962.

The credit for finding the child and returning him is due to Harel, who acted as stubbornly and resourcefully as usual. Those under him had their tactical disagreements with him but loyalty to him was absolute. In retrospect, I wager that Harel became personally involved in this affair because, although in his lifestyle he still remained the ascetic plumber who sat and drank tea in my mother's kitchen, the media plaudits following highly visible success in the Eichmann operation drew him. The temptation to win this praise again, as well as the desire to fulfil Ben-Gurion's wish, compelled Harel to put so much effort into the pursuit of an abducted child.

Whatever my criticisms of him, Harel had a deep, almost uncontrollable urge to succeed in complex operations, in 'impossible missions' conducted under his personal command. I do not think any of Harel's heirs have had his level of intuition and operational skill. In these, he surpassed us all.

Chapter 14

The Sword over Our Heads

Few remember today the affair of the German scientists in Egypt, which preoccupied Israeli politicians, intelligence and security forces, and the Israeli public for about two years and led directly to Harel's resignation as head of the intelligence and security services. To my mind, it also played a role in the political developments that eventually led to Ben-Gurion's resignation.

On 22 July 1962, Egyptian President Gamal Abdel Nasser announced a successful experiment in Egypt: the launching of four surface-to-surface missiles of two different types. In his announcement, Nasser emphasised that the missiles had a range that reached 'south of Beirut', leaving no doubt that Israel was their target. According to the Egyptian president, the missiles were 'designed and manufactured by Egyptian engineers'.

July 22nd is a major holiday in Egypt, marking the day when the 'Free Officers' coup ended the Egyptian monarchy. In 1962, the tenth anniversary of the coup, a celebratory military parade was held in Cairo, featuring the missiles on their platforms in front of cheering crowds. Nasser's announcement and the display severely shook the Israeli intelligence community. Less than twenty years since London and other cities were battered by German missiles, we felt that an existential threat had materialised under our noses.

Even at the time, those in the know were aware that Nasser was not telling the truth when he claimed that the missile had been developed by Egyptians. It soon became clear that the Egyptian missiles were still in the early stages of development, and were not yet equipped with a navigation system that could home in on a target. What was not clear was whether Nasser knew this when he made his announcement, or whether he was being misled by the project leaders, all of whom were Germans.

It is presumed that the first campaign against the German scientists in Egypt began with President Nasser's 22 July boast. But contrary to much of what has been written about this affair, it is wrong to think that the Israeli intelligence community was in a coma, awaking to action only with the announcement. If and when the archives of the IDF and Mossad are opened, it will become clear that, as early as 1951, we were aware of Egyptian efforts to recruit German experts and engineers. At first, they attempted to establish an industry to produce jet engines and supersonic fighter jets, then to develop the capacity to produce surface-to-surface missiles. It is true that at first neither the IDF nor Mossad took a sufficiently serious view of these efforts, perhaps because they underestimated Egypt's ability to advance them or perhaps because of scant information. In any case, the issue was not treated with high priority.

The turning point came in the late 1950s. An intelligence source tried to pass on to Israeli authorities 'important information for Israel' regarding negotiations between Egypt and European companies to build a factory in Hilwan, near Cairo, to produce advanced fighter jets. At the time, I was working in Shin Bet. People in Mossad, headed by Harel, did not volunteer information that I did not need or that was not related to my area of responsibility. And I did not request such information. I have always believed that classified information should reach people purely on a need-to-know basis. Therefore, I do not know the scope or quality of the information we received. I also do not know what motivated Ben-Gurion to write in his diary, as early as February 1962, that is, about six months before the missile test in Egypt, that he had a conversation with Harel about an 'Egyptian missile'. Ben-Gurion did not specify Harel's source. It may have been Wolfgang Lutz (an Israeli agent who became known as the spy on the horse because of the opulent lifestyle he led in Egypt, where he owned a ranch and riding school. He later changed his name to Ze'ev Gur-Arieh and reached the rank of major). He was a member of military intelligence Unit 188. In any case, Ben-Gurion's diary entry in February 1962 reinforces my belief that our intelligence community was aware of Egyptian projects before the missiles were experimentally fired in July of that year.

Nonetheless, you would be hard put to find anyone who was in the intelligence community who would say that the Egyptian missile launch did not shock us, and all would concur that Mossad, whose head had devoted all his time and energy in the previous months in pursuit of Yossele Shumacher, was deeply traumatised by the event. Military intelligence did not hesitate to let Ben-Gurion know that they blamed Mossad for this failure. It is very possible that these allegations played a part in the tensions between Harel and Meir Amit, then head of military intelligence who replaced Harel at the head of Mossad. It was a tension that continued to Harel's death, almost forty years later.

Yossele was returned to Israel in July 1962, and Harel immediately shifted into high gear to concentrate all efforts on the Egyptian military projects. The comprehensive and complex operation, designed to put an end to these projects, was given the code name Damocles, from the Roman story of the dictator Dionysus and his adviser, Damocles.

For Operation Damocles, Harel made Paris his forward command centre, with his right-hand man Yosef Porat closely at his side. He also deployed two senior members of Mossad, Yosef Raanan, head of Hamoked, the European branch of Mossad's Tzomet division (in charge of recruiting and running agents), and Haim Eilam, head of Colossus, Mossad's operational unit in Western Europe.

In short order, the operatives got wind of a company by the name of Intrahandel, with offices first in Frankfurt and then near Egyptair's offices in Munich, that was purchasing raw materials and spare parts needed for the fighter and missile project. Known as Intra for short, it was headed by Heinz Krug, former director of the Jet Propulsion

Institute in Stuttgart. In Egypt, the project was led by scientists Wolfgang Piltz, Dr Paul Garca, a radar and electronics expert, and Professor Eugen Zanger. All three were first-rate experts who co-produced the V-1 and V-2 missiles during World War II, which killed thousands and caused enormous damage. The three were employed after the war in a jet propulsion institute in Stuttgart from where they were recruited by Egypt and went to work there.

At that time, we learned that the Egyptians were developing two types of missiles: Al-Zafar medium range (up to 300 kilometres) and Al-Kahar longer range (600 kilometres). We also knew that the project was still experiencing major engineering difficulties, particularly regarding navigation to their destination.

In early August 1962, Harel demanded that my staff help reinforce Colossus. I sent Shalom, Tavor and Malchin to Paris, and later also Aharoni. All four, as related earlier, participated in the capture of Eichmann.

Harel was a strict adherent to compartmentalisation regulations, even trying to conceal from me where he was sending my people. Even Avraham Ahituv, head of Shin Bet's operations at the time, did not always know what Harel's emissaries were doing in 'his territory'. Harel demanded frequent and complete reports from the 30–45 people deployed in the operation, but he himself rarely reported his actions and decisions, which explains the paucity of documents on this operation in Mossad archives. I opposed Harel's *modus operandi*, but did not try to intervene and voice my opinion. From my experience with him during the Eichmann operation, I knew that he would not welcome my view that there was no need to employ such a large number of operatives. My responsibility was reduced to supplying logistics and people for operations in Germany. But members of my staff working in Germany occasionally updated me on their actions during the series of operations they carried out in the early 1960s.

Only once at that time did I go to Germany and personally take part in the surveillance of the Intra offices at Schillerstrasse 21 in Munich. The building housed a noisy nightclub on the ground floor, which made it very easy for our observers. The intelligence information that my men gathered enabled the commander of Unit 188, Yosef (Yoske) Yariv, to plan an operation to send letter-bombs to German scientists in Egypt. Among them was one intended for the head of the missile project, Piltz. Unit 188's man in Egypt, Lutz, sent them to the targets. To our regret, the envelope destined for Piltz was opened by his secretary and lover, Hannelore Wende, who was blinded by the explosion.

In September 1962, Shalom played a leading role in capturing Krug, Intra's director, and bringing him to Israel, in an operation that resembled in many aspects the capture of Eichmann. Harel had come to the conclusion that Krug was the man with the most knowledge about the missile projects and that it was time to 'get his tongue' – the expression security services use for interrogating a suspect. The operatives did a masterful job of reconnaissance and were resourceful in coming up with a good plan. The idea was to make sure that after he disappeared, Egypt would be suspected of having abducted him and taken him there because he had refused to travel there of his own free will for work.

In mid-September, Krug was seized near his home and smuggled to France. We did not want to smuggle a kidnapped German citizen through Germany. He was hidden in several places in southern France before being flown to Israel. His interrogation lasted about three months, from early October to the end of December 1962. Although I knew about his interrogations, I did not meet him or follow the investigation. When it was over, it was clear that he could not be returned to Munich. I don't know what exactly happened to him. Years later I asked the person who was supposed to know what exactly happened. As in other cases, that closed and silent man answered: 'Don't remind me of the forgotten.'

To cover up Krug's disappearance, Harel carried out a ruse with the help of Aharoni, who was born in Germany and spoke perfect German. Aharoni became Krug's double, equipped with appropriate documents, and went off to South America, to create the impression in Germany that Krug was alive, but hiding. The story that spread was that Krug had abandoned his family in Germany (he was married and the father of a daughter and a son), obtained forged documents, and had run off to Brazil or Argentina. Mossad even planted evidence that Krug was running a business there in wholesale agricultural produce and implied that behind it all was a woman, supposedly Krug's lover, who had followed him to South America.

The most shocking information the interrogators squeezed out of Krug was that the Egyptians had recruited Otto Joklik, a world-renowned Austrian chemist specialising in radioactive isotopes, to work for them. Krug said Joklik had pledged to supply Egypt with radioactive materials, including highly toxic cobalt 60, to use in 'dirty bombs' in the Egyptian missile warheads.

Perhaps less shocking but no less important was Krug's divulging that the person in charge of manufacturing the missile guidance system was a German electronics engineer, Dr Hans Kleinwachter. He headed a team of fifteen engineers and technicians in a lab in the south-western German town of Lorrach. Kleinwachter's home was only a mile from the lab. Although Egypt had offered to move him and his team to Egypt, he declined, saying it would be easier to work from Germany.

In October 1962, during Krug's interrogation, Joklik offered his services to Israel, appearing suddenly at the offices of our country's reparations delegation in Cologne. He said his conscience bothered him. It is likely he was not misled by our efforts to create the impression that Krug had been abducted by Egypt and run off to South America and instead assumed that Israel had a hand in the mysterious disappearance – and feared he might face a fate similar to Krug's.

At that time, Ahituv had already replaced Yehuda A. as head of the branch in Germany and he asked Yehuda A. to meet Joklik and get a reading of the man and try to determine the quality of the information we might obtain from him. That meeting took place on 25 October at a hotel in Amsterdam, after which Joklik, accompanied by Yehuda A., arrived in Israel on 7 November, and was interrogated for a week by our experts and nuclear scientists. They concluded that he was dependable and he returned to Europe as a Mossad agent, with a handsome monthly salary of $1,000 (today equivalent to more than $9,000). His code name was Incidental Traveller. I never met him but was kept in the loop about him.

Joklik provided us with a wealth of information, most of which checked out and was verified by other Israeli sources and senior Israeli scientists. Among other things, he confirmed what we had learned from Krug's investigation – the centrality of Dr Kleinwachter to the project. Harel initially intended to abduct and interrogate Kleinwachter in an operation code name Cipher which was to be similar to the Krug operation. At the end of 1962 and the start of 1963, Kleinwachter's lab and home in the town of Lorrach were under 24-hour surveillance. Harel intermittently stayed nearby in Basel or Mulhouse, and, as was his habit, ran the operation from various cafés.

But after intensive surveillance, he came to the conclusion that abducting Kleinwachter was not feasible. However, it was essential to ensure that the Egyptian missile projects failed, and stopping the production of their guidance systems was crucial. Kleinwachter was the brains behind the system, and the conclusion was clear: he must be eliminated. Harel later said he explained Kleinwachter's role to Ben-Gurion, who told Harel, 'He needs to be finished off.' Equipped with that approval, Harel and his men planned Kleinwachter's assassination under Operation Kotzan (Hebrew for a prickly plant). This Operation Kotzan, which turned into a disaster, was the only part of the German scientist affair in Egypt in which I participated directly.

At that time, a sharp dispute had already erupted between Harel and then Deputy Defense Minister Shimon Peres. Harel considered the Egyptian missile project a major existential threat to Israel. Peres thought it was not particularly dangerous, convinced that Egypt was greatly exaggerating its abilities and progress in making the weapons operational. He believed the problem could be solved through the mediation of then West German Defence Minister

Franz-Josef Strauss, with whom he had an unusually warm and friendly relationship. Peres complained to Ben-Gurion that Harel was 'creating panic'. He also claimed, perhaps relying on military intelligence, that Joklik was an untrustworthy charlatan. But Peres ignored political factors that severely limited the chances that West Germany would actively stop its scientists in Egypt. Confrontation with Egypt over this could well lead Egypt to retaliate by establishing diplomatic ties with East Germany, and to other Arab countries following Cairo's lead. Such a move would be very harmful for West Germany both politically and economically at a time when Bonn's policy was to break relations with countries that formally recognised its communist neighbour.

In December 1962 and January 1963, Harel kept demanding more personnel from me to strengthen the teams in Europe. I sent all my stars to plan Kleinwachter's abduction. I flew to Paris in early January to assess the situation. I consulted with our people in Paris, then drove to Mulhouse in northern France and met Harel in one of his cafés. As usual, he urged me to order the most expensive thing on the menu. Shalom and Malchin joined us and presented their scenarios to me, and my impression was that they were impractical. Harel listened in silence. The only plan of action suggested to me was to block Kleinwachter's car with our car from which our assassin would shoot him through his window and escape.

I could sense that everyone felt under pressure. One should never operate under pressure. Covert operations must be done in a very orderly fashion, with detailed and meticulous plans for every possible scenario and mishap. Under pressure, they fail. I said to Harel: 'Give me a few days, I'll take a look around Lorrach and come up with a plan.' Harel agreed, but added: 'If we can't find a way to kidnap him, he will have to be eliminated.'

In January 1963, I crossed the border from Mulhouse to Lorrach, accompanied by Shalom and Eilam, all of us traveling with foreign passports. At the border crossing between France and Germany, we were asked if we were heading to Freiburg for a conference on nuclear reactors. We had no idea such a conference was taking place, but we responded in the affirmative and drove on, without scrutiny.

I surveyed Lorrach on foot in freezing cold weather and observed Kleinwachter's home and lab. I met Harel's operatives, who were sitting, freezing, in cars. Most roads were laden with snow. Every vehicle on them was in danger of getting stuck.

There was only one cleared road that led to Kleinwachter's home, which was close to his lab. I concluded that the plan to block his car was highly risky. Even if the assassination itself succeeded, our men could easily get stuck in the snow while trying to escape via side roads and were almost guaranteed to be stopped by German police if they attempted to get away on main roads. In my opinion, it would be much safer for a sniper to shoot him from about fifty metres away using a rifle with a silencer, and then make his way to a rescue car at a pre-determined location.

Harel did not like my idea and sent me back to look around again, which I did, but it didn't change my assessment. In a café in Mulhouse, I told him: 'Now, in mid-January, Kleinwachter is not going anywhere. Let's wait a few weeks, until the snow melts and the roads open up. I can get it done with three people. We don't need more. No one will catch us.'

But Harel was stressed, he felt everyone was sitting on him, blaming him and Mossad for the earlier intelligence failure. He needed a success immediately, not in a few weeks. He thanked me and said he had another mission for me. I knew he was angry at me. Taking a person off one mission and assigning him to another was his way of expressing dissatisfaction. I think it was the first time he was not satisfied with me, but I didn't care much. I was convinced that I was right.

In keeping with the division of responsibility during the time, it was clear that if someone was going to be eliminated, the assassin would come from the Mifratz ('Gulf') unit under Yitzhak Shamir. The unit sent us an operative for the task. He joined one of my observations, and I immediately decided he was idiot, with a lousy sense of direction. I had no doubt that with two of my good men, Shalom and Malchin for example, we could carry out the assassination much better than the man from Mifratz. I discussed this with Harel, and again asked him to give me two or three weeks to prepare a plan with three people. But Harel turned me down. Instead he sent me to Paris to meet Yaakov Kruz. 'He [Kruz] has received a message from the King of Morocco who wants our help. Talk to Yaacov, go to Morocco and see how the king can be helped.'

I told Harel that of course I would do so, but I wanted it to be clear that I did not intend to go to Morocco purely to offer advice to the king on his personal security, but rather wanted to try and establish with the Moroccan intelligence and security services the kind of ties we had with Iran and Turkey. He was in favour of this.

I don't know if Harel's rejection of my offer to plan Kleinwachter's killing was, as he said, because he wanted to move ahead without delay, or because it diverged from the proper procedure of leaving such matters to the Mifratz unit. Or perhaps he was just angry at me. In any case, I drove to Paris, for the new mission which I will describe later.

In early February, when I was away from the scene, the Katzan operation to eliminate Kleinwachter got under way. The assassin was joined by Aharoni, who drove the car. They came close to Kleinwachter's car just as he was trying to extract it from a deep snow drift, the tires spinning, which only caused the wheels to dig deeper into the snow. In short, he was a sitting duck. The assassin pulled out his pistol, opened the car window, and pulled the trigger. The bullet misfired. Kleinwachter pulled out a gun. Apparently after the explosive letter intended for Piltz and Krug's disappearance he feared his life might be in danger. He aimed at his would-be assassin. But he was a scientist and not a gunman. The operative knocked his hand, the bullet went off course; Aharoni and the operative did not wait another moment and fled the scene. Of course, the failed assassination attempt made big headlines in Germany and Switzerland. Most commentators opined that the would-be killers were Israeli agents, and this increased suspicions that Israel had a hand also in the mysterious disappearance of Krug.

A few weeks later Mossad suffered another serious failure. In late February, Heidi Goercke, the daughter of a German electronics engineer expert in electronic navigation systems named Jens-Paul Goercke, was approached by two men who knew that her father worked at Factory 333 in Egypt with Piltz. (Factory 333 was the code name for the base in eastern Cairo, where more than a thousand people worked on the development of the missiles, including about 250 German scientists, engineers and technicians.) They urged the young woman to convince her father to leave Egypt and return to Germany, hinting that if he didn't, bad things would befall him, and perhaps his daughter as well. After another attempt at contact, Heidi Goercke suggested a meeting at Les Trois Rois hotel in Basel, where Theodor Herzl had stayed and was famously photographed overlooking the Rhine from the balcony there during the Zionist Congress in 1901.

On 2 March 1963, a Mossad agent using the cover name Yosef Ben Gal and Joklik, who introduced himself by his real name, met her as planned. The two acted most incautiously, unsuspecting of what they should have assumed: Goercke had set a trap for them. They showed up at the meeting without back-up and spoke freely. It didn't occur to them that the Swiss police were recording them. When they left the hotel, they were both promptly arrested and charged with threats and extortion. With the help of crack lawyers, they denied during their trial that they had threatened Goercke, claiming that they had tried to 'persuade her without any implicit or explicit threats'. Switzerland probably wanted to avoid involvement in the whole affair. In any case, the two received fairly light sentences and were released from prison within months.

The double failure, in Lorrach and Basel, soon brought to an end the era of Harel as head of Mossad and Shin Bet. More on that later.

Chapter 15

Secret Relations with Morocco

Morocco gained independence from French rule in 1956 and instituted a monarchy headed by one of the leaders who had fought for liberation from France, Sultan Muhammad bin Yusuf. When he became King Muhammad V, he pursued a clear anti-Israel policy and took steps to restrict emigration to Israel. Despite this, the *aliyah* (immigration of Jews to Israel) continued to be assisted by Mossad, which operated in Morocco through efforts headed by Ephraim Rosen-Ronel.

In 1961, Hassan II, the son of Muhammad V, came to power and pursued a completely different policy towards Israel. In secret negotiations with Israel, Morocco agreed to allow any Jew who wanted to leave for Israel to do so in exchange for a payment of $250 a head, which was made through the Joint Distribution Committee (JDC), an American-Jewish organisation.

In late 1962 or early 1963, a message was received via the JDC that Hassan II wanted Israeli aid in building a personal security system. At the time, the Moroccan king was in conflict with Nasser. Hassan II refused to recognise Egypt's hegemony in the Arab and Muslim world, and Nasser in turn accused the Moroccan monarch of pursuing an overly pro-Western policy. The king received threats to his life and took them very seriously. Four years earlier, Faisal II, King of Iraq, had been assassinated, and there had been many attempts to assassinate King Hussein of Jordan, all of them inspired by Egypt.

I understand a bit of French but knew not rely on that knowledge in Morocco. I was accompanied by David Shomron, who was born in

Istanbul and attended a school where French was the main language of instruction. Carrying foreign passports, we boarded a Moroccan airline flight from Paris to Rabat. Near the plane's ramp when we disembarked, two representatives of the Moroccan security service were waiting for us, holding signs with the names written on our passports. We were taken in a Mercedes straight from the airport to the royal palace, an impressive complex of several magnificent buildings in a traditional Islamic style.

It was my first time in an Arab country and I was very curious. I looked out at the landscape and although Rabat was relatively modern, the fact that Morocco is a Muslim country was inescapable. We arrived in the middle of the month of Ramadan, and we passed the King's encampment set up in the courtyard for the observance. We were told that at the end of the fast each evening, the king welcomed distinguished guests there.

Shomron and I were assigned an apartment in one of the palace buildings and told our meeting would be that night. For close to four hours, we sat in the guest hall, forced to fast. Our stomachs were rumbling when the hall doors opened at 10.00 p.m., and servants entered, with huge amounts of food, including at least half a dozen kinds of grilled meats, to be eaten, as customary, rolled into rice with one's fingers, with no cutlery. Two men soon introduced themselves to us: General Muhammad Oufkir and Colonel Ahmed Dlimi.

Oufkir, was an impressive man: thin and tall, a Berber, his dark face hewn like desert rock. He was highly decorated by France for achievements in battle in World War II, when he was part of the Free French forces in North Africa (which did not accept the authority of the Vichy regime). Dlimi was also powerfully built. We also introduced ourselves, I in English, Shomron in French. Oufkir only spoke French, but Dlimi was fluent in both languages.

As servants continued to flood us with food, the conversation flowed as if we were old acquaintances. It was conducted mostly in French, and I rarely needed a translation. When I spoke, Shomron translated my words. During the conversation which lasted late into the night, I asked our hosts about the structure and hierarchy of Moroccan security services, and they gave detailed answers.

It turned out that Oufkir was not only in charge of Morocco's equivalent to Mossad and Shin Bet, like Harel, but that he was also in charge of Morocco's military intelligence service. Dlimi was his deputy, particularly for internal security matters in the Moroccan equivalent of Shin Bet.

I, too, provided full answers to their questions, explaining t my role as head of Shin Bet's operational headquarters. We also discussed Nasser and trends in Egypt. I gave them the latest information we had, including Nasser's plans to assassinate Hassan II. It turned out that Oufkir and Dlimi knew most of what I relayed, but they were glad for the confirmation and impressed by our intelligence capability.

While eating with my hands, I gathered my courage and with a bit of chutzpah I turned to Oufkir and suggested that if they wanted effective and courageous partnership, we should set up regular meetings and determine a series of issues for joint action. The Israeli side would help guide and train security for the king and others as part of these ties. Not only did Oufkir and Dlimi not fall off their couches in shock, they responded with enthusiasm. It should be noted that Oufkir, as a Berber, did not consider himself an Arab or part of the Arab world. Eventually, this would lead to his assassination.

Late at night, we summed up and detailed what was agreed between us, and I wrote down the summaries for myself. At this early stage they even decided to choose a team of security personnel to be trained – not in Morocco but in Israel.

By the end of the meeting, Oufkir was calling me 'Rafik,' a word that connotes 'friend' in Arabic. When it was over, our hosts left to brief the king in his tent. Shomron and I stayed awake. Oufkir and Dlimi returned to us around 4.00 a.m. to inform us that the king had approved everything we had discussed – and that he would welcome us soon into his tent. We were told to bow but not say anything to the king. And so it was. We came to the king's huge tent, he passed by us, we bowed a little, he shook our hands, and said 'thank you' in French.

That was the end of my mission. We exchanged confidential phone numbers with Oufkir. No document was signed, but I had no doubt that the agreement would be honoured by both parties. We stayed another day in Rabat to tour the city before returning to Paris.

From Kruz's office in Paris, I sent a long report on our meeting to Harel and Naftali Keinan, head of Tevel, Mossad's foreign relations unit. With Kruz, I already started to plan in general terms the next moves with the Moroccan services, then returned to Israel, to my position at the head of Shin Bet's Division 10.

Colonel Dlimi arrived in Israel a week later,. For obvious reasons, he stayed at the Mossad's training institute, known as the Midrasha. For the most part, I acted as his host. I invited him to dinner in our small apartment in the Tel Aviv suburb of Moaz Aviv. Dlimi brought me typical Moroccan slippers, delicately embroidered and curled up at the toes, which I used for twenty years. I took Dlimi touring around the country. During his visit, the first delegation of security guards and commanders arrived and their training was assigned to my division.

All this took place during Harel's tenure, on the eve of the crisis that led to his resignation and the appointment of Meir Amit as his successor. Shortly after Meir took over at Mossad, Oufkir paid the first of a number of visits to Israel. At the time, I was still head of Shin Bet's Division 10, providing operational services to Mossad. This included assisting with training for the Moroccans on security issues.

Ben-Gurion and other senior officials were kept briefed on our cooperation with Morocco in general, and with Oufkir in particular. Neither I nor others involved ever heard a word of praise or thanks for what we were doing, but I knew the top political echelons were definitely in the loop and considered the connection with Morocco – the first of its kind with an Arab country – to be very important. True, we already had contacts with Turkey and Iran, which were Muslim, but they were not Arab countries.

Cooperation the with Moroccan security services, which began in this way in 1963, lasted for many years, with Mossad having a representative office in Morocco. Between April 1963 and April 1964, that is, until the end of my tenure as head of Division 10, several dozen Moroccan security service personnel trained in personal security, in cycles of ten or twenty people each time. They were housed in hotels in Tel Aviv, and most of their training was at the Midrasha, which at that time still served only as a guest house for foreign visitors to Mossad. Over the years, at least 200 security guards from Morocco were trained in Israel.

Rehavam Zeevi was active in training the Moroccan service for border protection between Morocco and its neighbours. He visited Morocco several times, planned their border security and helped them set up the Moroccan border patrol, along the lines of Israel's border guard.

The close cooperation with Oufkir, Dlimi and the Moroccan services led in 1965 to our entanglement in the murder of prominent Moroccan opposition leader Mahdi Ben-Barka, which I will discuss later in detail. This harmed our relations with the French. But intelligence ties with the Moroccans paved the way for Foreign Minister Moshe Dayan's talks with Hassan Tuhami, Egypt's deputy prime minister, in Morocco in 1977, under the newly elected government of Prime Minister Menachem Begin. On the eve of his departure for Morocco, Dayan thoroughly read Mossad's files on our special relationship with Morocco. He learned of the king's willingness to help us, his discretion, and was assured also that Moroccan security detail could be trusted with his safety while there. The meeting between Dayan and Tuhami led the way for President Sadat's historic visit to Jerusalem in November 1977.

I am not in the habit of taking credit for the work of others, and will not do so here either. I had no part in the political moves that established and strengthened ties with Morocco, or in Moshe Dayan's trip to Morocco. But I allow myself to note with satisfaction my part in initiating Mossad's contacts with the Moroccan security services. Like with the capture of Eichmann, I did not receive official recognition of this work from the Israeli government.

Chapter 16

A New Boss and a New Role

The End of an Era: Isser Harel's Retirement

The failure of the assassination attempt against Kleinwachter in Lorrach and the arrest of the two agents in Basel (detailed in Chapter 13) were laid at Harel's door. He exacerbated the situation with an act that was untypical for him. On his return from Europe in early March 1963 and his efforts there to stem German missile aid to Egypt, he convened the editors' committee of the daily press, and briefed them on what had happened in Germany and Switzerland. Then, without the prime minister's knowledge, he provided three senior journalists with documents and secret information about German scientists involved in Egypt and encouraged them to travel to Germany to investigate the matter as journalists and to publish their findings. The results were sensational headlines about the German-aided missile programme in Egypt. I believe this riled Ben-Gurion and led to Harel's resignation.

When one of the three journalists, Yeshayahu (Shaikeh) Ben-Porat, a journalist for the leading *Yedioth Ahronoth* newspaper returned to Israel, Yitzhak Navon, Ben-Gurion's political secretary, approached him and learned that Ben-Porat had been fed information by Harel to get his investigation going. Navon was shocked and reported this to Ben-Gurion. Two or three days later, Harel's resignation was announced.

The incident was the culmination of a growing confrontation between Ben-Gurion and Harel over the Egyptian missile project.

Its origins lay in the difference in the assessments of Harel, based on the information he had, and that of Meir Amit, the head of military intelligence. While Harel considered the Egyptian missile programme an imminent threat to Israel, Amit, based on some of the same information but analysed by his people, had concluded that it would be at least five years before the Egyptian missiles could pose a realistic threat and that it was possible that the Germans were promising much more than they could deliver, essentially extorting money from the Egyptians. A military intelligence report to this effect landed on Ben-Gurion's desk, just as Harel was en route back to Israel from Europe.

Amit's views were strengthened by Deputy Defense Minister Shimon Peres, who convinced Ben-Gurion that West German Defence Minister Franz-Josef Strauss, with whom he had close ties, would quietly and discreetly thwart the missile project in Egypt so that assassinations were unnecessary and would only tarnish Israel's image and complicate its relations with friendly governments.

Ben-Gurion attached great importance to Peres's assessment, holding him in high esteem for his deft negotiations with France to obtain a nuclear reactor for Israel, and for having initiated and overseen the launch of the Shavit 2 missile in 1961, which although only partially successful was considered an important achievement. Furthermore, it is probable that Ben-Gurion also did not want to jeopardise the security ties between Israel and West Germany, which became increasingly significant during that period.

Harel, feeling under pressure to gain support for his view, turned to his friend Golda Meir, then foreign minister. She was a bitter political rival of Peres, who, she felt, undermined her by his independent activity in France, then Israel's main ally. Harel asked her for permission to launch a public campaign against the German scientists in Egypt and she agreed.

Why did Harel turn to the foreign minister and not to the prime minister and defense minister, to whom he was directly subordinate? The answer is clear: he figured that Ben-Gurion would refuse his request and follow the advice of Peres, who favoured covert and quiet diplomacy through West Germany. Indeed, Ben-Gurion was furious at Harel's initiative and at his insubordination in going to Meir for approval rather than to Ben-Gurion himself. Some in Ben-Gurion's circle urged Harel to apologise, but he refused.

The rest as they say is history. Harel submitted a letter of resignation to Ben-Gurion stating:

> Given the significant differences of opinion between you and myself in the problem of German scientists working for Egypt's war effort, with all that entails, I consider it my duty to resign from my position as head of Mossad and the Security Service.

Ben-Gurion replied that he was rejecting the resignation, and invited him to present his views to the government, but added, 'It is possible that your opinion will be accepted by the government or the Knesset, and you can continue your work under another prime minister.'

The implication was clear: 'It's you or me.' In the body of his letter, Ben-Gurion demanded that Harel present the government with evidence for his view, namely who the sources were, the findings of his investigations, the names of the journalists he persuaded to go to Germany. But Harel did not respond to the invitation to appear before the Cabinet, and sent Ben-Gurion a letter saying that his resignation was final.

All this took place on 26 March 1963, on the eve of Passover. Ben-Gurion wanted to appoint Amos Manor as head of Mossad, but Manor was on his way to celebrate the holiday in Kibbutz Ma'agan. There were no cell phones in those days; there were radio telephones only in the cars of the chief of staff and some senior officers. Ben-Gurion's office contacted me to track down Manor, but I too could not locate him. Ben-Gurion, unwilling to leave Mossad for even an hour without a head, ordered: 'Bring Meir Amit.' Thus, Amit was appointed head of Mossad, in addition to heading military intelligence, and showed up at Mossad HQ immediately after *seder* night as its new head.

Manor was very hurt by Amit's appointment and let Ben-Gurion know his feelings. 'The old man' tried to backtrack: he attempted to woo Amit from Mossad by asking him to continue as head of military intelligence and promising him that he would become the next chief of staff of the IDF. But Amit had fallen in love with his job at Mossad, and announced that he would remain there, and that his deputy, Aharon Yariv, would succeed him as head of military intelligence. This soon prompted Manor to resign as head of Shin Bet, and he was replaced by his deputy, Yossef Harmelin.

Although Harel's resignation had no effect on Shin Bet, it deeply shook Mossad and prompted a revolt among some senior officials who resigned in protest. A day or two after Harel left, I had a meeting at Mossad. The secretary's eyes were red from crying. There was a psychosis of grief and depression in the place, like in a Greek tragedy. There were those who declared, 'We will bring him back,' and there were some who initiated a collective resignation, hoping that this would force Ben-Gurion reinstate Harel. The revolt was led by Raanan, head of Mossad operations in Europe, and a letter of resignation was sent to Amit, signed by several Mossad staffers in Europe, including Yitzhak Shamir, Malka Braverman, Mishka Drori, Zvi Z., Ephraim Ronel-Rosen and others. Amit did not accept their resignations, but soon after Shamir, Raanan, Drori, Ronel-Rosen and Zvi Z. retired.

To Amit's credit, it must be said that he overcame the trauma caused by Harel's resignation, and succeeded in rebuilding Mossad, reorganising it and replacing those who retired with good people. However, to this day the internal structure of Mossad is no different from the one Harel designed and built.

Immediately after slamming the door shut on Mossad, Harel set up a private investment fund called Haran, drew a respectable group of investors and raised millions of dollars, a huge sum in those days. But the business failed, and within a few years the investments dwindled to nothing.

With Mossad in Europe

Amit was appointed acting head of Mossad on the day of Harel's resignation, 25 March 1963. Until September 1963, he served simultaneously as acting head of Mossad and head of military intelligence. He left much of the work at military intelligence to his deputy there, Yariv, and devoted most of his time and attention to Mossad. Unlike Harel, he did not hold the title commissioner of security and intelligence services, and did not deal at all with the Security Service, which was henceforth under the sole authority of the head of the service. From the time of Harel's departure and to this day, the separation of powers between Shin Bet and Mossad has been maintained.

A few days after Passover, Amit summoned me to his office at military intelligence. We did not know each other very well, only from cooperation between Division 10 and military intelligence, and he asked me to brief him on the work of the division. A few weeks later, he invited me to meet him again, this time for lunch in a restaurant in Tel Aviv, where we were joined by Rehavia Vardi, a long-time acquaintance, with the rank of colonel, who had worked in various departments within military intelligence including as commander of the 154th Intelligence Unit (later Unit 504), responsible for recruiting and running a network of Arab agents on our behalf in Arab countries.

The conversation was friendly; Amit shared his thoughts about structural changes for Mossad, and said Vardi would be joining Mossad as head of Tzomet (Hebrew for 'junction') which operates espionage activities against Arab countries. Vardi had suggested Amit recruit me from Shin Bet to Mossad as head of its operations in Europe, based in Paris, which included operations of Tzomet in Europe, where much of the recruitment and operation of Arab agents was carried out. In fact, Vardi had made my heading the office in Europe a condition for his agreeing to take over at the helm of Tzomet.

The offer came as a complete surprise to me. To say the least, I did not jump for joy. The job would require me to relocate with my family to Paris for at least three years. I was relatively newly married, with two young children, Yael, aged four, and Sharon, aged two. We had purchased a plot of land in the Tel Aviv suburb of Afeka to build our house. I was busy, satisfied with my work. My first reaction was 'What do I need this upheaval for?' My second thought only intensified my reluctance: it would not be a step up in rank and it would involve a pay cut.

I do not remember exactly what I replied to Amit, but he immediately understood my reservations and rushed to assure me that my rank and pay would not be diminished. 'I need a positive answer from you – immediately, now. We must put an end to that whole Egyptian–German missile project and the person who must deal with it is the head of operations in Europe. And I want you to be the one to do it.'

I knew that until then, Amit had considered the missile project unimportant. So why had ending it suddenly become so urgent? I didn't ask Amit directly then or later. But I surmised that once at Mossad, Amit was exposed to all the material Mossad had collected on the project, and he concluded that although it did not pose an immediate existential danger to Israel, its continued existence could do so in the future.

I asked Amit for some time to weigh the offer and discuss it with my wife. He agreed, but stressed that he very much hoped for a positive answer. Mulling over the offer at home, Miriam and I considered the benefits of a few years in Paris. We would learn a new language, go to museums, see new places and the children would be exposed to another culture. Financially it also made sense. With Mossad paying for our accommodation in Paris, we could rent out or sell our apartment in Maoz Aviv, which meant we would have more money to build a house on the land we had purchased in Afeka, difficult to do on a regular government salary. Before giving my answer to Amit, I also consulted with Manor, my direct commander, who encouraged me to accept the offer. At that time, we agreed that my successor at the head of Division 10 would be Shalom.

About a week later I told Amit I'd take the job. He thanked me. I told him, 'I want you to know that I plan to set up an operational unit in Paris that will work for me in Europe. I won't be able to get up in the morning, if I don't have a such a unit.'

'By all means, set it up,' Amit said.

'I need people,' I said.

'Take whoever you want,' Amit replied, flipping through the paperwork in front of him.

I was due to leave for Paris in early March 1964 and start the job a month later. Only a few people in Mossad knew about my new position as head of Hamoked as the European unit was called, and I continued until then as head of Division 10. In October 1963, I wrote to Raanan about my replacing him. It turned out that no one had bothered to tell him, and my letter caught him by surprise. When he returned to Israel, he retired.

The summer of 1963 was a turbulent time. In June, Ben-Gurion resigned, and Levi Eshkol succeeded him as prime minister and defense minister. In September, Amit was officially appointed head of Mossad, Yariv replaced him as head of military intelligence and Harmelin shortly took over at Shin Bet.

I spoke to Harmelin and told him that Amit had approved my plans to revamp the operational unit in Europe. I gave him a list of five people from Division 10 whom I wanted to take with me to Paris. The most senior of them was Malchin. I sent him to Paris a few months before my arrival, and he began rebuilding the infrastructure of Colossus, Mossad's operations unit in Europe.

At the same time, I spent many hours preparing for my new assignment. My main focus at first was to be the German scientists and I was briefed on this by Zvi Reuter, a Holocaust survivor, a lieutenant colonel in military intelligence who was loaned to Mossad during Harel's period, and Rafi Meidan, whom I later transferred to Europe to help with this matter. I also met Raanan, of course, and went to Paris to meet the personnel at Tzomet there and then toured some of our other branches in Europe.

Miriam and Rafi Eitan during celebrations of their fiftieth anniversary in 2011.

Rafi as sculptor.
An artist and his creation.

Rafi at the grave of his brother Reuven, who died in childhood, when the grave was renewed.

Rafi, David Ben-Gurion (in local costume) and the Prime Minister's son, Amos, during a visit to Burma, 1961.

Rafi and Fidel Castro head their teams at a business meeting in Havana.

Handshake with Fidel Castro.
Rafi's business partner Elhanan Fess can be seen over Castro's shoulder.

Rafi attending a Passover *seder* with the Jewish community in Havana, April 2001.

During a special Knesset session addressed by French President Nicolas Sarkozy. On Rafi's left are Ehud Barak, Tzipi Livni and Ehud Olmert.

Rafi in conversation with Chancellor Angela Merkel of Germany in March 2008

U.S. President George W. Bush is seemingly happy to meet Israel's Pensioner Affairs Minister, perhaps forgetting Rafi's role in the Jonathan Pollard spying scandal.

תון שבועי ■ 18.3.87 ■ גיליון 224 ■ 56 עמודים ■ המחיר 3 ש"ח (כולל מע"מ) ■

כותרת רא

נחיתה קשה: דיוקנו של האלוף עמוס לפידות

דוד סופר ונחום וסקביץ': האלבינים החדשים

האמריקנים לישראל: "פולארד הוא רק קצה־הקרחון"

הביאו את המרגלים

The cover of the *Koteret Rashit* newspaper of 18 March 1987, at the height of the Pollard scandal, with Uncle Sam announcing: 'We Want the Spies'.

Rafi with President Shimon Peres at a reception.

Pensioners' Party members of the 17th Knesset: (*from right*) Yaakov Ben-Yizri, Health Minister, Rafi Eitan, Pensioner Affairs Minister, Moshe Sharoni, chairman of the Labour, Welfare and Health Committee.

The Minister for Pensioner Affairs addresses the Knesset, 11 May 2008.

During a Cabinet meeting. On Rafi's left Ehud Barak, former Prime Minister but now Defense Minister in Ehud Olmert's government.

Siblings (*right to left*) Ami, Oded, Rafi and Rina
at Rafi's seventieth birthday celebration, at home, 1996.

Miriam Eitan.

All this convinced me that it was necessary to restructure Tzomet in Europe, which dealt not only with recruiting and placing Arab spies in Arab countries, but also with liaison with intelligence services in foreign countries and with operational support in Europe to Mossad in general. Each branch in Europe reported to a different desk manager of Tzomet back in Tel Aviv, not to the head of Tzomet in Paris. The result was that often the European head of Tzomet in Paris was left out of the loop of operations in other European cities or heard about them via Tzomet in Tel Aviv. This meant that the head of Tzomet in Paris was more of a coordinator than a commander of European operations, going around to various branches once a month or so. I told Amit I would not replace Raanan unless I was given complete operational control over the branches in Europe. I wanted the tasks of staff officers to be determined according to each issue being handled – one for the German scientists, one for operations, others for recruitment and placement of spies in various Arab countries. I also wanted to develop archives in Europe, to end the dependence until then on the archives in Tel Aviv. Amit accepted my proposals and I implemented them in full. As was expected, changing the role of the head of Tzomet from coordinator to commander led to some conflict with the desks in Tel Aviv, a conflict which endured for most of my stay in Paris.

To implement the personnel changes, I recruited people I thought would be good for Hamoked from Shin Bet and military intelligence. To handle matters with Egypt, I recruited Yaakov Brown and Avraham Yoffe from Shin Bet, and Zev Liron from military intelligence.

In January '64, about two months before I left with my family for Paris, I met Peres by chance. I told him about my mission, about the goals I had set for myself, and of course I mentioned the matter of the German experts in Egypt. Peres showed great interest. I knew he had a good relationship with West German Defence Minister Franz-Josef Strauss, but in our conversation, he revealed to me some details I had not previously known and added, 'If you think Strauss can help us with anything, call me. I will help you as much as I can.' I thanked him and promised to ask for help if I needed it.

Our family arrived in Paris on 10 March 1964. After a short stay in a hotel, we moved into a beautiful and spacious rented apartment. Paris is rightly considered a city of pleasure, a city of culture, music, museums, spectacular architecture. But my years there were not a period of much fun. I worked like a dog, from 9.00 a.m. to 9 or 10 p.m., since most meetings of my staff with agents and spies took place in the evenings, and I waited in the office for their reports.

My basic approach to work was to leave the field work to the people in the field, while I pulled the strings behind the scene. When I did go out into the field, I mostly stood on the side-lines. This was warranted by the nature of my job: I was the head of a very large array of agents, and I had to control them. In the field, you can only do one operation, while from the office you can keep an eye on dozens of operations – of which there were between fifty and eighty a week every year after I became head of Hamoked. One or two days a month, I visited a few branches in Europe and, once a month, branch managers would come to Paris for a meeting.

I took part in none of the entertainment of the City of Light. Miriam rightly complained that I did not spend enough time with my family, except during summer holidays. I also had no leisure to study French systematically, and to this day I can manage to read a newspaper in French and know some basic phrases but cannot conduct a real conversation.

Miriam found Paris hard as is clear in her description of life there.

Testimony of Miriam

> In April 1964 we arrived in Paris . . . I did not know the city. I did not speak a word of French. I had two toddlers to care for, aged four and two. I had no idea where anything was. I had no one to ask. And Rafi worked until late in the evening, busy in his office. We stood, the children and I, facing the filthy glass. It was raining outside; there were tears inside.

Rafi's job was sacrosanct. It would not have occurred to me to ask him to help me at home or with childcare, let alone pay me much attention or pamper me. Rafi was an open-minded, liberal man, perhaps even a feminist, but his behaviour was supremely chauvinistic.

Compared to my past, life in Paris was supposed to be easy and enriching. I was happy about the prospect of moving. No one forced it on me. But the reality was not simple. Although we had help and I was able to go out in the mornings to the Alliance Française, the famous French language school, the rest of the day I was imprisoned in my home.

Because of the nature of Rafi's work, we lived in complete isolation. We did not make contact with local people. Not one French guest visited our apartment during our years in Paris. I had no friends. Rafi did not understand the language, so we could not go to the theatre and other cultural events together. But it was not all because of Rafi. I was probably still carrying around me some of the emotional effects of my widowhood from my first husband, Yair, who died when I was pregnant with Yael. It was something that kept me from making connections, and this loneliness played into the conditions regarding social interaction that Rafi's position dictated. His success at work was our mutual mission. I never set foot in his office, but I knew everything – he hid almost nothing from me. But that did not prevent the loneliness, and in truth, in the end, the children and I were the ones who paid the price of his success.

The first years in Paris were good years in our relationship, and that was paramount. But the loneliness increasingly encroached. Rafi's absences got longer and longer – sometimes he was away for a few weeks, sometimes for several months. In the meantime, we had another son, Yuval. We lived in a secluded area, I would be taken by car to the supermarket once a week, but apart from that I saw no one. Me and three kids, alone, in a city of millions. I constantly worried that if

> something happened to me outside the house, no one would know, and the children would be left completely alone. These were difficult years. And if I complained to Rafi, his response was always: 'You caught me right in a very tense period.'
>
> After almost seven years in Paris, I breathed a sigh of relief when we returned home to Israel.
>
> But it was all a long time ago. Since then, a lot of water has flowed under the bridge.

As for me, I concluded that my main duties in my new position were:

- Supervise and manage the recruitment and operation of spies, primarily in Egypt and Syria, and secondarily in other Arab countries;
- Strive to establish intelligence ties with Arab and Muslim countries;
- Activate Colossus to advance the goals of Mossad in Europe;
- Maintain operational contact with foreign intelligence services.

On the last task, I found excellent allies in some European intelligence services who cooperated with us. Sympathy for the Jewish state motivated them, but it was not only that. For example, we were asked by one European intelligence service to provide material on the MiG-21 flown to Israel by an Iraqi pilot recruited by Mossad. We were able to tell them that even before they requested it, we were in the process of translating the aircraft's instruction manual and would send it to them very soon, and told them we would be happy to answer any further questions after they received it.

Most of my first months as the head of Hamoked in Europe were spent organising procedures for operations in general, and for Colossus in particular. As mentioned earlier, about two months before I came to Paris, I appointed Malchin to head Colossus and in consultation we brought some top-notch staff from Israel to work with him. By the end of my first year, I was overseeing about 150 people throughout Europe, including the Colossus unit, which I reinforced with people I brought in from Israel to ensure the security of our operations personnel, to empty drop boxes and to maintain and guard safehouses, among other tasks.

I invested a great deal of effort in identifying places and ways to best place potential agents in Arab countries. It later became clear that in this I had a lot in common with Markus Wolf, head of the East German intelligence service, a prominent spymaster during the Cold War (who, by the way, was Jewish, and never tried to hide his origins). Many years after he no longer engaged in espionage, Wolf told me that one person planted in the right place could bring in more intelligence than an entire brigade. And he knew what he was talking about. It was Wolf who recruited Günter Guillaume and sent him in 1956 – along with his wife – ostensibly as refugees to West Germany. Guillaume joined the Social Democratic Party, rose in the ranks to serve as a senior aide to party leader Willy Brandt, and in 1969, when Brandt was elected chancellor, Guillaume continued in his bureau.

There was one glitch during my initial period in Europe: we had strong suspicions against one of the people who paid our spies, and he stole several thousand dollars. I fired him. He filed a complaint against me at Mossad, but there was no follow-up. Naturally, spies don't give out receipts when they are paid, so the case officers in charge of paying them must be trustworthy and above suspicion that they might not be handing over all monies due to the spies they control. Whenever there was a suspicion, I was not prepared to compromise. Fortunately, there were very few such instances.

Most case officers began their careers in military intelligence and included immigrants from Iraq, Lebanon, Syria and Egypt, whose mother tongue was Arabic.

The Palestine Liberation Organisation (PLO) was established in June 1964, and in January 1965 Fatah carried out its first operation. Following this, we focused on Palestinian organisations as targets. I suggested to Amit that we obliterate all of Fatah's leadership. In those days, Fatah and Arafat had not caught much attention in the world, and their elimination would not have created much of a stir. But Amit, who may have consulted with Eshkol on this matter, replied in the negative. Some forty years later, in a closed discussion of the National Security Council under Major General (Reserves) Uzi Dayan in 2001 or 2002, Shabtai Shavit, then head of Mossad, mentioned my proposal and commented: 'It's a pity we didn't do it then. Perhaps we would have prevented the situation we have reached now.'

The solidarity with Israel that Jews around the world – and Gentiles in large numbers, too – felt at that time was exceptional. The establishment of the state, our victories in the War of Independence and the 1956 Sinai operation, and – I allow myself to mention – the capture of Eichmann and his trial in Israel, all created admiration for Israel on a scale not known today. This helped us in our actions. I want to note that no one who assisted us from these motives ever asked me for favours in return to advance their business, nor to the best of my knowledge did they do so for any economic gains.

Skorzeny: Low-hanging Fruit

In my first year as head of Hamoked in Europe, the number of messages and telegrams exchanged with Tzomet headquarters in Israel rose to about 200 a week, compared to about thirty a week in the year before I joined. As mentioned, I invested most of my efforts in 1964–5 in two areas: German scientists in Egypt, and identifying and planting agents in Arab target countries. Our efforts led to impressive successes in both areas. Even before the end of 1965, the scientists' affair gradually worked itself out and so did its urgency. Due to our activities, at the outbreak of the June 1967 War, no guided missiles were available to the Egyptian Army.

As is well known, an agent who later worked in Mossad's service, Ashraf Marwan, who was recruited in 1969 and was married to Nasser's third daughter, gave us warning of the war on the eve of Yom Kippur. Subsequently, there were allegations that he may have been a double agent. I don't know but it is possible. It often happens when it comes to Arab agents, they play a double role, giving each side what they think that side wants to hear, and receiving payment from both parties (and sometimes more than two . . .).

Our activity was highly appreciated at Mossad HQ. On 7 July 1965, Amit wrote to me to let me know how impressed he was that useful and successful operations had increased by 45 per cent in my first year as head of Hamoked, which he termed 'a legendary' increase and added: 'We all know most of them were "born" under you.'

If our operations could be published, they would deserve not a chapter but a thick book. The operations involved not only our own staff but also statesmen, businessmen, industrialists and others. There were two interlinked operations that were archived under the code name Countdown in Mossad's archives. For the sake of brevity and because I do not remember all the details, I will confine myself to a general description, and only of actions in which I personally took part.

In late 1963, about six months before I left Shin Bet for Paris, we learned from various sources about the success of Egyptian contacts and intermediaries in assembling and recruiting a new group of thirty to forty German engineers and technicians, experts in inertial navigation of surface-to-surface missiles, at least ten of whom had already arrived in Egypt. One of our sources was Yitzhak Navon, Ben-Gurion's former political secretary (and later the fifth president of Israel). Navon, who had an intelligence background from his days in the Haganah, was on a ship from Europe to Israel when he heard that a group of workers from Helige, headquartered in Freiburg in West Germany, had been recruited to work in Egypt. Helige was considered one of the most advanced companies in the world for inertial navigation systems for missiles. Navon, who knew from the information on Ben-Gurion's desk that the inertial navigation of missiles was the critical issue delaying the Egyptian project, immediately notified Amit.

During this period, our German branch, headed by Avraham Ahituv, was hampered in operating against the German scientists because of security measures put in place by Kleinwachter, head of the team at Lorrach developing the missile navigation system, after the assassination attempt against him and the disappearance of Heinz Krug, whose fate was unknown to the Germans. Those measures included hiring Herman Adolf Vallentin, a devoted Nazi and former member of an SS commando unit, to guard and head security for the German scientists working on the project. We nicknamed Vallentin 'the teacher'. He met each scientist on arrival in Egypt and had a free hand from the Egyptians to do all that was necessary to ensure the scientists' security and that of the project.

At the end of May or in early June 1964, I initiated a meeting in Paris to discuss all the plans and tasks of Tzomet and Caesarea, Mossad's operations unit, in Europe. Among the participants were Amit, Vardi, Yosef Yariv, who in late 1963 had become the head of Caesarea. Yariv was a personal friend, but we disagreed over tactics regarding the German scientists in Egypt. Naturally, in his new position, he pushed for violent actions against the scientists, from sending threatening letters to explosive packages, among other deterrent actions. I argued that violence would attract the attention of the German authorities, lead them to us, and bring failure. I suggested that we approach the European suppliers of the Egyptians, who were known to us, and try to convince them not to provide components to the Egyptians.

Arguments of this kind are typical of security and intelligence services, with some supporting what is today called 'low signature', and was then called 'smart treatment', compared to 'high signature', or 'noisy treatment'.

In my life I have solved some problems with noisy treatment, but when circumstances allow I prefer smart treatment. In this case, I thought that noisy treatment would not prove to be justified. German scientists and experts continued to flock to Egypt and the project was progressing, despite the fact that Krug had been abducted, Kleinwachter had been subject to an assassination attempt which he survived, and Hannelore Wende was blinded by an exploding letter. So I thought we should change tactics.

I argued that we could not prevent a German citizen from accepting a job offer from Egypt, or any other country. But we could convince him not to accept an offer by putting a better one in front of him. The way to do this was to present the situation and its consequences to the German authorities, and to make them act – quietly but effectively – so that the scientists would turn down offers from Egypt, because they received other, better offers. And those who had already signed contracts would receive compensation.

Amit sat with a frown, struggling to decide between the two approaches. As far as I could tell, he was more inclined to Yariv's methods, but refrained at the time from making a clear decision, though Yariv's plans were halted, at least temporarily.

A few days later, Amit and I met Ahituv, who supported my approach, and then shared an original concept.

> I've been mulling over an idea for some time. I didn't mention it before now because it felt too unclear, but now I've gathered more operational intelligence and I think it's sufficiently formed. You are the first I'm sharing this idea with: let's recruit the 'the teacher' and convince him to work with us.

'How can we recruit him? He already works for Kleinwachter and his gang. What can we give him that they will not give him? And he's a Nazi, hates Jews . . .'

'*We* will not recruit him,' Avraham replied.

'Not us? So who?'

'His commander in the SS, Obersturmbannführer Otto Skorzeny.'

Skorzeny, who was born in 1907 in Vienna of German parents, served during World War II first as an officer in Hitler's personal security unit and later headed the SS commando unit that in July 1943 whisked Benito Mussolini from captivity in the Apennines, for which Hitler personally decorated him. He also led the abduction, in October 1944, of Miklos Horthy Jr, the son of Hungarian Admiral Horthy, to force the father to relinquish power in favour of Ferenc Szálasi, the leader of Hungary's pro-Nazi Arrow Cross Party.

After being acquitted in a war crimes trial in 1948, Skorzeny eventually settled in Madrid, where he set up a small metal-processing factory. In 1953, Skorzeny went to Egypt to train units of the Egyptian Army in commando warfare. There he met Nasser, who was very impressed with him, and considered him a personal friend.

Ahituv's idea of recruiting Skorzeny may have sounded fantastical, but Ahituv was not one for fantasies and I never rejected an idea out of hand. It was worth trying to recruit former Nazis, some of whom feared they might share Eichmann's fate. I did not intend to recruit people who committed mass murder, or who were actively involved in the persecution and extermination of Jews. There were, however, quite a few people who held various positions in the government or in Nazi forces, who might serve our purposes.

I would like to make clear that it was not a matter of forgiving those Nazis or Nazi accomplices who might work with us. But Ahituv, I and others at Hamoked considered it our duty to do everything possible for the security of the State of Israel. The existence of the state was not taken for granted at the time. This was before the Six-Day War in 1967. The Arabs, led by Nasser, were constantly talking about the 'second round' in which the State of Israel would be destroyed, and we had to take their threats seriously and do all we could to thwart them. Therefore, I had no hesitation about employing Nazis who could help us ensure the security of Israel.

When Amit and Yariv came to Paris again, Ahituv outlined his plan. Yariv didn't believe it would work. Amit felt it was dangerous to employ someone like Skorzeny. Only I unreservedly supported Ahituv's proposal.

'I believe there is a nine in ten chance the man will work with us,' I said.

'What makes you believe that?' asked Amit. 'What exactly will you offer him?'

'Freedom from fear,' I replied. 'Since the capture of Eichmann and his hanging in Israel, Nazis have been trembling with fear.'

Amit approved the operation without enthusiasm.

From then on, Ahituv coordinated all the moves and I approved them, but unlike Harel I did not try to put myself in charge of Ahituv and, when the time came, I did not intervene and left direct contact with Skorzeny in his hands.

I will not go into all the meticulous work of Ahituv and his men and others in the Colossus unit that led us to Skorzeny, the revered commander of Oberscharführer (Staff Sergeant) Vallentin. Among those involved was 'Nazi hunter' Shimon Wiesenthal.

The operation went into high gear in the autumn of 1964. I met Ahituv, who, as mentioned earlier, spoke German as a mother tongue, as he was about to leave Frankfurt for Madrid to meet 'the monster' (as we called Skorzeny among ourselves). Joining us was an excellent field officer from the German branch, a tall and elegant man with a European appearance, who had made contact with Skorzeny's wife, Countess Ilse von Finckenstein, charmed her and persuaded her to have her husband meet up with Ahituv. Together we discussed in detail what Ahituv should say to Skorzeny, and especially how. I suggested, and Ahituv immediately concurred, that there should be no hint of a threat. Skorzeny would assume that our ability to harm him was limited: he was not charged with genocide, he lived in Madrid and was protected by the Franco regime. Unlike Eichmann, who never fought in battle, Skorzeny was a skilled fighter who knew how to defend himself. Any attempt to harm him would be highly risky.

According to procedures, I was meant to report Ahituv's departure for Madrid to Tel Aviv, but I didn't for fear that Amit, who liked to be present during operations likely to be of historic significance, would decide to come too. It's a natural tendency, but I trusted Ahituv completely and didn't want Amit to command or disturb him. I reported to Israel about the meeting in Madrid after it had already taken place. I received an angry response: how dare I hide from Amit the matter of the meeting in Madrid! I replied that due to time constraints, I couldn't report to him in advance. I don't know if he believed me, but I got no further flak about this.

The operation to recruit Skorzeny ended surprisingly quickly and was completely successful. On the pretext of a conference of former SS members, Skorzeny invited Vallentin to Madrid. When they met, Skorzeny did not ask him or solicit him, but simply ordered him to cooperate with a 'foreign intelligence service', as Ahituv advised him. He told Vallentin that a new Germany was in the works and involved intelligence cooperation with a foreign intelligence service interested in information about Egypt's missile project.

Vallentin listened and saluted, with a Nazi gesture, of course. He had only one request: for complying with Skorzeny's order, he asked to be promoted retroactively to the rank of officer. Skorzeny, of course, had no problem complying with this wish, and so Vallentin, almost twenty years after the end of World War II, fulfilled his dream of becoming an officer in the SS.

Our first meeting with Vallentin took place in early October in Madrid. Vallentin's purported recruitment to a foreign intelligence service was carried out by another field officer, a tall and handsome young man of Australian descent, and David Kimchi, then head of the psychological warfare department at Mossad (later head of the Tevel department and deputy head of Mossad). Both were native English speakers. I came to Madrid on the eve of the meeting with Vallentin to impart my knowledge on European intelligence services. These officers did an excellent job of recruiting Vallentin. Just as he was an effective security guard for German scientists and experts, so Vallentin proved himself a diligent agent of the purported foreign intelligence service and showed great resourcefulness in the tasks given to him. We soon had complete, detailed lists of all the scientists, engineers, and technicians under contract with the Egyptians.

Only after the Six-Day War, did we tell Vallentin who he was really working for. It did not bother him at all, and for several years he continued to work for us, fully aware that his employers were from Mossad.

Our collaboration with Skorzeny was not limited to Vallentin's recruitment. Until his death from cancer in 1975, Skorzeny provided us with a lot of information about Egyptian activity in Europe, and also visited Egypt once or twice and brought us information from there.

Contrary to my suggestions, Amit and Eshkol did not agree to one of Skorzeny's requests in exchange for his service: to arrange for the Israeli media to report prominently that his autobiography had been translated into Hebrew and copies distributed among IDF commando units. At the time, Skorzeny was facing charges in Germany and he believed this would help his case as evidence that he did not persecute Jews. We were faced with a real dilemma: Eshkol and Amit believed that even if we used his services, we should not lend a hand to defend this senior Nazi. A compromise was found that satisfied Skorzeny: Kimchi saw to it that a London newspaper published an article about the translation of Skorzeny's book into Hebrew.

In mid-October 1964, Operation Countdown began, with the aim of ending, or at least severely disrupting, the Egyptian missile project. Amit this time decided on a combined strategy with both noisy treatment (handled by the Caesarea unit) and smart treatment (which I favoured). This meant both non-violent means to sever ties between Egypt and European suppliers and at the same time a warning letter to any German who signed on to the Egyptian missile project. In addition, Kimchi prepared a major campaign in the German and world media that insinuated that Helige's involvement in the Egyptian project amounted to planning a new Holocaust for Jews, this time in their homeland, with the German government ignoring the situation.

The warning letters provoked nervousness and anger from the West German authorities.

In early December, Amit decided to transfer all of Operation Countdown to the Caesarea unit, that is to concentrate on the noisy treatment. I vehemently opposed this, demanding that the operation fall under me as head of Hamoked in Europe. Amit came to Paris, and after heated discussions, I persuaded him to give up the noisy approach. He rescinded his previous order, but took command of the operation, and remained in Europe to participate in it himself.

On 7 December, the first meeting was held at a secure hotel in a European capital with Thomas, an engineer and the team leader of the twenty-nine engineers and technicians who had recently signed employment contracts with the Egyptians. Gideon Rothschild, who identified himself as a representative of the Israeli government, conducted the negotiations with Thomas. Amit, Ahituv, Rafi Meidan and I sat in a room one floor above and listened to the negotiations. Meidan translated for Amit and me (Ahituv did not need the translation). Rothschild promised Thomas that his teammates would receive compensation, and that we would provide them with alternative jobs in Germany. At my behest, he offered Thomas a hefty advance on the compensation the Germans would get. As I expected, this offer made a strong impression on Thomas, who understood that we were serious, and that we could pay the sums we were offering.

At the end of the meeting, Thomas took the bank draft from Rothschild and went to Freiburg, where he convened his group and got a green light to continue negotiations with us. After discussions that lasted several days, a final agreement was reached.

In mid-December 1964, Amit returned to Israel, leaving me fully responsible to continue the operation to its end. At this point, I called in Peres, Deputy Minister of Defense, who, before I left for Paris, had stressed to me his excellent relations with West German Minister of Defence Franz-Josef Strauss. Peres's intervention was essential to the successful completion of the operation. To manage the secret contacts with the Germans, I appointed Meidan, a very charming man, who spoke German fluently and knew German culture to the core. I instructed him what to ask of Strauss, and he did a great job. Strauss, for his part, acted with typical secrecy and efficiency.

In all, thirty-four experts cancelled their employment contracts with Egypt. Thirteen of them went on to be employed by Bölkow, a company which later merged with Messerschmitt into MBB. As a token of appreciation for his contribution to the settlement, the

Israeli government sent Ludwig Bölkow twenty Uzi submachine guns. Twelve experts continued to work at Helige which received new orders from the German government, and for the rest we arranged jobs in other enterprises.

Practically speaking, Operation Countdown ended the affair of German scientists in Egypt. The low-level expertise of the Egyptians involved in missile production made it impossible to complete the project on their own, without European help.

During 1965, as a follow-up to Operation Countdown, we identified and visited all the companies in Europe that we considered potential candidates to cooperate with Egypt's missile development efforts. On my strict orders, we refrained from any threats, stressing instead the danger to Israel that the missiles posed in order to dissuade them from supplying Egypt with the experts, raw materials or spare parts the Egyptians needed to develop their missile programme. Needless to say, we did mention the Holocaust of the Jews of Europe. Some company executives were sympathetic; others realised that they should not mess with us.

As a result of our efforts, when the Six-Day War broke out in June 1967, surface-to-surface missiles were not available to the Egyptian Army.

On the night of 4 June 1967, a day before the war broke out, I immediately went down to 'the pit', the central military command headquarters, and asked late Air Force commander Major General Mordechai Hod, to bomb three sites near Cairo: Factory 333 (the base where missiles were developed), and two missile assembly and launch facilities. I did not consult with anyone and did not ask for permission, but Hod – with the knowledge of IDF Chief of Staff Lieutenant General Haim Bar-Lev – complied with my request in part. For operational reasons, Factory 333 was not bombed during the war, but the other two facilities were destroyed.

Chapter 17

The Ben-Barka Affair

Our cooperation with the Moroccans was considered a significant achievement not only within the intelligence services, but also at the most senior political level. This achievement, however, involved controversy around the abduction and murder in Paris of Mahdi Ben-Barka, leader of the outlawed Moroccan left-wing party, National Union of the People's Forces. In 1962, Ben-Barka was accused of conspiring against King Hassan II, and went into exile in Switzerland. In 1963, after expressing support for Algeria in the territorial conflict that erupted with Morocco, he was accused of treason and sentenced to death *in absentia*.

About two or three months before the abduction, on 29 October 1965, Naftali Keinan, the head of Tevel (Mossad's foreign relations unit) in Europe, told me that he had met in Morocco with the king and General Muhammad Oufkir, their head of intelligence with whom we had prior contact. They asked us to help them locate and follow Ben-Barka and a group of his supporters, opponents of the king, who lived in Geneva.

After Ben-Barka was murdered, the French press kept publishing imaginary details about the affair and Israel's purported involvement in it. Our service was not involved in any way in the planning of his abduction and murder (which the Moroccans considered the execution of a sentence from Ben-Barka's *in absentia* trial) and these came as a complete surprise to us.

But the affair had far-reaching consequences internally in Israel due to the rivalry at the time between Harel and Amit. Harel had become the prime minister's adviser on intelligence and security issues. Deputy head of Mossad Yaakov Kruz leaked to Harel the details of the Moroccans' request for assistance in the Ben-Barka affair. Harel showed this material to his boss, hoping it would bring down Amit, his successor at Mossad.

The prime minister and senior politicians did not take any action against Amit, but the matter made its way into the Israeli press through a marginal pornographic weekly called *Bull*, which published a huge headline about 'Mossad's involvement in the assassination of Ben- Barka'. Police officers and Shin Bet personnel raided newsstands and confiscated all the copies of the weekly they managed to get their hands on. *Bull*'s editor and deputy editor were arrested and prosecuted for censorship violations. But the French press continued to publish details about the alleged involvement of Mossad in Ben-Barka's assassination.

Amit continued to serve as head of Mossad until August 1968, when he was replaced by Zvi Zamir, but as early as 1965, Harel retired from the post of prime minister's adviser on intelligence and security. Kruz was forced to resign not long after the Ben-Barka affair.

It was a time of crisis in the country's intelligence system. Sitting in Paris, most of what I knew about it stemmed from my correspondence with colleagues in Mossad and Shin Bet. These included private exchanges with Amit. In one message in September 1965, before the Ben-Barka affair, he poured out his heart over Harel's appointment as prime minister's intelligence and security adviser, an appointment made not only without Amit's knowledge and consent, but also – and not by chance – just when Amit was abroad on work-related business.

In other letters, he gave me background information that it was at Harel's insistence that Eshkol set up a committee of inquiry to look into the Ben-Barka affair. Amit was convinced we would all emerge from it unscathed

The Yadin–Sharaf Committee, named for its two members, former Chief of Staff Yigal Yadin and Cabinet Secretary Zeev Sharaf, began its deliberations in early 1966. It was asked to answer three questions:

1. Were proper reporting procedures followed? Specifically was Eshkol kept properly informed by Amit and was Amit kept informed by his people in the field (that is to say Keinan, myself and my people)?
2. Did the field act in accordance with Amit's instructions and had these been approved by Eshkol?
3. Did the head of Mossad have overall political discretion?

With regard to the first two questions, the two members of the committee did not have any comments or objections. They looked at transcripts of Amit's conversations with Eshkol and all the reports from the field. When the committee members wanted to bring me and Keinan to testify, Amit told them that it was unnecessary, since he took both ministerial and direct operational responsibility for everything his people did on the ground.

Only regarding the third question did the Yadin–Sharaf Committee in fact issue a ruling: it recommended heretofore limiting the term of office of the head of Mossad – including the current one – to five years. This verdict was directed against Amit. At the time, it meant he had less than two years left as head of Mossad, and he did retire in August 1968, at the end of a term of exactly five years. However, it should be noted that if the same committee had found fault with Amit's conduct, he would have been dismissed from Mossad immediately.

The period was a very stressful one for me, with pain all over. At the end of one of his letters to me, Amit advised me, 'Rafi, take care of your haemorrhoids . . .'

Years later, a British journalist called Stewart Steven published a book, *The Spymasters of Israel*, in which he devoted a chapter to Ben-Barka's kidnapping and murder. It included a lot of inaccuracies.

Chapter 18

New and Unlikely Foreign Contacts

Early Negotiations with Egypt

I mentioned in a previous chapter that on the eve of my appointment as head of Hamoked in Europe, I discussed with Amit my future tasks as well as my work plan. In our discussions, I mentioned that I wanted to find ways to talk to the Egyptian intelligence services. I relied on the fact that, although like the Moroccans the Egyptians are also Muslims, their identification with the Arab nation is not complete and absolute, and that they had no actual conflict with the State of Israel.

I knew, of course, that in his book *The Philosophy of the Revolution*, published in 1959, Nasser wrote that one of the three circles to which Egypt belonged – and in which it saw itself as playing a central role – was the Arab circle. In the meantime, however, many things had happened, including the disintegration of the loose union between Egypt and Syria, as well as greater tension between Egypt and Jordan, and with other Arab countries. My impression, shared by others, was that Nasser had come to attach greater importance to another circle – the circle of non-aligned states.

Amit was not enthusiastic about my idea, but he did not rule it out. As usual, he advised exercising extreme caution, pointing out the sensitivity of the issue. He believed that Nasser had never given up on his aspiration for hegemony in the Arab world and was thus compelled to take a strong anti-Israel line. Consequently, as long as Nasser remained in power, the chances of starting a dialogue between Egypt and Israel were very low in Amit's estimate.

With the assistance of Tevel, which was in contact with friendly European intelligence services, in July 1964, I met a man by the name of Mark – I don't remember his full name – who regularly helped Mossad. Mark pointed me to an insurance agent, known to his friends as Max, who was an avid supporter of Israel. Max had a client called Steve, a businessman with close ties to Egyptian Air Force Colonel Ism al-Din Mahmoud Khalil, who played a key role in Egyptian military procurement in Europe, including for the missile project. Many purchases for the Egyptian military were made through Steve.

After clearance from Rehavia Vardi, head of Tzomet, which, as mentioned earlier, handled espionage against Arab countries, Mark arranged a meeting for both of us with Max at my hotel in Zurich. I told Max outright in our conversation that I was a member of the Israeli intelligence community, and that we wanted to reach Khalil through his friend and client Steve, to 'create a hot line' to Nasser. (A year earlier, in 1963, a 'hot line' had been established for quick communication between Washington and Moscow, to help prevent the outbreak of World War III due to a mistake or misunderstanding.) Max told us that Steve also handled Khalil's private business, and even dealt with Nasser's property and assets outside Egypt, including land in British Columbia, Canada. Max believed that Steve had recently run into difficulties. His business with Egypt has slumped recently and Steve worried that Israel might well know of the services he provided to Cairo, and consequently feared that the world-renowned long arm of its secret services might target him for assassination

In conclusion, Max thought that it would not be difficult to arrange for us to meet Steve. Knowing Amit would want to assess Max before we could move forward, I suggested we pay for Max to travel to Israel to meet one of our intelligence chiefs. Max told us that he already had plans to visit Israel in September. As in the case of Skorzeny's recruitment, this time, too, I reported to Amit the fruitful conversation with Max only after the fact and incurred his wrath.

But he did agree to meet Max and after they met in September Amit allowed me to continue the operation.

Khalil, a former head of Egyptian Air Force intelligence and head of the missile project, was considered one of Nasser's closest associates at the time. From the intelligence we collected on him, we knew that he was clever, cunning, pleasure-loving when he was in Europe, accustomed to drinking a certain brand of whiskey at lunch and another brand in the evening. We also knew his health was not good and that in the previous year he had suffered from both a nervous breakdown and from stomach pain.

After Amit's meeting with Max, I moved the operation into high gear. For our direct contacts with Steve, and later with Khalil, I chose Meidan, who had been the head of the German scientists' desk at Mossad headquarters in Israel until I brought him to Europe to work directly with me. Between January and July 1965, Meidan met no less than seven times with Steve, sometimes at Max's house in Zurich, or alone in hotels in Zurich and Paris. After each meeting, in which the parameters of a relationship with Egypt were discussed, Steve would fly to Egypt to brief Khalil, who in turn briefed Nasser, and Steve would return to us with their answers.

In October 1965, ahead of a state visit to France of Egyptian Vice President Marshal Abdel Hakim Amer, accompanied by General Khalil, a written summary based on our talks was drawn up in discussions with Eshkol and Amit. This summary, signed by a 'consultant', without an explicit name, was forwarded to Egypt.

The following are the main points raised during the talks, in the non-binding written summary sent to Egypt:

- Establishment of a 'hot line' between Eshkol and Nasser, in order to prevent violent clashes that could lead to an uncontrolled crisis and even war;
- Israeli assistance to Egypt in obtaining a large loan from a European bank. Israel was willing to transfer to an Egyptian bank account in Europe an immediate loan of \$25–30 million, at an annual interest rate of five per cent;

- An Israeli–Egyptian barter deal in the above amount for the supply of wheat from Canada to Egypt, and an Israeli purchase of 100,000 bales of Egyptian cotton;
- Free passage of Israeli goods (but not Israeli ships initially) in the Suez Canal;
- Right of Israel to fly over the Straits of Tiran;
- The release of the Israeli spy Wolfgang Lutz ('We always knew he was Israeli and not German,' Khalil later revealed to Amit), and the release of prisoners from 'the bad business' who were still imprisoned in Egypt.

Things were beginning to take shape, so much so that Deputy Defense Minister Zvi Dinstein, who succeeded Peres, called me to say he was about to make a deposit of the first millions for the Egyptians to a Swiss bank and asked me to press the Egyptians to agree to raise the interest rate on the loan to 5.5 instead of 5 per cent a year. At the same time, Steve approached us and asked – actually begged us – to obtain a grant or loan for him of $1.5 million required to save some real estate property in Canada, owned by him or a senior Egyptian figure. Though our intervention, he received the funds, but I do not know how much it cost Israel, if at all.

On 1 February 1966, Amit and Khalil met face to face at Steve's home in Europe. Their conversation lasted about three hours, and Amit told me that it was conducted politely and in good spirits. However, the Egyptians expressed concern that Israel would seek publicity about the contacts, harming Egypt's position in the Arab world. 'All our contacts in the past, in the early 1950s, became public,' Khalil complained. Amit tried to allay those fears by pointing out that in the past, contact was conducted through mediators and they were the ones who leaked the information. 'This is the first time we have had a direct conversation, without intermediaries,' Amit pointed out to Khalil.

Khalil suggested that a small Israeli delegation meet an Egyptian team on 12 February to conclude the negotiations on the points under discussion and bring them to Nasser and Eshkol for their approval.

The Israeli delegation was to be composed of Amit, Dinstein and a senior representative of the Foreign Ministry. But the meeting never happened because of disagreement over where to meet. The Egyptians wanted the meeting to be in Cairo, but Harel, as security adviser to Eshkol, was adamantly opposed to the venue. His rationale: Amit and Dinstein, two people who know Israel's most hidden secrets, must not go to Cairo. He suspected the Egyptians of setting a trap for the two by insisting on Cairo. We suggested Athens instead, but the Egyptians, saying they feared leaks, would not agree.

No further meeting was held with the Egyptians, putting an end to the operation.

Amit blamed the failure of the operation on his rival, Harel, who was unwilling to accept the thought that his hated successor might receive credit for starting a dialogue between Israel and Egypt, which might even lead to peace.

I refused to give up and in a desperate attempt to breathe life into the dying operation, I tried in various ways to advance the issue of European lending to Egypt. I reached out, through our Ambassador to Rome, Ehud Avriel, to the German Jewish banker Eric Warburg, and asked him to arrange a guarantee from the German government for a $150 million loan from the Warburg Bank in Frankfurt to the Egyptian Central Bank. The Germans were unwilling. Avriel then suggested approaching the ruler of Yugoslavia, Tito, for help in resuming talks with the Egyptians. But Amit, apparently after consultation with Eshkol, rejected this idea out of hand.

Until the Six-Day War, there were exchanges with the Egyptians, but to no benefit. I did set up a telephone 'hot line' in a safehouse that I rented in Paris, staffed 24 hours a day and equipped with a voice recorder. We sent the last message to Egypt on this line, on the orders of Amit, on 19 May 1967, at the beginning of the crisis that led to the Six-Day War. The broadcast included a speech by Eshkol in which he declared that Israel did not want a war, along with a personal message from Amit to Khalil proposing a mutual thinning out of Egyptian forces in the Sinai and Israeli forces on the Egyptian border.

When I received the text of the message to pass on from headquarters in Israel, I told Amit that I thought the message would be counter-productive, and that Nasser would conclude from it that Israel was fearful, thus encouraging him to threaten us with war. I failed to sway Amit, so I conveyed the message to Khalil in Cairo, with a copy to Steve. On 23 May, four days after the message was sent, Nasser blocked the Straits of Tiran, a move that Israel considered a *casus belli,* and led directly to the outbreak of war.

The secret contacts with the Egyptians lasted almost two years. I personally did not meet Khalil, but every aspect of the operation went through me. The millions of dollars promised to Egypt were not transferred to them, because the payment was conditional on the signing of an agreement which was never concluded. Throughout the operation, the Egyptians doubted our intentions and feared we were plotting to publicise the contact. However, I believe that Nasser wanted the contact because he feared Israel militarily and that he did not want go to war with Israel but lost control of events.

So where did we go wrong in the operation with Egypt? As is evident from letters I wrote at the time, I think we should have limited contact at first strictly to a 'hot line'. Only after such contact was well-established, more ties – first economic and then political – might have been forged. Also, in letters at the time to Amit, I urged that we be content with a meeting on the operational/expert level, not with such senior officials as the head of Mossad and a political figure like Dinstein. From the moment we pushed for a high-level delegation, Nasser became defensive and perhaps even anxious, for fear of a leak that would damage his image in the eyes of his Arab allies. A lower-level meeting would not have led to the objections Harel also raised over sending senior officials into the lion's den in Cairo, and Eshkol would therefore have likely approved such a meeting.

In retrospect, the operation failed as a result of Amit's personal ambition, Harel's intrigues, and Nasser's apprehension.

A Jewish General in the People's Republic of China

Another subject Amit discussed with me as I prepared to head Hamoked in Europe, was the need to look for ways to connect with the People's Republic of China.

Until 1950, there were two large Jewish communities in China, in Shanghai on the east coast and in Harbin in the north. Most of Harbin's Jews immigrated to China from Russia in the early twentieth century. Shanghai was inhabited mainly by Jews from India and Iraq, but in the 1930s a large wave of Jewish immigrants arrived, most of them from Germany and Austria. In 1950, after the Communist victory in China's civil war, a law was enacted that required all Chinese residents who held foreign citizenship (single or dual) to give up foreign citizenship or leave China. Most Jews preferred to leave China, emigrating mostly to the United States, Canada and Australia, and a minority settling in Israel.

Long before I left for Europe, I had met in Israel a former Harbin resident, Aaron Prozensky who was looking to import from Hong Kong a small device invented there that could be attached to a car fuel pipe and save about 15 per cent of fuel consumption. I thought it was a good deal. I set up a company, together with partners, and since as a civil servant I was barred from engaging in private business, I registered my shares in the company in my wife Miriam's name. We bought 10,000 devices from Hong Kong, easily sold about a hundred of them and thought we were on our way to getting rich. But it turned out that the devices caused the cars to catch fire. Luckily, no one died, but the company went bankrupt and I lost a bit of money.

From Prozensky I learned about a prominent Jew in China by the name of Morris Cohen. He was a British-Canadian who had contacts in top government circles in Beijing. He was on the list of people I wanted to contact when I got to Paris, but my first year in Europe I was drowning in work on other more pressing matters. In early summer 1965, I saw a photo in a newspaper of the Chinese Politburo, with Cohen in the front row with the Chinese leadership. It prompted me to contact Prozensky, who gave me the phone number of Cohen's sister, Leah, a widow who lived in Manchester. Coincidentally, I was in London at the time. I called her, introduced myself by my real name, and asked if she could help facilitate a meeting with her brother, telling her I wanted 'to hear from him about the situation of Jews in China'. She told me her brother would be visiting her in a month, and invited me to be in touch then. I immediately wrote to Amit (it was 9 June 1965) to tell him of my plans to initiate contact with China via Cohen and he approved these first steps.

Morris Cohen, a son of Jews from Poland, was born in 1887, emigrated to Canada when he was sixteen and eventually went into the real estate business there together with some Chinese immigrants, and learned Chinese in the process. He impressed them with his physical prowess when he single-handedly overpowered a would-be robber who tried to hold up the diners and the owner of a restaurant where they were all eating. When Sun Yat Sen, the first president of the Republic of China, came on a visit to Canada in 1913, Cohen's Chinese friends proposed he be Sun Yat Sen's bodyguard. A warm bond developed between the two. During World War I, Cohen served with the Chinese personnel supporting the British Army. He went to China after the war as a military adviser to the Chinese army at Sun Yat Sen's request. Cohen continued under Sun's successor Chiang Kai-Shek, rising to the rank of brigadier general. Simultaneously, he started a private business, representing Western companies in China. After World War II, he served under Mao Zedong as a consultant to the Chinese intelligence services.

When I first met Cohen at his sister's, he was 77 or 78 years old, received a monthly pension from the Chinese, and was representing large British companies in China, travelling frequently to China and in close contact with the communist authorities.

I described him in a letter to Amit and Vardi after my first meeting as: 'Upright, despite his age, with a clear, forthright voice, accurate in his words and quick in his perceptions . . . He is one of the few

Westerners in the world with direct access to the top echelons of the Chinese government.' I reported that I introduced myself as a member of the Israeli intelligence community, and explained that I wanted to explore with him the possibility of ties between Israel and the People's Republic of China.

Cohen was surprised by the idea. He told me that China was unlikely to view ties with Israel as in its interest, given its relations with the Arab world and many countries in Asia and Africa. But in his opinion, there were senior figures who felt some closeness to Israel because both countries had struggled for their independence in recent years. So there might be a chance of leveraging this sympathy to create a covert connection between the two countries' intelligence services.

He said he would be happy if at the end of his life he was given an opportunity to serve the Jewish state and promised to raise the matter with a senior Chinese figure he was due to meet soon in London. He stressed the need for utmost discretion, and we agreed that from then on, I would use a code name, Albert. Indeed, that is how I was referred to also by his sister, Leah, who sent on my messages to him.

In July 1965, I accompanied him on a trip to London, where he was scheduled to meet a Chinese commercial delegation buying radar devices. The delegation was headed by a man called Lee, head of the China Export and Import Institute, who held an important position at the top of the party and government. He told Cohen that there was no chance of open contact between China and Israel but did not comment at all on the possibility of discreet contact between the two intelligence services. Cohen assumed that Israel's interest in such ties was relayed by Lee to his superiors in Beijing.

Cohen agreed to travel to China in September 1965, having requested a meeting with Prime Minister Zhou Enlai, the number two in China after Mao, and in charge of foreign relations. I suggested that Cohen meet with Amit before he went to China. Cohen advised us to make a list of topics likely to prompt China's interest in contact with Israel. He was clearly referring to military technical information, which China could not get from any other country in the world.

Miriam and I hosted Cohen at our home in Paris for dinner when he was on his way to Israel. There, he visited Ben-Gurion in Sde Boker and had a lively conversation with him, and also met Amit before setting out to China, where, as planned, he met Zhou. On his return, I saw him in Manchester, and he told me that Zhou was willing to consider ties, but only on condition that Israel transfer military technology to China. I immediately reported this to Amit, but, as expected, the Israeli government was afraid to upset the United States, and rejected the Chinese terms. Less than a year after the Six-Day War, we sent Cohen to China once more, offering cooperation on military matters. Silence was the only response, one which Cohen explained to me, was their way of telling us no. Thus ended the China chapter in my life.

Morris Cohen died ten years later, at the age of 88. I stayed friendly with him, visiting him whenever I was in Britain, I always greeted him by saying: 'How do you do, old putz?' To this he would reply: 'This is not a joke anymore, now I'm nothing but an old shmuck.'

Chapter 19

The France–Israel Relationship

In early 1966, a few months after the Ben-Barka affair, Keinan, the representative of the Tevel unit in Paris and our liaison with the French intelligence services, began to notice a new, unfriendly tone in communications with his French colleagues – not just in letters or messages but in oral conversations too. Keinan's French contacts said they had been advised to 'work in a more restrained manner than hitherto' with their Israeli counterparts. Until then, there had been regular exchanges of information with the French on intelligence issues. But from the spring of 1966, this close cooperation gradually ceased, including activities of the Ministry of Defense's shopping delegation headed by Moka Limon.

I had no doubt, as I wrote at the time to Vardi and Amit, that the orders to cool relations with us came directly from the President Charles de Gaulle's office. The rumours and media reports of our involvement in the Ben-Barka affair angered de Gaulle, who had no tolerance for the activities of foreign elements he felt violated France's sphere of interest. As I have already explained, we vigorously denied any involvement in the Ben-Barka affair. But it is not inconceivable – although we had no evidence – that French investigations in Morocco made them suspicious of us. In any case, in all my years in Europe, I was never asked a direct question on the subject by any French official.

De Gaulle went beyond stopping intelligence cooperation. In addition, he kicked out all Israelis training or studying in nuclear reactors and in nuclear industries in France. He was aware, of course, of his country's nuclear cooperation with Israel and knew who provided us with the reactor in the late 1950s, and who helped us set it up and operate it in the southern Israeli town of Dimona. The Israeli reactor became active on 1 January 1960.

By the spring of 1966, there were no more Israelis working in France at reactors. I heard rumours that French citizens of Jewish descent were being expelled from their positions in the French nuclear industry. I did not put much effort into verifying these rumours, which may have had a factual basis.

The Israel–France romance, which started in the 1950s, was based on a common interest in containing Nasser, but dissipated quickly. De Gaulle's about turn on Israel hit us in June 1967, when France imposed an embargo on arms shipments to the Middle East, just as we were being threatened with war by our Arab neighbours. For the Arabs, the embargo was insignificant, because their main arms supplier was the Soviet Union, but for Israel, whose main weapons until then came from France, the embargo caused great trepidation.

At the end of May 1967, in the midst of the days of waiting before the Six-Day War, after Nasser announced the closure of the Tiran Straits to Israeli shipping, and when we still did not know about the impending French embargo, I sent an urgent telegram to Amit, Vardi and Israeli, urging that Israel make every effort to appease de Gaulle. I noted that the only person who had a chance of succeeding was Ben-Gurion, who, although he had resigned from power, was still revered by the president of France. I came to this conclusion after a conversation with a colleague in the French secret service, who told me: 'De Gaulle is furious with Israel, and in case of war initiated by Israel, he will stop all military and security assistance to punish it.' He suggested that if Ben-Gurion showed up in France and wanted to see de Gaulle, the French president could not help but welcome him. I conveyed this advice, but due to time constraints, it did not come to fruition.

However, the Israeli military attaché in Paris told me that during war the arms embargo that de Gaulle imposed was not enforced against Israel. Our friends in France, and we had many of them, made sure to fill new orders quickly. This was later confirmed to me by Limon, head of our procurement delegation in Paris, who added details. During the fighting, Limon issued about a hundred orders for ammunition and spare parts, mostly for our fighter jets, most of which were placed in France. All the orders were fulfilled with just one exception. On an order of 500 rocket motors for air-to-air missiles for a particular type of aircraft, we were provided with 'only' 350.

French officers, including some I met at an Israeli embassy reception on 10 June, expressed much admiration for the strategy, speed and efficiency shown by our forces during the Six-Day War. Their praise may have been the result of friendships that developed over the years, and perhaps was tinged by the anti-Arab sentiments that simmered among some of the French security establishment, especially those who harboured resentment towards Egypt for its aid in the past to Algerian rebels.

Not long after the war, in the summer of 1967, I wrote to Haim Israeli (head of Ben-Gurion's office) and Amit that the occupation of the territories opened up an opportunity for us to make peace with all Arab countries. We could not return the West Bank to King Hussein of Jordan I wrote, because he would insist on including Jerusalem, which we would not be willing to give up. I urged that we should approach the Arab people living in the West Bank and let them establish an independent political entity, with Israel retaining only vital security areas, as outlined in the Allon Plan. I continued to hold these views. As is well known, nothing came out of such ideas, neither mine nor others', neither then nor later.

One of the consequences of the Six-Day War was that we suddenly faced the enormous potential of recruiting Arab agents in Gaza and the West Bank. It is no exaggeration to say that in the post-war months, we were inundated with possible agents. Sorting through them all was a huge job that lasted several months, and which yielded a considerable number of effective agents. One of the agents, an Egyptian student we recruited in Europe, was caught in Egypt, sentenced to death and, I am sorry to say, executed by hanging, a tragic incident barely mentioned in our newspapers.

Hoping to find in Egypt a partner for dialogue the day after the war, I tried to contact Khalil in Cairo, sending him a letter via Steve. In addition, we approached an Egyptian citizen living in London and asked him to travel to Cairo and explore with Khalil the possibility of renewing the hot line. However, both received negative answers: It turned out that Khalil was considered an ally of Marshal Amer, who tried to instigate a military coup against Nasser. Consequently, Khalil was removed from his senior position.

I would like to end this chapter with two comments, one regarding Nasser's intentions on the eve of the war, and the other regarding Mossad's contribution to victory in the war.

To the best of my knowledge, and based on what we knew at the time, Nasser did not want a war. He aspired to a political victory achieved without war. At least in the first days of the crisis, blocking the Straits of Tiran against Israeli shipping to demonstrate strong Egyptian sovereignty over the straits would have sufficed for him. The Israeli government also did not want a war. Had the superpowers, the United States foremost among them, been willing to take real steps to resolve the crisis, the war might have been avoided. But the powers stayed on the side-lines, and Egyptian public opinion flared, inflaming Nasser. Syria goaded him to take an increasingly militaristic stance, leading him to deploy more and more forces in the Sinai. He was prompted to send the head of the army, Marshal Abdel Hakim Amer, to Amman and Damascus to coordinate operations with Jordan and Syria.

Under such conditions, with Arab forces deployed at our border and with no buffer between us and our enemies, with most of the Israeli economy paralysed due to the call-up of reservists, we had no choice but to go to war.

Mossad's contribution to the victory was primarily in the cumulative intelligence that it provided about Arab armies, and the types of weapons they purchased in the Soviet Union and Europe. Second, thanks to Mossad's work, the danger of the missiles was removed. The fact is that in 1967 the Egyptians did not have surface-to-surface missiles. Third, it was Mossad that provided the highly significant information that the Soviets would not intervene in the war. This was a great relief to Eshkol and Dayan, and contributed to their decision to go to war.

Chapter 20

Israeli Agents in the Arab World

One of Harel's qualities was his vision and ability to think and plan for the long term. Thus, as far back as the mid-1950s, he initiated a long-term move: identifying and recruiting young people to Mossad who were descendants of families from Arab countries.

Ten talented young people were selected, among them only one Jew and the rest Shi'ite Muslims. At Harel's behest, scholarships were arranged for them (including living expenses) at various institutions of higher learning in Israel. They studied in Israel for three to four years, completed academic degrees, returned to their country of origin and became the mainstays of our relationship with the local authorities and intelligence services there. It was clear to both sides that this was a worthwhile long-term investment. Of course, no one in Israel – nor one of the countries involved, nor in foreign intelligence services – then foresaw the fall of the regime in that country, and its replacement by a radical Islamic regime.

I continued to keep in touch with two of the former students for decades: I met one of them while he was studying at the Faculty of Agriculture in Rehovot. He met a Jewish woman while in Israel, she returned with him to his country, and these days they live in London. Their three children grew up as Jews. At one point, I went into business with him in Cuba.

The second student, who operated under the code name 'Jimmy', stayed in his country and married a Muslim woman. Over the years, I used to call him occasionally, of course not from Israel, but when I was in a foreign country.

The two students in question were not recruited to Mossad. The first connected us with his brother, who held a senior position in his country, and through him many transactions were made with that country. Jimmy we only used for technical matters. We did not need intelligence from him.

In January 1965, Israeli spy Eli Cohen was captured in Damascus. To this day, there are various versions as to why he was captured. According to one version, Cohen was discovered when the Syrians imposed a 24-hour wireless silence on their military to test a new Soviet-made communications system they were introducing. Cohen did not know about it, so continued to broadcast as usual, which caught the attention of the Syrian counter-espionage service.

Another version links Cohen's capture with the IDF's very successful operation in November 1964, when precise aerial bombing and artillery fire severely damaged the Syrian effort to thwart Israel's national carrier project by diverting the sources of the Jordan River. The IDF's precision hits on the Syrian targets prompted Damascus to suspect Israel had a highly placed spy who had provided exceedingly accurate information.

Cohen's hanging in Damascus was a tragic event, which affected all of us, especially Amit, who made tremendous efforts to save Cohen's life. Amit travelled to Paris, contacted officials close to the Syrian authorities, and expressed a willingness to provide Syria with valuable medicine and high-quality civilian equipment, and even information about Syrian dissidents – all to no avail.

When I came to Hamoked in Paris in 1964, our agents in Arab countries, recruited under Harel, provided us with initial information about the formation of the PLO in January 1964 under the leadership of Ahmad Shukiri. Simultaneously, a young engineer by the name of Yasser Arafat established Fatah in Yemen. Two men associated with it were Khalid al-Hassan and Hani al-Hassan. They were two Palestinian brothers who came to Europe as students and became businessmen. Thanks to his connections, one of our agents met Hani al-Hassan and became friends with him and thus infiltrated the leadership of Fatah (which then comprised only a few hundred people).

Another of our agents became our foremost source information about the people closest to Arafat in Fatah's upper echelons, among them Halil al-Azir (Abu Jihad), Salah Khalaf (Abu Iyad), Farouk Kedumi and others. The agent's reports reached me through Sami Moriah, Tzomet representative in Europe, whom I had put in charge of this effort.

Based on the information from the agent, in early 1965 I recommended (orally) to Vardi and Amit that we deal with Fatah aggressively, by planting a bomb in the hall where a Fatah conference was to open or by using a skilled sniper to eliminate Arafat and Abu Jihad. My proposal to hit the leadership of Fatah was rejected then and also later, when I raised it again after the Six-Day War. To be honest, I did not object vigorously when my idea was rejected. After all, I also could not yet know how important Fatah would become in the future. At the time, the Palestinian issue was still a low priority, ranking after Egypt, Syria and other Arab countries.

At one point in 1964, we learned that Hani al-Hassan was having a romantic relationship with the wife of one of the agents. We feared that the agent's wife would reveal to al-Hassan what she knew about her husband. After some hesitation, I summoned the agent for a private conversation and told him what we had discovered. To my surprise, he knew about his wife's relationship with al-Hassan. I demanded that he be vigilant in his contacts with Fatah, and prepare to return to Israel with his family. In the spring of 1967, the families of the two agents following the activities of Fatah returned to Israel. One continued to work under Vardi on Tzomet's Palestinian Desk, until he died of a heart attack in the 1970s. The other was transferred to Shin Bet and served there until his retirement.

As a result of all the information we collected, we had quality intelligence in advance about most of the Fatah cells that tried to infiltrate Israel in the half year after the Six-Day War, and prepared ambushes for them along the Jordan River.

At the end of June 1967, Yasser Arafat, under a false name of course, visited the territories Israel had seized in the Six-Day War, and spent some time in Ramallah. Shortly afterwards he sent a message to Hani al-Hassan in which he said, 'Now, after the defeat of the Arab countries in the war against Israel, it is our turn to fight.' Some of the cells organised in Europe, others in Jordan, underwent short training, were equipped with weapons in Jordan, and were sent on missions to Israel. Hani al-Hassan himself came in August 1967 at the head of a cell, nut was caught with his comrades and imprisoned.

About a month later I returned to Israel on holiday. At that time, Vardi was trying to recruit al-Hassan, and at his suggestion I accompanied him on a tour designed to show al-Hassan the 'Zionist enterprise'. But the recruitment attempt failed. Unlike other sources who worked for us, al-Hassan's motivation and commitment were high. Then we had an audacious idea: free al-Hassan and use him as a goodwill ambassador to the Palestinians.

Within the intelligence community, opinions were divided on the matter. There were those who thought that under certain conditions, it would be possible to reach peace with the Palestinians. Others argued that this could only happen in a united Arab world, because as long as divisions continued, each Arab faction and country would want to prove it was no less zealous than the others. Amit and I thought it might be possible to make peace with the Palestinians without Jordan as a partner on the basis of the Allon Plan. Vardi was much more pessimistic.

At that time, Arafat was already considered the most prominent Palestinian figure, while Ahmad Shukiri, then chairman of the PLO, was already on his way out. Although Arafat did not show the faintest sign of a willingness to give up his ambition to eliminate the 'Zionist entity' (as the Palestinians then called Israel) during various appearances in Arab communities in Europe that we followed, we wanted to explore the possibility that he would be more moderate in secret contacts than he was in his public appearances. With the consent of Eshkol, we prepared a message in Arabic to Arafat which said in essence: 'An opportunity has been created for dialogue between our two peoples, and you are invited to open negotiations with Israel for peace.' Al-Hassan was freed and flown to Europe with the message. He was given a telephone number that Arafat could call to start negotiations. After a week, we received a short response: 'With blood and fire Palestine will be redeemed. That is the answer of the *rais* [literally, head, in Arabic].'

In retrospect, we probably should have anticipated this failure. However, when trying to make secret contact with an enemy, it is almost impossible not to fail.

So it was in 1967, and since then nothing has changed. Later, when I served as the prime minister's adviser on the war on terror and stated in a press interview that we had a hundred years of terror ahead of us, I knew what I was talking about. I knew that there was no chance of reaching a dialogue and peace with Arafat and the top leadership that surrounded him, some of whom still lead the PLO and Fatah at this time of writing (2019).

In view of Arafat's negative answer, I again suggested carrying out targeted attacks against the leadership of Fatah. As I have already said, Eshkol and Amit did not give their approval.

An agent I personally recruited in the post-Six-Day War period was an Egyptian who contacted our embassy in Paris, asked for information about Israel, and was referred to me. I met him at a café in Paris, and as early as our first conversation asked him if he saw himself as an Arab or a European. His response was 'I live in Europe.' I did not hesitate long and asked him directly if he was willing to help the State of Israel. His answer was yes. I referred him to my assistant, who integrated and handled him. For nearly twenty years, he helped our efforts due to his many contacts, providing us with information on various people, on attitudes, and also brought us intelligence and military information.

New Technology

As mentioned, throughout the Six-Day War in June 1967 until the end of that year, the French cooperated with us. Despite the embargo announced by President de Gaulle, we received everything we requested, including airlifts of most of the military equipment we asked for. But, at the end of 1967, explicit instructions were issued again from the Elysée Palace to freeze security ties with Israel. I assume that in the months after the war, de Gaulle gradually discovered the extent of the security ties that continued with Israel, and it angered him. One way or another, from the beginning of 1968, we again began to receive messages from the French services, through Keinan, who had direct contact with them, to slow down activity. In fact, we were required to freeze centres of covert and intelligence activity on French soil. It is worth noting that the French service personnel were embarrassed by this, emphasising to Keinan that they had no choice. 'The instructions come from upstairs,' they told him, indicating from de Gaulle himself or his immediate entourage.

At the start of 1969, Hamoked moved to new headquarters. My family moved to a rented house with a garden and a large lawn in a nice neighbourhood of villas outside the city. After a struggle with bureaucrats at Mossad, it was agreed that Miriam would work part-time organising the archives of Hamoked and I acquired a small Fiat car for her. In July 1968, when the period of overlap at the head of Mossad between Amit and Zvi Zamir began, I announced my desire to return to Israel but it was not until the mid-1970s that I finished my job in Europe and came home.

In mid-1969, I coordinated a special effort to improve the technological and electronic equipment available to us. At that time, many active agents were already working for us in target countries, and we urgently needed sophisticated and up-to-date transmitters, of a kind not yet manufactured in our laboratories in Israel. We also needed state-of-the-art intelligence equipment, which we knew was already in use at various United States intelligence agencies. So I went to the United States with Malchin for a two-week tour of factories that specialised in producing the equipment we needed. The tour was held with the blessing of the FBI, which knew that Malchin and I were from Israeli intelligence. The acquisitions in the US significantly advanced the types of technical equipment we used from then on.

One incident on our shopping tour is worth mentioning. We visited Dr Zalman Shapiro's factory in Pennsylvania. The factory was classified, and before the visit, the FBI man who accompanied us asked us to register in the guest book not as members of an Israeli intelligence organisation, but as scientists. I registered, therefore, as 'Raphael Eitan, chemical engineer'. In the late 1970s, an American investigation was conducted into a certain amount of plutonium that had allegedly disappeared from the plant. Several years passed, and in the midst of the Pollard affair (which I will discuss later), the FBI tracked down everything Raphael Eitan had ever done in the United States. They discovered the visit of 'Raphael Eitan, chemical engineer' to Shapiro's factory. They leaked the story to the *Washington Post*, which published an article under the headline: 'From a factory that Rafael Eitan visited twice, a quantity of plutonium has disappeared. Is there a connection between the two?' I photocopied the article and hung it in my office when I was chairman of Israel Chemicals, as 'proof' that I was a chemical engineer.

The truth, which was not known to the FBI or the *Washington Post*, is that Dr Shapiro did not provide us with a single milligram of plutonium.

Chapter 21

The End of My Road at Mossad

In the late 1970s I retired from Mossad. Before I detail the circumstances of my retirement, let me say unequivocally that I did not retire because I thought I had exhausted my potential, or because I was getting bored. On the contrary, I decided to leave after much deliberation and with deep sorrow.

As previously mentioned, the Yadin–Sharaf committee recommended limiting the term of office of the head of Mossad to five years. In the case of Amit, this recommendation was implemented, but his successor, Zvi Zamir, and most subsequent Mossad heads – Yitzhak Hofi, Nahum Admoni, Shabtai Shavit and Meir Dagan – served for more than five years. The summer of 1968 marked five years since Amit's official appointment as head of Mossad. Eshkol decided to appoint as his successor Major General Zvi Zamir, General of the Southern Command in 1962–5 and IDF attaché and head of the Ministry of Defense delegation in Britain and Scandinavia in 1965–8. During their overlap they visited me in Europe and I held a party in my home in Paris to honour Amit and welcome Zamir. I knew Zamir from pre-state days, when he was my instructor in a Palmach Marine Corps course. I remembered him as a positive and nice person of my generation. We did not have deep personal ties, but we had met socially and Miriam and Zamir's wife Rina were friends from before the time when he met her.

Zamir's appointment as head of Mossad was not a surprise to people in Mossad, but there was a sense of disappointment. Towards the end of Amit's five-year tenure, I suggested that he make Vardi his deputy or nominate him as his successor. After all, Vardi was the most experienced and skilled man in Mossad regarding Arab affairs, which was a focus of our activities. But Amit did not recommend anyone to the prime minister, perhaps because he didn't believe anyone in Mossad could equal him. Maybe I am wrong, but my feeling then was that that deep down Amit wanted to prove that, after him, Mossad would be less efficient and productive. I have no other explanation for why he did not recommend Vardi. I believed then and still do that Vardi would have been as good a head of Mossad as Amit.

Zamir won the position mainly due to his close relationship with Golda Meir, who recommended him and pushed Eshkol to appoint him. It is possible that the aura and prestige that enveloped IDF generals in the period after the Six-Day War also played a role in the decision.

We were not only disappointed that an outsider was being imposed on us, but also that Zamir had never served in intelligence. I tried to take comfort in the thought that his being a former Palmach man, like me, promised a certain closeness, and indeed there was. Zamir appreciated me at first and did not hide it, but very soon our working relationship began to sour.

For the first two or three months, things went smoothly, although Zamir, unlike Amit, did not reply to my letters from Paris. Eventually he did so, but the style was very different from Amit's. There was none of the intimacy and friendship that characterised Amit's letters. Next, there were missives from him regarding changes in responsibilities that I, Vardi and the branches in Europe had previously held. Until then, for example, the decision on how to approach a potential agent – directly or indirectly – had been in my hands, subject of course to a discussion at headquarters. For a civilian, approval from Vardi was sufficient and he would brief Amit. Only in the case of a diplomat or military person was it necessary to obtain prior approval from the head of Mossad. All this changed – for the worse.

Zamir reduced powers and complicated processes. It would have been understandable if Zamir wanted to make his mark by introducing broad changes and new types of action to improve the organisation. But his touches were small, bureaucratic. They involved intervening in routine activity, performed until then automatically, that required no intervention.

He delayed permissions for action and rescinded Vardi's authority to grant permission. Then he deprived me of the authority to determine how to approach potential agents, demanding to be personally involved in the decision. These measures created bottlenecks, delaying our work and sometimes paralysing it completely. I told Vardi I couldn't work this way. On average, for every hundred people we approached, fewer than a half dozen eventually became effective spies. So requests for a green light to begin an approach were frequent, but with Zamir's new rules, it became impossible to move forward effectively. I must also admit that I personally need maximum freedom to operate well. When I don't get it, I go elsewhere.

Although Zamir's management annoyed me, at this point I chalked it up to the birth pains of a new Mossad head. But this kind of micro-management continued throughout his time as head of Mossad. During the failed operation in Lillehammer, when Mossad killed an innocent Moroccan waiter, Ahmad Bushiki, mistaking him for the terrorist Hassan Salameh, head of the Black September operation, Zamir was on the ground, making decisions on the execution of the operation, not just Mike Harari of the Caesarea unit. The escape plan for our people was completely wrong. It endangered them and led to their arrest. I am absolutely convinced that this would not have happened with Vardi, with me or with Malchin.

The mistake in identifying Salameh was unfortunate, but such things happen in our type of work, and compared to other secret services, Mossad did not make many such mistakes. The failure lay in the amateurish escape plan. All the perpetrators should have fled the area within half an hour of the assassination at the very most. How was it that they left behind hired cars and safehouses that became traps? It happened because it was Zamir, not Harari, who determined the escape plan.

I do not remember exactly when I realised that I could not work with Zamir. These kinds of grievances start small before flaring up.

One incident that raised my ire occurred in early 1969, when Zamir established a new unit for planning and operational coordination at Mossad. He did not include Nachik Navot, whose job was to coordinate between all the units of the institution in the initial planning of an action. Navot wrote to me about it, and I wrote to Zamir and warned him of his mistake, but at first he did not answer at all, and at most gave me indirect and vague responses.

By this point, it was no longer possible to consider any operation without Zamir's approval. Yehudit Nessyahu, who was with us in the safehouse where Eichmann was held, was assigned by Zamir to the new planning and coordination unit, headed by David Kimchi. I began receiving instructions from her, and it was clear to me that she did not understand at all what she was writing. Also, no one told me that from now on, my orders were to come from her and not from Vardi.

In one case, our handler was to meet with an Arab 'volunteer' (what we called walk-ins who came to us voluntarily and were candidates to become agents), who approached us in Germany. I ordered that the meeting be held in a neutral place. For no logical operational reason, I got a message from Nessyahu (whose nickname was 'the dancer') to meet the volunteer in a specific place which I feared would endanger our handler. I complained about it to Vardi in a letter:

> I do not want to receive operational instructions from The Dancer & Co. I think they are unprofessional, and my empirical experience shows that their advice is not worth a penny. There is also a principle of how to operate our branches. One can't mess around. They must receive operating instructions from only one source.

When we recall this period, Miriam reminds me that I was not only restless and frustrated, but that the situation took a toll on my health, and I underwent heart tests. I was eating myself up and felt abandoned, with no one in authority whom I trusted. I am usually a practical person, and don't easily take things to heart, but I had a hard time dealing with the situation. If Yariv or Vardi had been appointed head of Mossad and not Zamir, I have no doubt that I would have had no problem accepting their authority, and I would have stayed.

Vardi advised me to 'bend a little', but that did not suit my character. However, there was never a direct clash between me and Zamir but by mid-1969 I began to doubt my future was with Mossad.

During one of Zamir's visits to Europe, we discussed my return to Israel. He offered me a job as head of the Caesarea unit, replacing Yariv who was about to retire. In principle I agreed, but demanded a number of changes, first and foremost the establishment of an operational unit similar to the Colossus unit, to be headed by Malchin and to serve the Caesarea unit. I also suggested some changes in the structure of Mossad. Zamir did not respond and one day, without informing me, he appointed Harari to head the Caesarea unit. It was clearly a response to me, typically indirect, and did not deal with the proposals themselves.

I considered my options and concluded that the time had come to leave. I did not want some amorphous position in Mossad, such as an assistant to the head of Mossad, or the head of the operational unit that I considered Malchin suitable to direct. I knew in advance that if I did not become a division head, I would have no chance of being appointed head of Mossad after Zamir. No one – neither inside nor outside Mossad – told me then that I had no chance of becoming head of the institution, but I came to that conclusion on my own, after sober analysis.

In the early 1970s, towards the end of my tenure as head of Hamoked in Europe, my successor, Shmuel Goren, a veteran security officer with the rank of colonel, arrived in Paris. We overlapped for six weeks, and developed an excellent relationship, then and afterwards.On 4 March 1970, I sent Zamir a farewell letter, outlining my disappointment at being passed over as head of the Caesarea unit, at my prospects for promotion, and explaining my need for new challenges.

In considering what I might do next, I consulted with Haim Israeli, Ben-Gurion's former bureau chief, and explained to him the reasons for my retirement from Mossad. Some time later he informed me that I could be appointed deputy to Yaakov Shapira, head of the Ministry of Defense's Procurement and Production Administration.

In August 1970, we returned to Israel and moved into our new home in the Tel Aviv suburb of Afeka. Zamir, who knew that I had started working with Shapira, invited himself to my office at the Ministry of Defense. For about two hours, he tried to persuade me to stay at Mossad as 'minister without portfolio', that is, a kind of assistant to him. I turned him down, although I was unsure I had done the right thing.

Even fifty years later, I do not know if I made the right move. It was not that I did not like his proposal, but I felt incapable and unwilling to serve as a 'yes man' to Zamir, whose work methods I disliked from his first day at Mossad. But in terms of my career, I may have made a mistake. Accepting the position would have been a natural stepping stone to eventually succeeding him as head of Mossad, but my need for freedom of action and independence outweighed my career aspirations. At the time, my refusal was followed by days of insomnia. My whole life had been dedicated to the security of the state – in the Palmach, Shin Bet and Mossad – and I expected it to be my future. And then Zamir came along, and emotionally and viscerally, I clashed with him; I could not continue to serve under his authority. Hence the frustration and the heartache ran deep.

I won't deny that for years I felt frustrated that I never reached the top of the pyramid. If Yariv or Vardi had become head of Mossad and not me, I would have been disappointed, but not frustrated, because each of them was suitable for the position. They both had dealt for years with the classic issues of intelligence – recruitment and operation of agents, intelligent use of sophisticated equipment, understanding of political issues and the ability to make operational decisions based on their insights. Zamir lacked all of these qualities, and in a manner visible to any professional.

My appointment as the head of the Bureau of Scientific Relations, in 1982, tamped my frustration. Although the bureau, known by its Hebrew acronym as Lekem, was a small organisation compared to Mossad, I made it a leading body in several areas within the Israeli intelligence community. These accomplishments helped heal my bruised ego.

In September 1972, when Palestinian terrorists attacked the lodgings of the Israeli delegation at the Munich Olympics, killing two team members and holding hostage nine athletes and coaches (all of whom were murdered subsequently), I was still working at the Ministry of Defense. I knew that Zamir was about to leave for Munich, called him and offered to accompany him. He replied in the negative.

Unfortunately, Zamir made one mistake after another in Munich. In Lillehammer and Munich, the truth was out: Zamir was not an intelligence man.

Chapter 22

Exploring a New Path

A Year at the Defense Ministry

On my return to Israel in the autumn of 1970, I began working as Shapira's deputy, on secondment from Mossad for more than a year to the Ministry of Defense's Procurement and Production Administration. This office coordinated the equipment orders of the IDF and the Ministry of Defense, placing orders in Israel, or for purchase through the ministry's delegations abroad. At the time, it was a major section within the ministry, with a staff of about 200 people. As Shapira's deputy, I learned all about Israel's military production sector and visited all the factories that supplied our military. I also participated with Shapira in all meetings and discussions on armaments and equipment, including IDF General Staff meetings on procurement and manufacturing matters.

It was a new world for me, interesting in itself, but since the work was primarily administrative paperwork that did not grab me, I took every possible opportunity for job-related jaunts outside the office. That's how I ended up going to Vietnam twice, in 1971 and 1972. The IDF lacked armoured personnel carriers at the time. The Americans had developed a new M113 vehicle, made of aluminium, that was much easier to manoeuvre and better protected against rocket-propelled grenades than the M3s we had been using. Many damaged M113s were left in Vietnam after the withdrawal of American ground forces, about to be sold as scrap metal. We decided to try to import them to Israel and revamp them (they became known in Israel as Zeldas). The

Americans approved the idea, but on condition that Israel not buy the damaged vehicles directly, but through a local company in Vietnam set up for this purpose.

Together with Moshe Lancet, our military attaché in Tokyo, we met in Saigon with Israeli industrialist Shaul Eisenberg, who already had oil businesses in Vietnam and Korea, and had been chosen by Shapira to set up a shell go-between company, through which we would get the weapons. It was a good deal for all: we got the APCs at rock-bottom scrap prices, Eisenberg got his commission as the go-between, and the Americans were spared the bother of dealing with scrapped weapons.

I don't remember exactly how many APCs we brought from Vietnam, but it was in the several hundreds. We also purchased parts of a crumbling bridge that was used about a year later, in the Yom Kippur War, by Arik Sharon's forces battling at the Suez Canal.

One of my visits to Vietnam lasted about a month, and the other about six weeks. During that time, I asked to join a helicopter flight to the city of Hue, near the border with North Vietnam, days before American forces evacuated. I watched the shocking spectacle of tens of thousands of Vietnamese surrounding the airport hoping to leave as well.

I left Vietnam feeling that the Americans were waging a futile war. I reached this conclusion after a Vietnamese general with whom I had become friendly asked me for help: 'I have two sons and I want to get them out of Vietnam. Please, get them Israeli passports and take them away.' He was the head of intelligence in the Vietnamese military. Embarrassed and overwhelmed, I mumbled that I would check and see. Of course, I did nothing. Departure from South Vietnam was then restricted, and the sons of a general had no chance of obtaining an exit permit. This incident led me to believe the Americans had no one to rely on in Vietnam, so their involvement there would end badly.

My relationship with Shapira was good, but from the beginning, I considered my work with him as a springboard to other positions.

During my visit to Vietnam, I made inquiries about the possibility of playing a role in Eisenberg's business, but, after talking to people who worked with him, came to the conclusion that I did not want a job with him.

My second visit to Vietnam was in early 1972. By then, the caches of surplus and damaged American military equipment had caught the attention of shady arms dealers from around the world, some of whom had served in terrorist or criminal organisations. It was not for me and I resigned from my job. Mossad, from which I had been seconded, agreed to give me unpaid leave for three years.

In the following years I took the plunge, depending on nothing but my resourcefulness and talents to earn a living for my family. I loved the independence, but in my heart of hearts, all the time I was in private business, I knew that if an enticing offer from the intelligence community came my way, I would be tempted to grab it.

Three Years with Amnon Barness

One person who knew I wanted to leave the Defense Ministry was Yigal Allon, then Education Minister. I told him I did not intend to go back to Mossad and wanted to get involved in business. When Allon visited Los Angeles shortly after our conversation, he was asked by Amnon Barness, a former Israeli businessman with extensive holdings in the USA, if he could recommend someone to help him develop his business in the hotel sector in Israel. Allon gave Barness two names. Mine was one of them.

Barness, about my age, was from an old Sephardic Jerusalem family on his father's side. His mother was born in Egypt of parents who came from Poland. He acquired Daylin, a commercial real estate company in America, which owned more than 700 supermarkets and department stores at its peak. In Israel, Barness then invested in setting up hotels and acquiring partnerships in existing hotels. Some time after his meeting with Allon in Los Angeles, he visited Israel, and we met. At the first meeting, Barness offered me the position of CEO of the business development company he wanted to establish in

Israel, despite my lack of previous commercial experience. The salary was three times what I received at the Ministry of Defense. I said yes on the spot.

During the three years I worked with Amnon Barness, we established one hotel in Eilat and two in Sharm el-Sheikh, one in partnership with Clal, and the other, Caravan Hotel, together with Ben-Zion Spector, whom we hired to run the hotels owned by the company. At one point, we purchased part of Edmond de Rothschild's Unico Bank. We hired a CEO with experience in banking and I was appointed a director, which gave me an opportunity to learn about that world. Later we invested in a slew of hotels, and also became partners in some of the business of Yekutiel Federman, the owner of the Dan hotel chain. Through Asher Yadlin, then chairman of the Histadrut's Workers' Company, we made a series of deals with Solel Boneh (International), including large construction projects in Iran.

Meanwhile, Barness continued his business in the United States apace. He acquired a network of private hospitals, as well as medical equipment supply companies. Most of these acquisitions were made with leveraged loans, not equity, which would cost Amnon dearly. For my part, I tried to set up a medical network in Iran, taking advantage of the good connections I had from the days of cooperation with the security services there, but I didn't succeed.

Barness was involved not only in business in Israel, but also in philanthropy. He poured about $5 million a year into an educational fund he established, a huge sum in the 1970s. Among its beneficiaries were Tel Aviv University, Ben-Gurion University in Be'er Sheva and the Weizmann Institute in Rehovot.

In 1975, about three years after I joined Barness's business, his company in the USA faced bankruptcy, mainly due to excessive debt and expansion beyond its financial capacity. An American judge granted the creditors' claims and appointed a liquidator to distribute the assets. I went to Los Angeles for two months, and helped the liquidator break up the company into small units and find buyers for them, mostly large investment banks. I was intensely involved in negotiations with the banks, and through this gained a great deal of experience in the financial side of the business.

The liquidation order was also applied to the Daylin assets in Israel and we had to put them up for sale. It was easiest to sell Unico Bank, which was acquired by a financial company which continued the bank's activity under the name Ubank. The sale of the bank brought Daylin a profit of about 100 per cent on the original investment, the largest profit of any Barness business in Israel, but all the profit – $3.5 million beyond the principal – was transferred to the American receiver.

My time working for Barness gave me experience that helped me run Israel Chemicals and later develop businesses in Cuba and elsewhere. I did well financially in my work with him. At the end of the liquidation of Daylin in America and Israel, the liquidator gave me a handsome bonus for my part in the process. It was enough to support my family for about a year.

The Yom Kippur War

I was working for Barness when the Yom Kippur War broke out, and had no more idea of what was coming than any other citizen reading the newspapers. As is well known, despite intelligence warnings flowing from all sides, neither the heads of the army, of the intelligence community or of the government believed that war was lurking.

On the night of Yom Kippur (5/6 October 1973), at 2.00 a.m., my phone rang. On the other end was Reuven Alloni, head of the Shlomo Region administration responsible for the parts of the Sinai under Israeli rule. 'Rafi, there's going to be a war. I've arranged three planes from Arkia Airlines, and I want you to fly with them to Sharm el-Sheikh and evacuate all the guests at your hotel,' he said to me. The hotel – the only one operating in Sharm at the time – was not mine, of course, but belonged to Barness' company. When I got to Sharm, the officers I met at the airport told me they were on maximum alert, and that there was a high probability that war would break out that day.

The guests – about a hundred men and women – were evacuated, and we landed in Tel Aviv shortly before 6.00 a.m. even before reservists were mobilised.

On Saturday the 6th at 2.00 p.m., after the war had already broken out, I called Shin Bet and offered my help, but they didn't know what to do with me. I then tried to reach the head of military intelligence, Eli Zeira, who agreed to meet me at 5.00 a.m. in his office the next day. When I arrived, I found him shaving. I asked him what I should do, and he didn't know what to say to me, but told me that Major General (Res.) Yeshayahu Gavish, whom I knew as a teenager in agricultural school and later in the Palmach, was about to be named commander of the Sinai area.

I asked for and received a transfer order to Gavish's area. After I arranged a kind of shelter with sandbags at our home for Miriam and the children and borrowed a gun from my cousin, I flew to Sharm el-Sheikh and checked in with Gavish, but he also didn't know what to do with me.

The next day Gavish called me and assigned me a task: 'Take some Jeeps, I will put a helicopter at your disposal. Chase and eliminate Egyptian commando soldiers who are stationed in the Ras Sudr area and are now roaming our territory.'

The Egyptian commando unit's mission was to conquer southern Sinai, reach Eilat and cut it off from Israel, and connect Egypt and Jordan. The Egyptian soldiers in the Ras Sudr area advanced south, along the coast, to the oil wells in Abu Rudeis, and from there to the town of El Tor to Ras Mohamed, the southernmost point in the Sinai Peninsula. We improvised a force of about fifty people, some Jeeps (I took four of them from our hotel), and a helicopter accompanied us for a few hours a day. With the help of the information we received from Gavish's intelligence unit, we located the Egyptian commando soldiers. After four days of activity in a relatively large area, we killed at least sixty Egyptian soldiers, most of them with sniper fire from the helicopter. One I killed myself with the gun I took from my cousin. Another sixty surrendered and were taken as prisoners of war.

At the end of the operation, I returned to Tel Aviv.

The failure of Israel to anticipate the Yom Kippur attack was due to the erroneous assessment of the situation. Intelligence information was plentiful, and it was even accurate. Colonel Yoel Ben-Porat, commander of Unit 848 (today 8200), charged with collecting information extracted by electronic means, did not receive permission from the head of military intelligence, Zeira, to operate the 'special means' in his unit's possession. In the early 1990s, when I ran into Zeira on a flight from South America and asked him why he had not aggressively activated the intelligence system at his disposal, he answered: 'I was convinced there would be no war.' I am sure that had electronic means been activated more fully, we would have discovered that the enemy was planning far more than military manoeuvring, as was the case in May 1973.

Our failures at the beginning of the Yom Kippur War stemmed from acts of omission such as the one described above and from stupidity, particularly of the political leadership – Prime Minister Golda Meir, Defense Minister Moshe Dayan, and Minister Without Portfolio Yisrael Galili – in commanding the IDF to refrain from any activity that could lead to Israel being blamed for starting the war.

There were additional acts of omission. Zamir failed to assess the intelligence accumulated within Mossad, and from Mossad's most important agent, Ashraf Marwan. Marwan, who held senior positions in the Egyptian government and began working with us in Europe during my tenure as head of Hamoked, was married to Nasser's daughter and was one of President Sadat's associates and confidants. About forty hours before the war, Marwan placed a call to a pre-arranged phone number, reserved for such a situation, and said in the conversation the code word 'chemical' for imminent war. That should have been enough of an alert. Marwan asked to meet the head of Mossad in London. Zamir took much longer than Marwan to get to London, so their meeting began only at 10.00 p.m. on 5 October in London (midnight Israel time), and due to various communication problems, Marwan's warning was transmitted to Israel only at

4.00 a.m., ten hours before the start of the Arab attack. Israel could have received that information many hours earlier, perhaps even an entire day earlier.

Although Marwan asked to meet Zamir, there was no need for a personal meeting between them. His use of the code word 'chemical' was clear enough. He could have been politely told to meet his regular operator, or with a senior member of one of Mossad's branches in Europe. Truth be told, even before the meeting in London, there was substantial information with Mossad and military intelligence that war was imminent. Zamir could have avoided wasting precious time flying to London and instead used that time better by pounding on tables to alert the government. It was his insecurity that motivated Zamir to travel to London himself, to see and hear Marwan face to face.

Zeira also made some disastrous mistakes. Not only did he refrain from using special measures to gather information electronically, but he did not heighten the security alert of military intelligence from 'low' to 'high' even when he received news that the Soviets were sending special planes to evacuate the families of Soviet military advisers from Egypt and Syria. Neither Zeira nor Zamir warned stringently enough that war was coming. Had they done so, the IDF could have deployed its forces better, and the chief of staff might have prevailed on government leaders to allow the air force to launch a pre-emptive attack.

I played no major role in any war after Israel's War of Independence in 1948. In the Yom Kippur War, more than in any other war, I felt the pain of not being part of the system and regretted my retirement. It's easy to be smart after the fact, but I'm convinced that if I had been in Mossad at the time, I would have raised a hue and cry, and demanded we prepare for war.

At the end of the war, I returned to my work routine in Barness's business.

In the years after the Yom Kippur War I was invited to internal discussions on the lessons of the failures in the days before the war and in the first days of the war. It was my opinion that the failures of intelligence lay at the feet of Zamir and Zeira. Keinan and Vardi agreed with me, and they were not the only ones.

Chapter 23

Rabin, Sharon and Me

After the Yom Kippur War, my ties with Ariel Sharon became stronger. More than once, when I drove to Sinai, I stopped overnight at his farm in the Negev which was then being built. He and his wife, Lily, were exemplary hosts, and I enjoyed staying with them. Sharon and I wanted to be involved in the leadership of the country and we talked a lot about this.

On 3 June 1974, Yitzhak Rabin was elected Prime Minister. In mid-1975, Rabin called Sharon and asked him to become his security adviser in three areas: world Jewry, national security, and settlement in Judea and Samaria (the areas of the West Bank captured by Israel in the 1967 War). Sharon accepted Rabin's offer and, knowing that the collapse of Barness's business meant I was 'open to suggestions', he offered me a position as his assistant in the prime minister's office. I accepted and began working there in July 1975. When Sharon resigned in the spring of 1976, I was left alone in the office of the prime minister's security adviser for several months, until Rabin's resignation in April 1977.

Sharon and I did not do much in our short tenure. My job was mainly as a technical assistant: I would schedule Sharon's meetings with Rabin. In October 1975, at Sharon's request, I presented him with a job description of my position as assistant to the prime minister's adviser, as follows:

- [The Assistant] will take care of permanent or temporary tasks assigned to him by the Adviser.
- Will participate in discussions to be chaired by the Adviser.

- Will accompany the adviser on his tours as determined by the Adviser.
- Will be a partner in matters in accordance with guidelines determined by the Adviser.

But I also advised Sharon on more significant issues, including sensitive national security matters. By virtue of my previous positions, my security clearance was higher than Sharon's and I could receive material and take part in some discussions that Sharon could not. In one case, I was allowed to give Sharon a summary of a discussion I was involved in only after first getting permission to do so from Rabin.

On the subject of world Jewry, I prepared a long and detailed memorandum for him in the autumn of 1975 with plans to mobilise human resources in the diaspora and to hold conventions in Israel of diaspora leaders. I also drew his attention to issues regarding Israelis living in the diaspora. In his position, Sharon did not pay attention to the diaspora, only to the IDF and the defence establishment, and to settlement.

Did he have any influence on Rabin's policy? Definitely not! Sharon resigned as security adviser in February 1976 because he realised that Rabin was not listening to him and rarely took his advice. He wanted to take part in all prime ministerial meetings with the chief of staff, defense minister, Mossad head, Shin Bet head, as well as government meetings where security issues were discussed, but Rabin wouldn't allow him to participate in discussions with secret service heads, and Defense Minister Peres refused to include him in his meetings with Rabin. Once in a while, Sharon was invited to discussions with the chief of staff or to Cabinet meetings.

It was clear to me that under these conditions, Sharon's time with Rabin would not last, so I was not at all surprised when, one day in February 1976, he got up from his desk, said, 'I'm tired,' and went home. I stayed as an 'assistant' to an 'adviser' who was no longer an adviser, for several months. The only reason was that I was not offered another job, and I needed a salary.

One day in the summer of 1976, the director-general of the prime minister's office, Amos Eran, told me that my unpaid leave from Mossad had ended, and that he had no position for me. It was a more or less gentle way to show me the door. I tried to meet Rabin, to get a sense of if he had anything to offer me, but he was unresponsive.

I met with the head of Mossad, Yitzhak Hofi, and immediately realised that he did not intend to offer me a position. On the spot, I informed him that I was retiring. According to the calculation of my number of years in Mossad, I was entitled to a pension at 72 per cent of my last salary. He approved a 70 per cent pension for me.

I left both Mossad and the prime minister's office on 1 July 1976.

I was asked then, and am still sometimes asked today, if it pained me to retire from Mossad. By nature, I do not tend to express my feelings and share them with others, and that was how I dealt with the matter. But today, more than forty years later, there is nothing holding me back from admitting that I was pained and bitterly disappointed over my retirement.

The frustrating process began when I turned to Rabin and asked him if he had anything to offer me. As usual he was blunt, and his answer was disappointing. Then I asked Hofi point blank: 'Do you need me.' His answer was 'No'. Unlike Zamir, Hofi was someone I could have worked with and if he had answered in the affirmative, I would have stayed. But his answer was clear: 'Your time is up. You are no longer needed here.'

It was a blow. An important chapter of my life ended. But I did not despair. I wanted to play a significant role again in national security, but I understood that until someone decided to use my knowledge, experience and talent, I would have to take care of myself and my family. My pension from Mossad was not enough to sustain the standard of living I wanted to provide for the family. Therefore, I decided to try my hand at private business once more.

Chapter 24

Fish, Turkeys and Politics

In the summer of 1976, at the age of fifty, I became self-employed for the first time in my life. I'd always been attracted to business, and I now had a chance to commit to it, with all my heart and soul.

To put it mildly, Miriam did not react with equanimity when I stopped getting a salary with all the extras. She characterises the years of 1976 to 1978 as my *Zorba the Greek* period. Those who have seen this wonderful film probably remember the funny–sad scene, towards the end of the film, when Zorba's complicated device to move trees from the mountain top to the harbour collapses and shatters. Making this comparison was Miriam's way of indicating that she thought I invested a lot of energy and hard work in schemes that often seemed to collapse on me. I think she exaggerates, but there is no dispute between us that it was a difficult time.

From work with Barness, I had business connections which I renewed after I left the prime minister's office and Mossad. For example, back in 1972 I had entered into a partnership with Irwin Semel, an immigrant from Brazil who settled on a kibbutz and with whom I set up a vegetable drying factory. In addition, we set up a commodities company called Rismax. Its customers were Israelis or Iranian companies and organisations, who came to us through the mediation of my friend Massoud Ali Hani. We were not particularly successful but even after the dissolution of Barness's Daylin company we continued to sell various products in Israel and especially in Iran. In Tehran, we equipped five hospitals with medical equipment imported from the United States, ranging from oxygen supplies to complete operating rooms. As suppliers we received a commission rate of about 4 per cent, a handsome amount when it came to deals of several million dollars. As part of this business, I visited Iran about a dozen times.

While I worked in the prime minister's office, Rismax was run by Semel but I remained a 50 per cent partner in the company. After I left that job, I settled in his office in Tel Aviv, though we did not even have a secretary.

In 1974, while in charge of Amnon Barness's hotels in Sharm el-Sheikh, I founded, with fisheries expert Yehuda Segev, the Tropi Fish company to catch fish in the Red Sea suitable for aquariums.

One day, Segev came to me with an idea. At the southernmost point in the Sinai Peninsula there are lots of tropical fish, and one of them, called the Emperor angelfish, is in high demand in the luxury aquarium market. If you could catch them and export them alive, you could get $500 or $600 a fish. At first I thought I hadn't heard right, but when I understood, I was in, and so Tropi Fish was born.

When I retired in 1976, I had time to develop Tropi Fish. We rented a building, where twenty asbestos tanks with a volume of 500 litres each were installed. I travelled to the United States and Britain to learn more about the aquaculture business and work out routes for shipping the fish. We got a loan from the bank, hired divers, put large aquariums in one of the bays in Ras Mohamed. We sold the edible fish we caught mainly to customers in Israel, while most of the ornamental fish were sold abroad. It was gruelling work. Segev and I would personally drive the live fish, each in a separate plastic bag, stored in insulated containers, from Sharm el-Sheikh to Ben-Gurion Airport, a distance of about 600 kilometres, a journey of seven to eight hours. Between late 1976 and mid-1978 I drove the route no fewer than fifty times. While driving we had to stop occasionally, to check the condition of the fish, and if necessary, add oxygen to the plastic bags where each was swimming. The fish were flown out to importers in Britain and America, who distributed them to additional countries.

Tropi Fish functioned well until 1980. We did not make any real profits, but we did not lose either. The truth is that the sale of ornamental fish only covered the expenses. The sale of the edible fish brought in a little more money. In 1978, Segev and I decided that this business was not for us. We sold 50 per cent of the company to two people, who ran it for the next two years. After the peace treaty was signed with Egypt, Israeli businesses in Sinai were liquidated. We received compensation, which was divided between Segev, the new partners and myself. My portion was about $35,000.

During the two-year period 1976–8, I also managed the liquidation of the Barness Group's business in Israel, selling off their hotels and caravans in southern Israel.

Another enterprise involved buying up herds of black goats. My friend Avraham Yaffe, who became director-general of the Nature Preservation Authority after serving as IDF southern commander, told me that it had been decided to eliminate black goat herds because they destroyed the forests in nature reserves. 'There will be tenders for the purchase of the herds from their Arab owners in Galilee and the Negev,' Yaffe told me. With financing from businessman Yossi Rieger and an Arab partner, we began bidding on the tenders. We won most of them, and trucked the herds to Jordan. This went on for about a year, until most of the black goats in the country were sold to Jordan or slaughtered.

At that time, I became interested in buying land in Samaria in the West Bank. I entered into a partnership with Micha Nathanson, who speaks Arabic fluently, and we bought up about 250 acres. We sold the land we had purchased to the Israel Land Administration at an average profit of about 15 per cent. In fact, we played a role as intermediaries between the Arab land sellers and the administration.

The partnership with Rieger gained momentum following the successful goat deal. We joined businessman Avraham Pilz and established a company to raise turkeys, in partnership with Moshe Tumarkin, considered the biggest expert in Israel in this field. At one point, we had the largest turkey coop in the country, with about

150,000 birds. Funding for the project was provided by Rieger and Pilz, and I contributed a very small percentage. But our business plan was not a good one. Our huge flock flooded the market for turkeys. There wasn't enough demand for them.

One day in late 1978, when I was serving as the prime minister's adviser on the war on terror, Tumarkin came to my office to have me sign as the guarantor on a loan of several hundred thousand dollars from the Farmers' Association. It turned out that he had borrowed the money to continue supplying food to the turkeys, hoping the project would recover. But his hopes were dashed, the project collapsed, and we lost a lot of money.

When that happened, I told the Farmers' Association the truth: I could not pay off my share of the debt, and if I was forced to pay it as guarantor, I would have to mortgage my house and perhaps lose it. One of the heads of the association showed understanding for my plight and expressed a willingness to write off the entire debt, provided I turned to the then Minister of Finance, Yigal Horowitz, and persuade him to give the Farmers' Association some relief and certain benefits it had fought to receive for years.

I called Horowitz, spoke to his heart, and a week later he came back to me and told me the matter had been dealt with. Our business received a convenient debt repayment schedule, and thanks to us, other chicken coops have also received easier repayment terms under the same conditions. Thus, our guarantee was revoked. But even after the cancellation of the guarantee, I lost a lot of money in the turkey business.

Finally, after a conflict of interest arose because of my employment as a full-time adviser to the Prime Minister, I decided to liquidate all of my joint business with Rieger and Pilz.

When I look back on the years 1976–8, I see them as a time when I gained expertise in aquaculture, and extensive experience in other businesses, some of which were a modest success and some of which failed. I did not become rich, but we did not suffer financial hardship at home. Still, it was a stormy period and I was away from home for days and weeks, at a great cost to our family life. Luckily, Miriam and I, with her help, knew how to overcome the crisis.

During that period, I also entered politics for the first time, as the right hand of Sharon in founding the Shlomtzion party. Although I had grown up in the milieu of the mainstream Mapai worker's party, even in my youth I did not believe in the socialist system, and I became even more convinced of the need for liberalisation of the Israeli economy after my return from London. But it was only after the 1973 Yom Kippur War that I turned away decisively from the Labour movement. The major influence in this turnaround was Yitzhak Shamir, one-time commander of the Lehi underground whom I knew from Mossad. During the period that I worked for Barness, Shamir, who had left Mossad, suggested I purchase for Daylin a rubber products factory he managed. After running the numbers past an accountant, I did not buy the factory, but I had many conversations with Shamir. He told me he was leaving the business world, in order to work with Menachem Begin to build up the Herut movement to challenge the Labour party, which had absorbed Mapai. We had a lot of deep discussions about the future of the country, and he convinced me that counter to the ideas I harboured for years – that Herut was fascistic – Begin was a true democrat and that the country would be more democratic under him than it had ever been under Mapai.

But my formal decision to leave Labour was preceded by the failure of Yom Kippur.

I knew Rabin well and valued him personally, but he found it difficult to control the government he headed in 1974–7, right after the war. The open tension between him and Defense Minister Peres impeded government activity. Added to this were various corruption scandals which cast a heavy shadow over the Labour party.

The person who got me to cross the Rubicon politically was Sharon. When we both worked in the Ministry of Defense, my ties with him became closer. Before the Yom Kippur War, he was already at the forefront of the effort to establish the Likud, a larger, more cohesive right-wing bloc. We spoke a lot about politics in later years when I stayed at his farm on my travels to and from Sharm el-Sheikh. We usually agreed that a change in government would be beneficial for the state and its democracy after nearly twenty years of Mapai rule in its various incarnations (actually fifty years, if one included the pre-state period).

I must admit that our agreement on this matter was also due to feelings of frustration we shared with each other: we were both feeling wronged for being expelled from the system, he from the IDF and I from Mossad. We were further alienated when Rabin refrained from giving Sharon a substantive role in determining his government's security policy.

When Sharon resigned as Rabin's adviser, he was identified with the Likud but not with any one of the half-dozen parties that made up the bloc. He debated between joining the Liberals, who were part of the bloc, or establishing an independent party. Lily, Sharon's wife, was convinced that he would be more successful as the head of an independent party, and the polls we conducted in late 1976 indicated she was right, predicting that a party led by Sharon could win between eight and fifteen seats (in the 120-seat Knesset). So Sharon decided to form and lead an independent party.

The final decision to form Sharon's party was made in early 1977. Sharon donated his house in Rehovot for an exhibition by prominent writer and painter Amos Keinan. At the end of the exhibition, we sat late at night Sharon and his wife, Weizmann Institute President Professor Michael Sela and his wife, Amos Keinan, Col. (Res.) Shmulik Pressburger, Miriam and me. Issues such as Greater Israel versus a Palestinian state were not yet the focus of much public debate at the time, but rather whether there was a need for a change of government, against the background of the Yom Kippur War and corruption scandals. It was Keinan who proposed the name of his daughter, Shlomtzion (peace on Zion), as the name of the new movement, and his proposal was accepted on the spot by all present. (Later, Keinan decided not to join Shlomtzion, considering it too right-wing.)

I was appointed chairman of Shlomtzion's management and worked at this from home, because my father was ill and needed constant supervision. Shortly afterwards, Shlomtzion's operations were transferred to Pressburger and a small staff who worked out of offices we rented in Tel Aviv. I showed up most evenings to lead grass-roots gatherings in people's homes to sway voters, and soon realised that this was not for me. I had to answer dozens of questions, some of them silly, and almost all of them repeated themselves every evening. I wanted to flee as quickly as possible.

The elections to the Ninth Knesset were held on 17 May 1977. The last polls before the elections predicted only two seats for us, and that was indeed the end result.

On the night of the election, we gathered in Tel Aviv, and like everyone in Israel watched the results come in on the one TV channel in the country at the time. We heard anchor Haim Yavin announce a 'revolution', and watched Begin's victory speech. I said to Sharon: 'Arik, don't waste a minute. Offer right now to add Shlomtzion's two seats to Herut. Without conditions, without demands.' Sharon listened to me, immediately called Begin, congratulated him, and said, 'Menachem, maybe we should join forces?'

'Tomorrow morning!' Begin replied enthusiastically.

The very next morning, I met Ezer Weizmann at Likud headquarters. He had conducted Likud's election campaign with great success. It was clear to Sharon and me that we would soon become an integral part of Herut. In light of the election results, there was no point in continuing Shlomtzion as an independent party.

In my capacity as head of the management of Shlomtzion, I became head of the division for national organisations and institutions on behalf of Herut. This included being in contact with the Histadrut Labour Federation, and with dozens of organisations that maintained links with Jewish communities abroad in Bulgaria, Romania, Morocco, Tunisia and so on, and with the World Zionist Congress in which I and Sharon participated as representatives of Herut.

For about two years, twice a week, on Thursday evenings and Friday mornings, I would sit in my office at Likud headquarters and deal with national organisational issues. In the second year, I became the head of management of Herut, because Michael Dekel, who preceded me in this position, was too busy in the Knesset. This forced me to devote much more time to party activities.

The country was taken by surprise when President Anwar Sadat announced in a speech to the Egyptian parliament his willingness to travel to Jerusalem and discuss peace with Israel. Within a few days it became clear that his intention was serious, and feverish preparations began for his visit. There were those who suspected it was a trap, but Sharon and I were not among them. We talked about it a lot and concluded that Sadat sincerely wanted coexistence with Israel, as well as stronger ties with the United States. I was filled with excitement at the sight of Sadat landing in Israel in November 1977 although I became sceptical about Egypt's goals over time as my views moved increasingly towards those of Likud.

In 1977–8 I was active in the Herut secretariat, attended meetings of the movement's bureau and central committee, toured branches, met with ordinary members. I must admit that more than once, especially in the first months, I felt like a stranger in this field. I didn't enjoy my roles at Likud headquarters. The reason I did them to the best of my ability was that I harboured the hope – one I did not share with others – that all this activity would serve as a springboard to becoming head of Mossad, or to some other senior government position. Indeed, in 1982, when Hofi was about to retire as head of Mossad, I spoke directly to Begin and asked him to consider me for the job. I also sent him a letter in which I listed my skills and plans for Mossad, were I to head it. I never received a response from him, but I got my answer when Nahum Admoni was named as Hofi's successor.

Chapter 25

Adviser for the War on Terror

Soon after he came to power, Begin appointed Amichai Paglin as the prime minister's adviser for the war on terror. But Paglin died tragically in January 1978 from injuries sustained in a car accident and for months the position was filled only temporarily.

In May 1978, I turned to Sharon (then Minister of Agriculture) and told him that I intended to seek that position. For a long time, I had been consumed, almost obsessively, with a desire to work once more in a challenging security position. I derived little satisfaction from business and my political activity was motivated mainly by the hope it would lead to a senior security position.

Sharon offered to submit my written candidacy to Begin. While I was drafting my letter to Begin, I received a phone call from Dr Eliahu Ben-Elissar, director-general of the prime minister's office, to ask if I was interested in Paglin's position. 'What a question? Of course, I'm interested,' I replied. 'What do I need to do?'

'We will send you forms, fill them in, and attach recommendations. I, of course, will do my best to see to it that you get the job.'

Some time after I applied, Ben-Elissar called to inform me, 'This evening at five o'clock the prime minister will speak with you.' Indeed, at exactly five o'clock the phone rang. Begin got on the line and said, 'Mr Eitan, I have decided to appoint you as the prime minister's adviser for the war on terror."

'I accept, Mr Prime Minister,' I replied. 'I thank you, and will try to fulfil the role in good faith.' A day or two later, on 11 July 1978, I received a letter of appointment for the position with an appendix defining my duties. These included assisting the prime minister in everything related to the war against terrorist organisations abroad and to inter-ministerial coordination on internal security issues related to terrorism, and direct contact with the heads of the secret services and relevant ministerial offices. It noted that that the role did not replace the roles or actions of existing security agencies or the authority of the prime minister over them.

On 13 July 1978, I reported to my office, which was within the Kiriya, the Ministry of Defense complex in Tel Aviv, and I met my deputy, Colonel Gideon Mahnayimi, whom I was friendly with from my time in Shin Bet. I explained that I intended to take up the post only in early September, after a long-planned trip with my family cross-country in the United States. To be honest, the position of adviser attracted me mainly because I thought it might be a stepping-stone to becoming head of Mossad. I was wrong about that, but I do not regret that I took this job.

The position of prime minister's adviser on the war on terror was created in late 1972, following the terrorist attack in Munich. The former head of military intelligence, Major General Aharon Yariv was the first to hold the post, and his high standing within the Israeli intelligence community enabled him to make the position one in which he, as adviser, participated in the Committee of Heads of Services, and in Cabinet meetings on all security issues. He also created a regular forum of representatives of the heads of Mossad, Shin Bet, military intelligence, the IDF Division of Operations, the Commissioner of Police and the Director-General of the Ministry of Foreign Affairs. This forum convened once a week to discuss operations in progress within Shin Bet and military intelligence and to decide and coordinate defensive matters related to anti-terrorism. In other words, he functioned as a sort of central command, with the authority to instruct the police or the IDF to take defensive measures in response to warnings or threats.

In early 1974, Yariv was elected to the Knesset and was replaced by Brigadier General Israel Lior, former military secretary to prime ministers Levi Eshkol and Golda Meir. Six months later, he retired, and Prime Minister Yitzhak Rabin appointed Major General Rehavam Zeevi, who left the post after Begin became prime minister, apparently at Begin's request, because the new prime minister wanted Paglin, whom he admired from their time in the Irgun. Paglin had been the Irgun's operations officer, the one who planned the explosion at the King David Hotel, the break-in to the Acre prison, and dozens of other operations.

However, according to several senior members of the Israeli intelligence community, Paglin acted like a bull in a china shop in his new position. He had never served in the army, never been a part of intelligence organisations in the State of Israel, did not know their work or their staff, and was aggressive to boot. In their view, he was nothing but an aging manufacturer of industrial ovens who lacked any idea of the complex activities of Israeli intelligence agencies and was unable to appreciate the experience they had gained during Israel's thirty years as an independent state. He didn't speak their language; he did not understand – or want to understand – the division of territory among them. The result was such antagonism with the various security forces that they stopped providing him with any information that was not directly related to defensive actions.

However, to his credit, Paglin had impressive technological knowledge. At his initiative, development began on an electronic system for protecting civilian aircraft from Soviet shoulder-fired missiles known to be in the hands of some Arab terrorist organisations. He was in constant contact with me regarding this, and I assisted him in contacting Sanders Associates near Boston, a company which was chiefly engaged in developing sophisticated electronic warfare products against radar installations.

Immediately on my return from my holiday, I contacted the three heads of the intelligence arms, and made it clear that I would do everything in harmony with them. All three of them, the head of Mossad, the head of Shin Bet and the head of military intelligence, came to my office to congratulate me personally on my appointment, and did not hide their joy that this time the prime minister's counter-terrorism adviser was one of them – from within the intelligence community.

My first initiative was to create a channel for accessing offensive missions of the three services, which had not existed under any of my predecessors. This meant that I was a secret partner in the plans and operations of Mossad, Shin Bet and military intelligence and was able to express my position to them and to the prime minister.

However, I do not want to create a false impression that this all ran smoothly. There is an inherent, almost inevitable, structural conflict between the prime minister's adviser on counter-terrorism and the heads of the intelligence and security services. As I predicted, the first friction I encountered was with Hofi, who vehemently opposed my demand for direct contact with international anti-terrorism services and organisations. He refused to let me meet the head of the CIA, Admiral Stansfield Turner, when he visited Israel. I complained to Begin about this and the prime minister ordered Hofi to have me meet the American guest. I was not satisfied with this and asked Begin to set general guidelines, which would clarify the prime minister's position on this issue. After Begin issued the guidelines, I spoke to Hofi and, to his credit, he was a rational man who understood my explanation that meetings with world counter-terrorism organisations were essential to my duties of coordinating international efforts in this area on behalf of the government.

Begin's instructions allowed me to make direct contact with all the organisations in Europe and the United States that fight terrorism. In essence, I set up a network of close connections that paralleled the Tevel unit of Mossad. This network included the American Delta Force, the British SAS, and similar units that operated in Germany, France, Italy and Japan. Our office had a staff of four others in addition to myself: my deputy, two aides, and a secretary. With the permission of IDF Chief of Staff Rafael Eitan (same name as me but no relation) I had access to military attachés in every Israeli embassy. In essence, I had a qualified person at each Israeli embassy whom I could use for day-to-day missions. The connection with Delta Force, for example, was handled for me through a counsellor at the Israeli Embassy in Washington by the name of Benyamin Netanyahu.

As I mentioned earlier, my predecessor, Paglin, had initiated a project to protect our civil aviation from Soviet-made Strela shoulder-fired missiles, already in use by Palestinian terrorist organisations, and I had been helping him with this. As soon as I took office, I set about completing a project to thwart these missiles, an effort that took three years. It is worth noting, we had the full cooperation of the FBI in this.

Among my priorities was significantly to increase the budget that the Ministry of Finance made available for the project, so I spoke directly to the budget director of the Finance Ministry, explaining the importance of the scheme. He approved the necessary funds. The electronic defence system initiated by Paglin is installed to this day in IDF fighter jets and helicopters. The heat-sensitive system was originally intended to protect civil aviation, but that did not happen. The system is based on an airborne laser that generates enough heat to divert heat-seeking missiles from homing in on the aircraft's engine heat.

In the early 1980s, I also managed to raise a considerable amount of money to fund equipment for detecting hidden explosives in suitcases and containers. These devices have been refined and have also been adapted for drug detection.

I would meet Begin once a week, or sometimes less often, as needed and according to his schedule, to brief him and receive his approval on various matters. The meetings were relaxed, lasting an hour to an hour and a half. Begin listened carefully, posed questions, and sometimes interrupted me with a remark, 'This I have already heard from the head of Mossad [or the head of Shin Bet], there is no need to repeat it.' Only on two occasions, did a problem arise from my briefings with him.

The first occurred in 1980 or 1981, before Operation Peace for the Galilee (the first Lebanon War).

From mid-1980 until the outbreak of the PLO war in June 1982, we carried out dozens of actions against the Palestinians. One day we received verified information that could have allowed us to eliminate Yasser Arafat using an explosive in a crowded place in a Beirut neighbourhood where he was to deliver a speech at a conference of his men.

At the time, Begin held the portfolio of defense minister in addition to being prime minister (this was after Ezer Weizmann left the government in May 1980, and with it surrendered his portfolio as defense minister). Such an operation, which could have killed Arafat with certainty, required the approval of the prime minister, but Begin was ill and lying in bed at the prime minister's residence in Jerusalem. In the middle of the night we – Northern District Commander Meir Dagan, who was in charge of military operations in South Lebanon, Northern Commander Yanush Ben Gal, Chief of Staff Rafael Eitan and me – sat around his bed. I explained that it would not be a surgical operation that would kill only Arafat or only a few people close to him but that an unknown number of civilians would also die.

The discussion in Begin's bedroom lasted over two hours. Eventually Begin refused his permission. 'I think Yasser Arafat should be killed, but only him, without killing innocent people,' Begin said. 'Since you can't assure me that innocent people will not be killed, I am not approving the operation.'

Every Thursday, I held a meeting in my office that included the head of operations from the IDF General Staff or one of his deputies, the head of military intelligence's counter-terrorism unit, a representative of the head of security within Shin Bet, a representative of the Tevel division of Mossad, the head of the police intelligence division, and the head of the Foreign Ministry's research division. The representative from military intelligence usually opened the discussion, reviewing the list of all current warnings, by regional division. Representatives of the other bodies would report on the defensive measures each had taken. I would decide on what sort of next steps should be taken depending on the nature of the warning, including deployment of additional forces or activating one intelligence arm or another. These coordination meetings lasted several hours and were in fact a sort of high command for defensive warfare against terrorism.

Every morning, when I got to the office, a list ten to twenty pages long awaited me on my desk, with all alerts received in the past day. Warnings were concentrated in the anti-terrorism branch of military intelligence, phoned in to me and to all relevant bodies in real time at all hours of the day and night. Depending on the circumstance, it was up to me to decide which body to activate and what actions should be undertaken. When there was an attack, I tended to go to the scene, and over time learned to distinguish between criminal and terrorist attacks.

My normal workday included meetings and discussions on technical issues and visits, at least twice a week, to areas where intensive terrorist activity occurred. Already then there was a problem with arms smuggling from Egypt to the Gaza Strip, which required IDF searches and sweeps, and I would occasionally join them.

The system I set up made sure that the wealth of information related to terrorism that was gathered flowed from one body to the other. I am convinced this flow of information helped thwart many attacks while they were still in planning stages.

However, under my watch, three members of the Haran family and a policeman were killed in 1979 in an attack for which we had no warnings. A year earlier, before my appointment, thirty-five Israelis were killed and more than seventy injured in an attack on a bus along the coastal highway north of Tel Aviv, one of the worst terrorist incidents in the history of Israel. In both cases, the terrorists came from the sea. The lesson was clear: the shores of the country must be secured against such infiltration. Therefore, I undertook to create effective protection of the shoreline from north to south. I obtained a special budget from the treasury of about $3 million over two years for this project, on which I worked with the Ministry of Defense's adviser for national planning, Major General (Res.) Avraham Tamir.

The Israeli defence companies Elbit and Rafael had already created an infrared instrument which scans the sea from the shore and identifies objects and vessels that emit any heat within a range of four or five kilometres. We placed the equipment on beaches at eight-kilometre intervals as well as radar stations at intervals of fifteen kilometres from each other. In this way, we could automatically catch the silhouette and the exact position of an approaching body on the computer screens of the control rooms operated by the navy, which took over implementation and operation of the project after the planning stage.

Usually, I dealt with projects like this of a military nature in the initial stages and then handed them over for implementation to the relevant bodies – the navy, Shin Bet or others. At that point, I was content to monitor the project's progress and provide technical assistance as needed.

As part of my growing ties with foreign services, I set up an international conference in July 1979 centred on a war-game simulation of a hijacking by a group of Palestinian and German terrorists. Those who attended included representatives from the American Delta counter-terrorism unit, the US State Department, and representatives of the nucleus of what was eventually to become the West German counter-terrorism unit, and a large group of our experts.

The idea for the conference came from Yaakov Katban, a doctor of psychology who was the adviser to West Germany police in counter-terrorism affairs, and Professor Ariel Marari, another psychologist, who served at the time as an adviser to a General Staff reconnaissance unit responsible for negotiations with terrorists. I liked the idea and turned to Aharon Yariv, who was chairman of the Jaffee Center for Strategic Studies (since renamed the Institute for National Security Studies) at Tel Aviv University, and he took over the organisation of the conference under the centre's roof.

The opening scenario of the exercise, prepared by Katban, Marari and the conference director, was kept secret and distributed to all participants in real time (as soon as the simulation began). It was as follows: a Boeing 707 TWA flight takes off from Tel Aviv to Boston and lands in Athens for refuelling and to pick up more passengers. Ten minutes after leaving Athens, the plane is taken over by a group of terrorists composed of some Palestinians and some Germans. The pilot is forced to fly towards Gibraltar, then to Damascus and then to Tripoli but each in turn refuse to let him land. With fuel about to run out, he is allowed to land at Algiers, on condition that he refuel and take off immediately. From there he returns to the Middle East, and at 18.07 (Israel time) lands at Mehrabad International Airport near Tehran. About an hour later, the kidnappers broadcast their demands: the release of sixty Palestinian prisoners from Israeli prisons to be flown (via Switzerland) to Algeria; release of five German terrorists; the release of Sirhan Sirhan, the assassin of Robert Kennedy imprisoned in the United States; and a ransom of $150 million to be paid by the United States, Israel and West Germany. The kidnappers allow a period of 24 hours to fulfil their demands, and threaten that after this they will execute a hostage every thirty minutes.

The operation codenamed Kingfisher began with the news of the hijacking, and continued with broadcasts from the airports which the plane approached, news flashes, etc. Participants were divided into various professional teams to analyse the developing situation, coordinate and supervise staff, deal with international media and with the relatives of the hostages. The exercise lasted about three days, and its conclusion was not clear and unequivocal because it was stopped at a late stage of negotiations with the hijackers at Tehran airport.

The conference and game were considered a great success and the Jaffee Center for Strategic Studies published a thick booklet entitled *Save* detailing it. In the 1980s, other similar conferences were held in Israel, various Western countries and the United States (sponsored by the FBI).

During this period, the Americans set up an international system that included Mossad and corresponding services in other countries to exchange raw information in real time regarding terrorism. In my position, I was entitled to receive information generated by this system, which was encrypted, and through Mossad I could address the system with specific questions or requests as necessary.

I had an active part in dealing with a kidnapping case that took place in Bogotá, Colombia. On the night of 28/29 February 1980, about 50 (!!) foreign diplomats and their wives, including Israeli Ambassador Eliyahu Barak and his wife, were abducted and taken hostage by M19, a Trotskyist underground organisation. My task was to receive information and pass on what was relevant to various bodies, maintain contact with my counterparts and brief the prime minister.

Two days after the kidnapping, our embassy staff in Bogotá, who were in contact with the local authorities, informed us that they had reached out to a Colombian Jew named Sami Yochai, who was trying to mediate between the Bogotá government and the kidnappers. I subsequently informed them of my decision to send Marari, the psychologist who specialised in negotiating with terrorists, to Bogotá. At that point, I decided not to reveal this to the Americans. I wanted to reserve for us maximum freedom of action and room for manoeuvre with Yochai, a businessman who was the Southern American representative of the Israeli communication company Tadiran. But he also had business ties with underground and criminal organisations in Colombia. Yochai, apparently in collaboration with Bogotá's chief rabbi, linked Marari to another Jew in Colombia by the name of Victor Shoshan, who put Marari in touch with M19 members.

The Americans were angry and insulted when they learned that we had not informed them we sent Marari, whom they knew well, to Colombia, considering it a vote of no confidence in them. But this is the sort of thing that occasionally happens even between countries with close cooperation, like ours with the United States.

Meanwhile, the Bogotá government managed to secure the release of the women and people who were sick from among the hostages.

Among them was also Ambassador Barak's wife. Marari met her and the information she provided was helpful in continuing negotiations he conducted with the kidnappers. Only at this point did we bring the Americans into the loop. The kidnappers originally asked for a huge sum of money, but Marari negotiated them down to $5 million to be paid by the United States. The other countries involved in the incident decided to share the burden, and Israel's portion was $200,000. And so concluded the incident.

For years I had worked to obtain information on Saddam Hussein's efforts to equip Iraq with nuclear weapons. The first time I dealt with the matter was in 1975, when I was Sharon's assistant. Part of my job was to comb through daily intelligence reports and draw the attention of the prime minister to important but not urgent issues. When the raw material I read lit a red light, I turned to the prime minister's military secretary, Brigadier General Ephraim Poran, who, like me, used to go over the intelligence material, and with his agreement, I wrote a short report to Rabin, with copies to the minister of defense and chief of staff. I pointed out the danger of an atomic bomb in Saddam Hussein's hands. I suggested to Rabin that he set up a team of experts to formulate a plan to prevent Iraq's atomic development.

I do not remember what Rabin's reaction was, and if he responded at all. He may have raised the issue in his closed-door talks with IDF chiefs and intelligence services. In any case, I left that position soon after. It was only when I became Begin's counter-terrorism adviser that I attended meetings that discussed security issues.

In February 1980, one such meeting raised the issue of the contract that then French Prime Minister Jacques Chirac had signed with Saddam regarding the supply of a nuclear reactor to Iraq, ostensibly for peaceful purposes. The conclusion was that we must be vigilant and take the necessary steps to prevent or delay the French–Iraqi deal. From that moment until the bombing of the reactor in June 1981, I regularly updated Sharon, then Minister of Agriculture in the Begin government, on all relevant information I received from the intelligence services regarding Iraq's nuclear development. Even then, in early 1980, Sharon believed that Israel would eventually have to bomb the Iraqi reactor and destroy it. That opinion grew stronger in subsequent months, on both the political and military levels. Sharon told me he suggested that Begin instruct the air force to prepare the bombing of the Osirak reactor.

Mossad requested, and received from the Americans, a series of satellite images of the reactor. The photographs confirmed the assumption that it was intended for military purposes. At the time, two Iraqi nuclear scientists working on the reactor were killed by Iranian agents in Europe, but Iran failed in its attempt to bomb the reactor from the air. During 1981, Israel exerted pressure on France and the United States to prevent the completion of the Iraqi reactor, but to no avail.

Towards June 1981, a number of dates for the bombing were set, but for various reasons, including leaks to the media, the strike was postponed time and time again. It is worth noting that former Defense Minister Ezer Weizmann vehemently opposed the bombing, and Shimon Peres, chairman of the Labour party, also tried to prevent it, claiming that his friend, François Mitterrand, recently elected president of France, promised to prevent nuclear supplies to Iraq.

Operation Opera, the bombing of the Osirak reactor, was carried out on 7 June 1981, by eight Israeli fighter jets, all of which returned home safely.

In 1986, as part of an investigation into France's role in the Iraqi reactor affair, journalist Yeshayahu Ben-Porat interviewed Chirac, who denied any responsibility for Osirak's military nature and Hussein's intention to equip Iraq with atomic weapons. The interview with Chirac was incorporated into a book called *Operation Babylon* co-written by Ben-Porat and Uri Dan. It was half documentary, half imaginary, but it caused a stir in media and political circles in France. In the book, the authors inflated my involvement in the affair beyond all proportion and attributed to me a central role in its planning and execution. Anyone who reads the book gets the impression that Sharon and I led the operation from 1975 until the bombing. The reality was very different. Except for my warning memo to Rabin in 1975 and the ongoing transfer of information to Sharon, I had no active part in the reactor affair. I knew about the bombing plan, but I did not know the exact date planned for the bombing.

Chapter 26

Lebanon and the Palestinians

For years, Lebanon was considered the least hostile Arab state to Israel. Lebanese villagers would wave to the residents of Israeli *kibbutzim* and *moshavim* on the northern border. The assumption – which proved to be wrong – was that only the fear of Arab reprisals prevented Lebanon from signing a peace agreement with Israel.

Since its independence in 1943, Lebanon has suffered from rifts and tensions among the many communities that make up its population. For various reasons, these tensions have intensified since the mid-1970s. Our natural allies were the Christians, who were in conflict with the Palestinians and fought with the PLO, the soldiers of Arafat, who made our lives miserable until they were expelled from Jordan in 1970. The PLO then moved north, so that instead of being on our eastern border with Jordan, they ended up in Lebanon, where they grew stronger and expanded, setting up an armed force more powerful than all the militias operating in that divided country.

True, even before Arafat's troops arrived from Jordan, there were Palestinians in Lebanon, but they lived in refugee camps, disorganised, without real power. Those who arrived in the 1970s saw themselves as the first to dare to act against Israel after the disgraceful defeat suffered by the Arab states in the 1967 Six-Day War.

The Palestinians, most of whom were Muslims, were regarded and regarded themselves as foreigners for whom Lebanon served as a base from which to attack Israel, until it was defeated and eliminated. In the political culture of Lebanon, such problems were treated with violence, as 1976 massacres in the Karantina district of Beirut and in Damour attest.

At that time, the Shi'ites formed a front with the Christians against the Palestinians. Gradually, they became a new force, solidifying its identity and defining its interests, which largely overlapped with the interests of the Christians. This was the picture as I saw it when I took over as Begin's counter-terrorism adviser in 1978.

When I took office, a kind of Palestinian mini state, which we called Fatahland, existed in southern Lebanon, extending south from western Beirut to the coastal towns of Tyre and Sidon and Palestinian refugee camps closer to the Israeli border. The Palestinians attacked us from there in various ways: infiltrating Israel by land and sea, launching Katyusha and mortar fire on Galilee, and even trying to come into Israel by air on hang-gliders. The also tried to infiltrate by crossing the Jordan River to slip in from the east (often they were captured by the Jordanians).

Although the Christians passed on intelligence regarding the Palestinians in western Beirut and southern Lebanon, this did not yield any results, and Israeli security heads often doubted the reliability of the information.

During my frequent visits to southern Lebanon accompanied by Meir Dagan, Commander of the IDF Southern Lebanon Region, in charge of our activities there, I met Major Saad Haddad, who headed a Christian militia that eventually became the Southern Lebanon Army (SLA), which operated independently of the Christian Phalangist militia, although there was loose coordination between them. Through Haddad we met the head of a group from Muslim villages in the area who told us they were fighting the Palestinians because, in their eyes, the Palestinians had become an occupying force, restricting locals' movement, and even levying taxes on them. As a result of this contact, Israel provided them with modest quantities of weapons, dozens of rifles, pistols and grenades, as well as explosives for their guerrilla operations against the Palestinians.

On 23 October 1981, I sent the Prime Minister a detailed memorandum on the situation in Lebanon, the war on the PLO, and the need to cooperate with various denominations in addition to Christians. It stated:

> The most serious political danger to Israel, now and in the foreseeable future, stems from the strengthening of the PLO's political status. The declarations of [Presidents Jimmy] Carter, [Gerald] Ford and [Carter's adviser Zbigniew] Brzezinski in American negotiations with the PLO and the meeting of [French Foreign Minister Claude] Cheysson with Arafat are only signs of a process that cannot be stopped in purely political and diplomatic ways.
>
> The PLO does not pose a physical risk to the State of Israel (in 1980, 19 Israelis were killed in terrorist acts), although some of these actions have a significant impact on public morale in the country.
>
> Liquidation of the PLO outpost in southern Lebanon
>
> This is the course of action which may, under the current conditions, lead to the most serious damage to the political status of the PLO. This action may achieve the following results:
>
> - A severe blow to the prestige of the PLO among the residents of the territories, thus aiding in the formation of anti-PLO elements as a possible basis for autonomy.
> - Increasing the PLO's dependence on Arab countries, thereby reducing its ability to manoeuvre in the inter-Arab and international arena.
> - Damage to the international status of the PLO, eliminating its territorial outpost that gives the image of a state and presenting it as a weak body.
> - Due to the loss of territorial control, reducing Fatah's control over other terrorist organisations and increasing conflicts between them.

Conditions for achieving the goals above are:

In order to prevent extreme negative reactions from the American administration and public opinion in the Western world, there must be a reason for the operation – a serious terrorist attack, shelling of border communities etc.

The operation must lead to the elimination or paralysis of the main combat force and the ranks of the Palestinian Field Command in Lebanon. It must therefore be swift and overwhelming, and prevent most of the terrorists from having the option to withdraw.

Every effort should be made to avoid civilian casualties.

Israel will not be able to hold on to the liberated territory for days. Therefore, the area freed from the PLO control must be large enough to form the basis of an independent Lebanese political entity, sympathetic to Israel. It is desirable to create a territorial continuity with the Christian area north of Beirut, recognised by the world as a legitimate, viable and independent political body (unlike the view of Haddad's enclave).

The elements for creating such a political entity must be prepared in advance. In its absence, the liberated territory will constitute a political vacuum, which will filled by UN forces, the government of [Lebanese President] Sarkis or the return of the PLO and the leftist front who control it today.

Israel must now assist – and urgently – in establishing a Lebanese political body, with symbolic military capability, which can declare itself the Free Lebanese Government, immediately upon the liberation of southern Lebanon by the IDF. It should accept political responsibility on the ground, and prevent the IDF from being seen as an occupying army imposing military rule. The IDF will be able to assist the Free Lebanese Government at its request, and for a limited period, to stabilise the region.

In order to create initial international recognition, it is desirable that the independent Lebanese body establish (with

> covert Israeli help) an office abroad, and conduct appropriate public relations and information activities, directed both internally (to Lebanon) and externally, to the Western world.
>
> Due to the urgency and importance of this matter, an inter-ministerial body should be immediately formed to manage and coordinate the preparation of the southern Lebanese entity and to guide it.

I will not list here all my activities as the prime minister's counter-terrorism adviser from 1978 until my removal from office in 1984 by Prime Minister Shimon Peres. But I will briefly mention a few issues that I dealt with during this period (in part since, in 1982, I also served as head of the Bureau for Scientific Relations, known by its Hebrew acronym as Lekem).

As part of my portfolio, I received a regular report from Mossad on its offensive operations in Europe, including those carried out before I replaced Paglin.

An important and impressive targeted assassination operation that foreign sources attributed to Mossad (it is well known that Israel in general and Mossad in particular do not usually admit or deny assassinations) was the assassination of one of the most brutal terrorists, Wadie Haddad, a founder and leader of the Popular Front for the Liberation of Palestine (PFLP). Among other actions, a branch of the PFLP had hijacked an Air France plane to Entebbe. According to the same sources, Mossad agents discovered that Haddad had a sweet tooth, particularly for Belgian chocolate. During a meeting in Germany, a Mossad agent gave him a small gift – a box of Belgian chocolate. Haddad devoured the chocolate the same day. A small amount of special poison had been added to the chocolate, and, according to foreign sources, it was enough to cause Haddad to develop leukaemia. He was hospitalised in East Germany where he died in March 1978.

After Haddad's death, we learned that his successor, Abu Ibrahim, who, like his predecessor, conducted operations from Iraq, had created five sophisticated explosive suitcases intended to be handed to innocent passengers on El Al planes. The explosives were to detonate when the plane was in the air to make sure there was no escape for passengers and crew. The suitcases were transferred to the Iraqi embassy in London and held there. After surveillance and other actions which I initiated, all five suitcases were uncovered, brought and unloaded in Israel. I leaked the story – without confidential operational details, of course – to Bob Woodward of the *Washington Post*, which garnered him huge publicity.

Although the security of El Al's offices and facilities at airports was the responsibility of Shin Bet, I dealt with this issue quite a bit. During one of my visits to Greece regarding this, I was summoned by the Greek prime minister. Greece only recognised Israel *de facto* and retained only a low-level diplomatic presence in Tel Aviv. The Greek prime minister sent a letter to Begin with me, promising *de jure* recognition if Begin won the next election. In fact, *de jure* recognition for Israel came only in 1990.

Sharon tasked me to head Lekem in 1981, shortly after he became minister of defense in Begin's second government. Lekem is the only intelligence service directly subordinate to the minister of defense.

At the end of 1981, the prime minister also tasked me to help Israel's efforts to retain control of Taba, a tiny strip of land south of Eilat. I will not go into the details of the complex controversy that plagued dozens of international law experts for years. Suffice it to say that, after looking into the matter, I became convinced that it would be better to reach a compromise with Egypt rather than take the case before the International Court of Justice in the Hague, as Egypt demanded. Begin, however, did not accept my opinion.

I turned to Uri Talmor, a reserve brigadier general with a rich background in management, economics and law, and asked him to gather relevant material. In March 1982, we prepared a summary of the material we had gathered in which we explained that there was no doubt that under the British Mandate, the border was moved north of Taba, and not in Taba itself as Israel was trying to argue. There was some doubt as to the boundary line in the days of the

Ottoman Empire, but even in this respect, the Egyptian position seemed more solid than ours. Despite this, Begin decided to take the dispute to the International Court of Justice. The court in the Hague eventually ruled against us, and in 1989 we were forced to hand over the entire Taba area to Egypt.

Many of my activities during this period were voluntary and motivated, among other things, by my political views. Thus, for example, I often visited settlements being established in Judea and Samaria, and gave lectures there. During most of my visits there, I also looked for suitable sites for establishing additional settlements, at the explicit request of Arik Sharon.

Peace for Galilee War

By May 1982, it was clear that Sharon, then minister of defense, favoured taking military action in Lebanon, but he had more than a smattering of opponents within the government. I was in the picture regarding both existing and planned actions in Lebanon, not only by virtue of my position but also due to my friendship with Sharon and our frequent conversations.

Immediately after his first meeting as defense minister with Christian Lebanese leaders north of Beirut in February 1982, he formulated in broad terms what was named Operation Oranim (Hebrew for pines) to occupy southern Lebanon to the outskirts of Beirut.

He set out three goals for the operation:

- Keep the PLO away from Lebanon;
- Conclude a peace treaty with a Lebanese government headed by a Christian president;
- Expel the Syrians from Lebanon.

Sharon sincerely believed this would ensure the long-term safety and security of Israel's northern settlements, which had been suffering for years from Katyusha rocket barrages that killed and wounded many victims and generally disrupted life in northern Israel.

After that visit to Lebanon, in February 1982, Sharon presented his views openly in the Defense Minister's Forum, which since Ben-Gurion's days occurs every Friday morning and is attended by army commanders and heads of intelligence services. Sharon regularly invited me to these discussions. During this period, the meetings usually opened with a briefing by the head of military intelligence, Major General Yehoshua Sagi, or the head of the research division, Brigadier General Aviezar Yaari, whose main focus was the PLO's growing power in Lebanon. Then other participants would speak, and, at the end, Sharon would express his views on the PLO in Lebanon. To the best of my recollection, everyone understood that sooner or later we would have to destroy this PLO 'mini-state' which was endangering Israel.

Lebanon was also a central part of discussions in Cabinet meetings. On 11 May 1982, I sent Sharon a letter which included the following wording:

> After the meeting today, I have reached the conclusion that we should think again about Operation Oranim. Hold your horses. Ministers are not with you on this subject. Even those who voted for an attack, and know that an air force mission is a reasonable action, are convinced that the urgency you feel regarding this is personal, not urgent for the country. In other words, Arik Sharon's private war.
>
> Operation Oranim will be a unifying force in the Arab world and will bring closer an all-out war with them, while today this world is increasingly divided. In other words, we are turning our military firepower against a force which is indeed annoying and thwarting a diplomatic solution, but who wants a diplomatic solution in Judea and Samaria, and in Gaza? In other words, our general military firepower is focusing on a secondary goal, at the risk of getting us into a mess, particularly with the Americans.

Until he received my letter Sharon was determined to invade Lebanon in May. He summoned me immediately to discuss it. Let me make clear, I agreed with the need to keep the PLO away from Lebanon, but disagreed with Sharon's timing for Operation Oranim.

'If the IDF invades only a narrow strip in southern Lebanon, you will not accomplish the goals you set for yourself,' I told Sharon,

> In order to accomplish those goals with a minimum of losses, you know as well as I do that from the first day of fighting you will have to capture Beirut airport with forces that will come from the sea. This means that from the first day you will need to control Beirut, and extend north and south, and you will be locked in the PLO infrastructure in southern Lebanon. But right now, you are forbidden from undertaking such a wide operation as far as Beirut. You need to wait until this festering boil bursts. What do I mean? Wait until Yasser Arafat activates his forces, his four armed brigades, the Katyushas and artillery concentrated in bases, tunnels and caves in southern Lebanon, which are just waiting for the *rais* to order the shelling of our northern settlements. Then the boil will burst and you will be able to do whatever you want. No one will say a word to you, neither in Israel nor in the world. Therefore, wait patiently and don't do it now!

The issue of timing was one I raised repeatedly, and not only with Sharon. In my weekly talks with Begin between February and May 1982, I stressed the importance of waiting until the whole world understood and accepted an IDF siege of Beirut. But I had the feeling, even then, that I failed to sway Begin on this matter.

Furthermore, in my conversation with Sharon on 11 May, I warned him not to rely too much on the Christian Phalange forces. I told him they were untrustworthy and fractured, basing this not only on my own acquaintance with them but also on the assessment of Dagan, who knew them much better. It was clear that Sharon was aware of their weaknesses but believed they could provide us with a territorial base for future warfare, and also hoped to extract intelligence on the PLO from them. Sharon listened, then said, 'Rafi, you are right.' He postponed the operation, but it was brought forward and launched immediately after our ambassador in London, Shlomo Argov, was assassinated by a faction of Fatah lead by Abu Nidal on 3 June 1982.

I was in Paris for meetings at the time. The next day, I was summoned home to attend a Cabinet meeting scheduled for Saturday evening, 5 June, at 8.00 p.m. at the prime minister's residence in Jerusalem. I landed in Israel two hours before the meeting. Before I rushed to Jerusalem, I was briefed on Israel's air force bombing of a PLO weapons depot at a stadium in West Beirut and retaliatory shelling by the Palestinians on our northern settlements.

In addition to Cabinet members, the meeting included Chief of Staff Rafael Eitan, the head of military intelligence, Yehoshua Sagi, head of Northern Command Avigdor Ben-Gal, and the heads of Shin Bet and Mossad. On the agenda was the question of the war in Lebanon. I soon realised that Begin was not waiting until Sharon, who was in the United States when the assassination occurred, returned to Israel. Begin had already decided that the IDF would invade Lebanon the next morning, 6 June.

Begin opened the meeting with moving words about the attack on Argov, noting that in the past he had warned that Israel would not restrain itself if there was one more assassination. Next, Sagi spoke, reviewing the situation in Lebanon and describing the PLO's military potential. All of a sudden, the door opened and Sharon walked in. When it was his turn to speak, he presented the three goals of attacking Lebanon, as he had in his presentation of Operation Oranim in the Defense Minister's forum. Sharon later told me that if it had been up to him, he would have waited before going to war, but by the time he arrived at the meeting, he already knew that the die was cast and saw no point in arguing with the prime minister about timing.

During the meeting, only two ministers posed pointed questions about the breadth of the invasion. Only one of them, Communications Minister Mordechai, had extensive military experience as a reserve brigadier general and former chief of Israel's armoured forces. The other was Deputy Prime Minister and Minister of Housing David

Levy. The rest went along with the flow. I was also silent, despite my scepticism over timing, mainly because I wanted to avoid a confrontation with Sharon

At the end of the meeting, I gave a ride home to then Minister of Education Zevulun Hammer, who had arrived at the meeting without his car. During our ride, I shared with him my misgivings about the timing.

'Rafi, how many dead will we have,' he asked me.

'Hard to predict,' I replied, 'but no less than fifty.'

Hammer sighed and did not say another word.

The next night, 6 June, with the war in full swing, Sharon explained that the invasion would extend between forty and forty-five kilometres into Lebanon to the town of Baabda on the outskirts of Beirut. The depth was determined by the range of Katyushas, and their removal to north of Baabda purportedly ensured peace for the inhabitants of Galilee.

During the first two weeks of the war, I left routine work at the office to my assistant in order to be available and free to move around within both Israel and Lebanon. Sharon allowed me to use an IDF helicopter for this from time to time. This made it easy for me to get to meetings at Northern Command headquarters, to Cabinet meetings when Begin summoned me, and to meetings of the chiefs of staff. I was very much at home among the top echelons in the IDF and defence establishment. I visited battle areas of Lebanon as I saw fit, and sometimes brought along a guest, among them conductor Zubin Mehta, former chairman of the Democratic Party in the USA Bob Strauss, and members of the Likud bloc.

Once the incursion into Lebanon began, the Cabinet met almost every day and I attended all those meetings. For the most part I made only a brief remark here and there on the issues discussed. If I wanted to raise an issue, I would, as was normal procedure, hand a note to the prime minister and ask for the right to speak. As far as I can remember, about one in three of my requests was answered in the affirmative.

Since I attended all Cabinet meetings, and at least some of the consultations between Sharon and Chief of Staff Eitan, I can testify that except in the two cases detailed below, Sharon did not circumvent government decisions and did not give the IDF instructions not previously approved by Begin and the Cabinet. Members of the Cabinet heard from experts about Arafat's tactics and strategy: his tactic was to unite not only Palestinian refugees but also the Sunnis, Shi'ites and Druze, in order to train and establish a bridgehead to fulfil the PLO's strategic goal – attacking Israel from the north. His stated goal was to eliminate the 'Zionist entity' and replace it with the State of Palestine, intended for Palestinians, without Jews. Given this, there was already agreement among Israel's leadership of the need to go into Lebanon under Sharon's predecessor as defense minister, Ezer Weizmann. There were differences of opinion on two matters. First, whether it was wise to go in as far as Beirut – Chief of Staff Eitan wanted to but Weizmann was against this. Second, the assessment of the Christian forces as allies fighting the Palestinians, with Mossad considering them trustworthy and military intelligence considering them a weak and unreliable force.

Sharon acted in accordance with his well-known strategic aims: removal of the PLO from Lebanon; removal of the Syrians; a peace agreement with a stable Christian government. Begin's dream was to reach a peace treaty with another Arab country, after Egypt. And it was Sharon's goal as well. As I have already indicated, it was Begin who ultimately decided the timing of the operation, and in my opinion, as well as apparently in Sharon's opinion, the timing was wrong.

Anyone who has ever been involved in warfare knows that war inevitably involves deviating from plans. The success of a war is not determined by how well one has stuck to original plans, but by whether its goals were achieved, regardless of how.

Maps were presented to Cabinet ministers, detailed maps, and maybe that was the problem. Although the democratic process requires the participation of the political echelon during battles, providing detailed IDF briefings that attempted to translate into maps what exactly was occurring on the ground in battle may have been misguided, maybe even fundamentally wrong. I am not, God forbid, questioning the intelligence of ministers Yosef Burg, Aharon Abu-Hatzira or Sarah Doron (all of whom had limited or no military experience). But what does Burg understand when you show him a military map? Reading such a map is a specialisation; they have a language of their own. The map isn't revealing the whole story, it only alarms the uninitiated viewer. Therefore, the controversy that took place years later over whether ministers were shown maps of what was going on in Lebanon is senseless. I can personally testify that they were shown maps, but what they understood of what they were seeing is hard for me to judge.

It is important to note that Sharon did not always explain exactly what the consequences might be of one move or another. He made decisions and acted on them, sometimes contrary to the opinion of the Cabinet or most of its ministers. But he did report his decisions, and, contrary to what others think, to my mind he did so within the normal framework of government conduct, and certainly did not deceive the Cabinet. Each and every phase was approved by the Cabinet, and Sharon answered every question posed to him in Cabinet meetings.

I can understand why some ministers felt that they had been deceived, that things were hidden from them. When a person realises *ex post facto* that he did not understand the implications of what was presented to him, he reacts in two ways, either by accepting that his knowledge was insufficient to understand what was happening, or by feeling he was deceived. It is natural, even subconsciously, to choose the latter option. But that's not what happened. Sharon, Chief of Staff Eitan, senior officers and other experts did not volunteer information, but if questions were asked, answers were given, including from Sharon. Anyone who understood anything about warfare knew that Operation Peace for Galilee was turning into the Lebanon War.

Two weeks into the war, I could already identify two groups within the Cabinet, The larger group was the one that had not yet realised we were in the midst of a war, one which would go on for some time if it was to reach its goal. They thought this was a somewhat extended version of Operation Litani (the month-long Israeli incursion into Lebanon in March 1978). The second, much smaller group consisted of those who immediately understood this was a war: Minister of Housing and Construction David Levy, Minister of Agriculture Simcha Erlich, Finance Minister Yitzhak Modai and of course Minister of Communications Itzchak Mordechai (a reserve lieutenant general and former deputy head of operations in the general staff). What about the prime minister himself? My impression is that Begin knew very well this was developing into a war, although he did not guess what the price would be.

Regarding Syria's presence in Lebanon, from the beginning it was decided to try and reassure the Syrians, via the United States, that we did not intend to confront them. Sharon believed – at least so he said in the Cabinet – that at this stage, a confrontation with the Syrians in the Beka Valley region of east Lebanon should be avoided. But it was also essential to refrain from pouring forces towards Beirut. After the first Cabinet meeting on that Saturday night, Begin immediately summoned American ambassador to Israel Sam Lewis and asked him to convey a reassuring message to the Syrians.

It was clear to me that in the end there would be no escape from a clash with the Syrians, and that Sharon knew this and even pulled in that direction, although he hoped to determine the timing of such a confrontation. More than once, when Sharon reassured ministers, I passed him a note that said, 'Arik, you are walking a tightrope,' because I was aware of the contradiction between what he was saying in Cabinet meetings and his true aims. However, it was my clear impression that in general Begin was aware of Sharon's intentions, although he was not aware of every move that Sharon planned.

The first significant move Sharon undertook in contradiction of the Cabinet's opinion, a move that angered Begin, was the air force's massive bombing of Beirut. I well remember a dramatic Cabinet meeting held at the Knesset. This was after President Ronald Reagan personally called Begin and demanded that Israel immediately stop bombing Beirut.

'Mr Prime Minister, this is a holocaust!' Reagan said.

'Mr President, I know very well what a holocaust is,' Begin replied angrily.

Nonetheless, he ordered a stop to the bombing. Despite the order, Sharon commanded the air force to continue bombing, and the Americans again complained to the prime minister.

During the Cabinet meeting at the Knesset, Begin sat at the head of the table, Minister Modai to his side. I sat beside Modai and on my other side sat Sharon. A heated altercation broke out between Begin and Sharon and I wrote down every word.

'I'm in charge of the army,' Sharon said.

'You in charge of the army? The whole government is in charge of the army, and the whole government orders you to stop bombing immediately. Now!'

The other time that Sharon deviated from government policy involved the IDF's 'creep' towards the Beirut–Damascus road, an advance that inevitably resulted in a collision with the Syrians. Syrian commando forces were roaming about on part of this road controlled by the IDF and Christian forces. The commandos were apparently there because the Syrians had failed to infiltrate the area with armoured forces. I don't think that Sharon wanted to start the fighting between the Syrians and our forces there, but incidents occurred, and Sharon ordered a general attack against the Syrians along the road, without permission from Begin and the government.

With the exception of these two cases, both of a tactical nature, there was no military action taken without government approval.

With Begin's explicit approval, Sharon assigned me the task of examining intelligence information to enable us to consider options for assassinating Arafat. At the same time, and with Sharon's approval, the army began working on Operation Saltwater Fish – to eliminate

Arafat. As the prime minister's adviser, I was not subordinate to the chief of staff. I set up a small team of my own to collect and examine intelligence from all the sources available to me, focusing on Arafat's movements and hiding places in West Beirut. But I was also formally attached to the IDF's operational team, and provided its head, Uzi Dayan, with my intelligence findings.

It was not easy to locate Arafat's changing hiding places. And even when we located him, new problems arose. We found out that he was hiding in the basement of a high-rise building, where innocent civilian families lived, which prevented our bombing it. Other times, it became clear to us that Christian intelligence, headed by Eli Hobeika, had simply deceived us and passed false information to Mossad about Arafat's presence at one site or another.

I will not pretend that I suspected at the time that Hobeika was an agent of Syrian intelligence, but I soon realised that he was a crook, a deceiver, one of the most despicable people I had ever met in my life. After the massacre at Sabra and Shatila, of which he was the key planner, he went to these camps and sold rice bags to the unfortunate survivors, at exorbitant prices. Unfortunately, Mossad relied entirely on Hobeika as a major source of intelligence and considered his information highly credible.

After we bombed several sites where Arafat was reported to be according to information provided by Mossad, and it turned out that Arafat was not there, I set up a meeting with Avner Azulai, Mossad's representative in the Lebanese Christian stronghold of Jounieh. I wanted to learn about his sources and evaluate their credibility. The meeting lasted about an hour, and when I left I was determined that from then on, we would not rely on information from Mossad regarding Arafat's whereabouts.

We finally solved the problem of intelligence information by having a special intelligence team available to Uzi Dayan, from which we obtained reliable reports. In addition, I added my former Mossad colleague Zvi Malchin to Dayan's team. Malchin had retired from Mossad in 1976, moved to New York and (known as Peter

Malkin) had become a sought-after painter there, but agreed to come on a mission to eliminate Arafat and exceeded all expectations in gathering intelligence. But Arafat continued to hide in high-rise buildings, which we did not bomb because civilians lived in them, so in the end we did not succeed in hitting Arafat, despite all the intelligence we had. After Israel took control of Beirut, I entered one of these buildings, where Arafat's headquarters were located, took some of the Mercedes cars in the garage and brought them to Israel. I reported this to the prime minister's office and the Ministry of Defense. After receiving permission from Israel's motor vehicle division, I drove around in one of them for a whole year.

I worked in Lebanon using a similar method to the one I employed as head of Mossad's operations in Europe. Through various connections, I met a group of Lebanese who moved back and forth between two parts of Beirut, and volunteered a lot of intelligence about the Palestinians in West Beirut. They, too, were part of the net I weaved for Operation Saltwater Fish in the early days of the Lebanon War.

When Arafat and his men were forced to leave Beirut and sail for Tunis, a sniper of ours, equipped with binoculars and a sniper rifle, saw Arafat's face well, and aimed his weapon at him. I will not detail how we managed to do this, but only say that the credit goes mainly to Malchin and military intelligence. It would have taken just one bullet to kill Arafat, but the sniper was forbidden to pull the trigger because we had promised the Americans who had brokered the agreement under which terrorist organisations left Lebanon that we would not harm Arafat or his forces during their evacuation from Beirut.

In subsequent years, there were those who considered it a failure that we did not eliminate Arafat in Beirut. My answer has always been that we refrained from bombing buildings where we knew Arafat was staying in order not to harm innocent Lebanese civilians living there. But there was a failure in the intelligence that Mossad gathered from the Phalangists in Jounieh.

Incidentally, Mossad failed to predict the results of Begin's meeting on 1 September 1982, with Bashir Gemayel, a week after his election as president of Lebanon and two weeks before the date set for his inauguration. Mossad told Begin that at the meeting at a hotel in the northern Israeli town of Nahariya, Gemayel would declare his intention to sign a peace agreement with Israel in due course. This is not what happened. Bashir explained to Begin that as an Arab leader, he must play down relations with Israel, and suggested ties similar to those Israel had with Iran under the shah, in other words intensive but invisible cooperation. Begin was bitterly disappointed, but I was not surprised given the dubious and elusive nature of our Phalange allies.

Another task that Sharon asked me to undertake during the war was to deal with Lebanese MPs whose vote in favour of electing Bashir Gemayel president of Lebanon was still in question. I was not the only one who dealt with this. Mossad did so as well. So too did Haim Lebkov, the founder and commander of the IDF's Druze unit, who focused on Druze parliamentary delegates.

I was forbidden from dealing with the Phalangists – Pierre Gemayel and his men – who were handled by Mossad. But the Christians had other forces and factions. One of them, was the Lebanese Forces, headed by Samir Ja'ja'. In his youth, he served the Gemayel family, but later set up his own militia, which took control of Mount Lebanon, operating hashish smuggling networks from the Beka Valley below. The smugglers paid Ja'ja' levies, which made him a multi-millionaire. The Lebanese Forces numbered about 700 fighters, about half the number of armed Phalangists, but the terror they inflicted on their enemies was no less than that inflicted by the Phalangists. I contacted Ja'ja', and he even visited our house near Tel Aviv several times. My goal was to explore with him the possibility of creating a Christian alternative to Gemayel's Phalangists, and the participation of the Lebanese Forces in our planned entrance to West Beirut. Sharon expressed reservations about this, because he feared creating conflicts with Bashir Gemayel, whose Phalangists ruled East Beirut. But I continued to maintain contact with Ja'ja', and even toured with him in his areas of control.

Military intelligence provided me with a list of members of the Lebanese parliament, and together with then-Major Amos Gilad, from their research unit, we compiled a list of those to be dealt with to garner the necessary votes for Bashir. In this mission, I collaborated also with Azulai from Mossad, in charge of relations with the Phalangists, and with his superior, Nachik Navot, head of Mossad's Tevel division.

Paramount was ensuring that the family of former Lebanese President Camille Chamoun and its allies supported Bashir Gemayel for president. Chamoun, who had served as president in 1952–8 and was pro-Western, thought he was more suitable to be president than Gemayel. After Bashir was assassinated, and his brother Amin Gemayel was nominated in his place, I suggested to Sharon that we consider supporting Chamoun, but Sharon rejected the idea. 'He's a has been,' he quickly responded.

As is well known, we supported Amin Gemayel, and he was elected president. Even then, I thought it was a mistake, based on information we received of his secret ties with the Syrians. We knew that during the siege of Beirut, he provided – for large sums of money – weapons and food to the besieged Palestinians. He was not the only one among the Phalangists to do so. Hobeika did the same. They did not do it to help the Palestinians or the Syrians or some other political faction, but purely for money. They were simply unscrupulous bastards, completely devoid of morals or values.

I set up an office for myself inside the headquarters of Northern Command in Lebanon and lodged in the mountain resort town of Aley, where the head of Northern Command also lodged. I would go to meet parliamentarians in a convoy of Jeeps, accompanied by reservists from our General Staff patrol. The very appearance of the convoy was enough for wavering parliamentarians to understand who Israel wanted for president of Lebanon. Among those I met was Khalil Azzam, head of the Sunnis in parliament, whom I had to meet late at night, because he did not want Israelis to be seen in his house. On one of my visits to Azzam, my good friend the actor Chaim Topol accompanied me. By then, the PLO had already left Beirut and we assumed Israel would manage to dislodge the Syrians from Lebanon. Therefore, I meant every word when I told Azzam that Israel did not plan to stay as an occupying army ruling over Lebanon, and that the Lebanese – all of them – should prepare to restore their country, to enact their constitution and to form a governing coalition with the participation of all ethnic groups. I was convinced it was possible. In accordance with their constitution, I said, the president would continue to be Christian, the speaker of the parliament and the prime minister would be Sunnis, and Israel would provide economic support, until Lebanon would once again flourish as it had in the past.

In all, I visited about fifteen parliamentarians, appealing to them to vote for Bashir Gemayel. Only in the case of one Shi'ite parliamentarian who just spoke Arabic did I need the services of a translator. It is important to note that none of the Lebanese I met in lobbying for Bashir asked me for money. Occasionally, I was asked to arrange a bureaucratic matter or for assistance of one kind or another. Camille Chamoun, for example, asked me to persuade Sharon to strengthen the position of his son, Danny Chamoun, vis-à-vis Bashir, who tended to ignore him. Azzam asked us to take care of his relatives in West Beirut and gave me a list of their names and addresses.

To illustrate the nature of the conversations I had with Camille Chamoun, here is a report on my conversation with him on 22 July 1982. Copies were sent to the prime minister, the defense minister and to the head of the Tzomet unit of the Mossad, Rehavia Vardi:

> Secret Meeting with Camille Chamoun (Beirut 22 July)
>
> Present were Shaul Tzur, head of military intelligence's unit on Syria and Lebanon and Rafi Eitan
>
> After exchanging greetings, Chamoun stated that he attached special importance to the meeting. He began with a broad assessment of the situation, the main points being:

- Operation Peace for Galilee – It was a mistake to stop it several times. If Israel had acted quickly, it could have entered Beirut within days and even eliminated the Syrian presence.
- The Beirut Problem – Sooner or later the terrorists will have to be forcibly expelled, political order is an illusion.
- The Syrians – The Israeli declarations that the Syrians must leave Lebanon must be upheld. Don't wait 'two years' to act.

Then, Chamoun moved on to the issue of the presidential election. He stressed that Israel must not interfere in any way as this would only provoke a reaction. Bashir Gemayel's candidacy had been decided by his father, Pierre Gemayel, and approved at the Phalangist headquarters. Bashir himself came to receive Chamoun's blessing, and he had told Bashir of his reservations. The vast majority of Muslims and quite a few Christian circles oppose Bashir's candidacy and form a parliamentary bloc that will not prevent him being elected. Chamoun noted that there is no Christian politician who truly wants Bashir as president, but his military power and the presence of Israel instil fear. Nonetheless, Chamoun told Bashir, if you insist on running, go ahead and try.

Chamoun said he has nothing personal against Bashir but from the point of view of Lebanese and regional politics 'Bashir is a disaster' (he was that blunt!). He has no new ideas and lacks the maturity to be president (Chamoun characterised him as an 'adolescent boy'). The Bashir of today will not be the Bashir of tomorrow. He will not be the same person if elected, and Israel will not derive any benefit from him. In this context, Chamoun noted that Bashir maintains regular contacts with the Syrians, and if the Syrians have to choose between Bashir's candidacy and his own, they will of course choose Bashir . . .

At this point, Chamoun announced that he himself was interested in becoming president. He has broad support and if there is a free vote, he is guaranteed the support of the vast majority of MPs (80 per cent). Although it was personally difficult for him to oppose Bashir (he is 'my political son', he said), he noted that in a situation of uncertainty, one should prepare an alternative candidate. Chamoun urged Israel to convince Bashir to withdraw his candidacy. In his opinion, Bashir should wait another six years and mature politically. Chamoun said that if he were elected president, he would make sure that Bashir got a position in the government that would prepare him be president in the future. He does not think Bashir will agree to give up his armed militia and integrate into the national Lebanese army.

Chamoun went on to analyse his position toward Israel were he to become president. He was amenable to full normalisation of relations, but a formal peace treaty is an issue. Lebanon is a member of the Arab League and everything that has happened to Egypt will also apply to Lebanon. He stressed the risk of an economic boycott, precisely because the Lebanese economy has always been built on economic relations with Arab countries (Saudi Arabia, the Gulf emirates and Iraq). Another difficulty would be the refusal of a Sunni prime minister to sign a peace treaty. In these circumstances, Chamoun proposes a security agreement as a first step, in which Israel will undertake not to attack Lebanon, while Lebanon will undertake not to allow any military entity to endanger Israel from its territory. There would be a joint oversight committee for the agreement and regulations would be formulated to facilitate normalisation.

Chamoun warned of a development that would surprise Israel. If there is no agreement about Bashir – and this will be clear a week to ten days before the election session [of the parliament] – it is customary to propose another candidate 'at the last minute' and even at that election session itself (albeit after approvals reached beforehand). Chamoun said he knows that President Sarkis is interested in proposing Gaby Lahoud. If so – Israel will end up empty handed.

> Chamoun concluded by stating that if the Muslims were united and Bashir found that he had no chance, he could be persuaded to withdraw his candidacy. However, if the Muslims were divided over Bashir, the picture might be slightly different. In another week he could clarify the situation after consulting with Muslim leaders who are his personal friends and were headed by the influential Saab Salam. He asked to meet again, to let us know the situation and his position.
>
> We emphasised to Chamoun several times that Bashir Gemayel has our trust and our support. We also asked him to address the issue of Beirut and the chance that the Phalangists would take part in the fighting. We explained that this could make it very easy for Israel in all respects. He replied that Bashir could not do so because of his military weakness and because he would lose the support he hoped to garner from the Muslims. According to him, Bashir sees his role as waving the Lebanese flag in western Beirut and nothing more. On the other hand, his position might change if he realised that he has no chance of being elected president.

My lobbying of the parliamentarians lasted about two weeks, until the convening of the parliament to elect Bashir. Even on the eve of Bashir's election as president, I continued to favour cultivating ties with other ethnic groups in Lebanon and not just with the Christians, in stark contrast to Mossad's position. In personal conversations with Sharon and in the defense minister's forum, I did not stop preaching for cooperation with the Druze in Lebanon. I believe that had it not been for the Sabra and Shatila massacre and its consequences for Sharon, he would have worked to establish a broad coalition in Lebanon, with the participation of all ethnic groups alongside Christians and Sunnis.

On the other hand, I erred – and in good faith I misled the prime minister regarding this – in saying that Bashir would agree to a peace treaty with Israel. It was easy to see that Begin was deeply disappointed when he emerged from his meeting with the then president-elect of

Lebanon in Nahariya on 1 September 1982. Only a peace agreement with Lebanon could have justified in his eyes our losses, which were mounting daily. It was heart-breaking to see him come out of that meeting, disappointment in his eyes.

Two days before he was to be sworn in, Bashir Gemayel was murdered in a building of the Phalangist headquarters in Beirut. I was in Tel Aviv and heard about the explosion on the radio news. I hurried to my office and put together a team to consider our response. Initially it was not clear if he was dead. Once we learned the truth, a few hours before it was made public, I called Sharon and said: 'Arik, now is the time to enter West Beirut.'

Sharon replied that he had the same thought and would discuss it with Begin. We both knew that even after the PLO left Beirut, there were still large quantities of weapons in the western part of the city and also many terrorists who stayed in hiding or went around as civilians. Our assumption was that with Gemayel's assassination, Begin would approve a plan to go into West Beirut to clear out what the PLO had left behind. Indeed, Begin approved the plan without bringing the issue up for discussion in the Cabinet.

The next day I flew to Beirut and joined the forces of Itzchak Mordechai who entered western Beirut from the north, from the port compound. At the same time, Amos Yaron's forces entered from the south. It was at this point that I got my hands on the PLO cars I have already mentioned, as well as a large amount of PLO documents, which we found in abandoned buildings in the city.

What we did not know then for sure is known to everyone today: a Syrian agent who had access to Phalangist headquarters planted the bomb that killed Bashir Gemayel. A rumour that has never been verified alleges that Hobeika, the head of Phalangist intelligence, had a role in the assassination, and that he allowed the Syrian agent to plant the bomb. It is almost certain that Hobeika worked for the Syrians, but I must admit that I have never deepened my research on the subject.

Sabra and Shatila

On 15 November 1982, two months after the events of Sabra and Shatila, and prior to my testimony before the commission of inquiry into the massacre chaired by Supreme Court President Yitzhak Kahan, I reconstructed and wrote down my schedule for mid-September 1982. In parentheses, I have included my retroactive assessment of the circumstances, which I wrote for myself twenty years later:

> *Tuesday 14 September* – The report of the assassination of Bashir reaches me from military intelligence (by phone) at 17.00 as I am on my way with Miriam from Afikim to Tel Aviv. I talk to Uri Dan, Arik's spokesman, and try to reach Arik by phone. Go home. A few minutes before 11 at night I talk to Amir Drori, who confirms that Bashir's body has been found and is surprised that we do not know he was killed in the explosion. Says he is preparing our forces for every eventuality. At night, I look for Arik and Azriel Nevo, the prime minister's military secretary. Arik has already reported to the prime minister. I suggest entering West Beirut to Arik, and through Nevo also to Begin. I raise the following issues: entry into West Beirut and an immediate replacement for Bashir.
>
> Arik under psychological pressure and concentrating on efforts for a resolution. (This was a note to myself and it meant that at the time, Arik did not decide yet about entering West Beirut or looking for a replacement for Bashir. He was at the stage of collecting information, not of making decisions.)
>
> *Wednesday 15 September* – 8.00 a.m. by helicopter to Beirut. On my own initiative, go to speak to Camille Chamoun and his group, as well as with Khalil Turbiah (head of a small independent Christian party). Return to Tel Aviv in the evening but leave my people in Beirut.
>
> *Friday 17 September* – Return to Beirut. Meet twice with Camille Chamoun, bring along Rehavia Vardi and Abrasha Tamir. (After learning of my meetings with the Christians, Mossad officials complained to the prime minister. I was

reprimanded and Begin and Arik demanded I cancel further meetings and return to Israel.) At night, before returning to Israel, slept at Drori's headquarters in Aley and heard nothing about what happened in the camps. In the morning, on my way to Israel by car, drive down to Amos Yaron's headquarters near Sabra and Shatila. At 9.00 a.m. sit with Amos Yaron, and hear nothing about a massacre in the camps. (In retrospect, even if Amos knew then about the Phalangists' entry into the camps, which was approved by the IDF in order to eliminate terrorists, no one there knew that something unusual and terrible was happening, beyond the instructions they received. In my opinion, none of our people expected that women, the elderly and children would be slaughtered.) At 10.00 a.m., return to Israel by car.

Saturday 18 September – Prepare a report on the meeting with Chamoun. Talk to Uri Dan and Arik. The issue of the massacre in the refugee camps is already surfacing. Both Uri and I, each separately, suggest to Arik that he immediately set up an investigation team. (Arik listens, ponders, but gives no answer.)

Beyond the diary, reconstructed about two months after the massacre, I had other assessments at the time. Following a conversation I had with a Christian resident in Beirut on 16 September, I passed on a letter from him and his wife to Begin and Sharon. In it, they explained the plight of Christians in Lebanon, arguing that it was Israel's moral duty to save them. They expressed fear of Israel's withdrawal from Lebanon. That Beirut resident was one of the first to warn us against Amin Gemayel, characterising him as totally under the thumb of the Syrians and a leading drug grower in the Beka region. He urged us not to rely on Pierre Gemayel and his son, but we did not listen to him because the Phalangists were the leading Christian forces.

On the same day, 16 September, Malchin, who I had added to my team, told me that he had toured some farm area and run into a group of Phalangists. He prevented them from putting two Palestinian children, 13 or 14 years old, up against a wall and executing them. He had no idea at that time what was going on inside the Sabra and Shatila camps.

Below are my assessments of the circumstances of the massacre in Sabra and Shatila, which I wrote as part of my testimony before the Kahan Commission on 17 January 1983:

> Testimony of the Prime Minister's Adviser on Terrorism – Rafi Eitan (a summary of the witness's records)
>
> Having read a number of public testimonies, Rafi Eitan finds it appropriate to present his assessment of the reasons for the massacre in the Sabra and Shatila camps.
>
> According to the witness, the massacre in the camps was planned, and approved by the political echelon that controls the Phalangists.
>
> The political background to the massacre included the following factors:
>
> The assassination of Bashir Gemayel agitated Pierre Gemayel, who feared that the sceptre of power which he had been striving to gain for many years should fall from the hands of the family. On 15 September, it became clear to Pierre that there was a chance that Camille Chamoun would run for president and win.
>
> Pierre Gemayel needed impressive actions that would win him the voices of swaying MPs, and perhaps even Sunni MPs like Saab Salam. Such measures were also needed to strengthen the Phalangists from within.
>
> In Lebanese political culture, acts of violence have a different effect than we are used to. In Lebanese history a violent act has often attracted people to the violent perpetrators.
>
> In the opinion of the witness, the Phalangist activity in the refugee camps was undertaken with the approval and guidance of the political echelon (Pierre Gemayel).
>
> In the opinion of the witness, in directing his companies to

carry out the massacre in the camps, Pierre Gemayel did not intend to harm relations with Israel. He did not expect that the matter would take on the dimensions it later did. In order to carry out the massacre, it was necessary to deceive the Israelis 'slightly'.

The following is a list of facts that support this assessment:

In direct contacts between the witness and Camille Chamoun on Thursday 16 September, Chamoun said he considered himself a presidential candidate with a reasonable chance of winning.

Camille Chamoun suggested to the witness that the Phalangists would harm a Muslim MP in order to dissuade Muslims from supporting him (Chamoun). In other words, the Phalangists were prepared to act violently to serve their internal Lebanese political interests.

After the assassination of Bashir Gemayel, there was an explicit order from Sheikh Pierre Gemayel to refrain from an uncontrolled rampage. Fadi Frem (commander of the military wing of the Phalangists) issued an order on behalf of Sheikh Pierre not to leave the camps – all indicating control of the situation and of their forces.

Most of the senior commanders of the Phalangists have a family connection with Sheikh Pierre. It is not possible for the massacre to have been done without the approval of the 'head of the tribe'.

Eli Hobeika was totally loyal to Bashir – a loyalty that passed on to Pierre and from him to Amin. The fact is that his place in the tribe is preserved to this day (even after the massacre).

Previous killings of the Phalangists:

Tel al-Za'atar.

The people of Frangia.

The people of Chamoun.

All of these were orderly and planned actions that served policy purposes.

> Summary
>
> Lebanon's 'political culture' puts pressure on parliamentarians in an indirect way that can be denied, getting them to accede to positions that accord with the position of those exerting the pressure; the need to strengthen and unify the Phalangists around Amin Gemayel's leadership after the assassination; all of these point to the possibility that the massacre in the camps was planned and executed to serve internal Lebanese interests.

I produced the document without consulting Sharon or anyone else. However, on 15 January 1983, that is, two days before my testimony before the commission, I summoned Samir Ja'ja', the commander of the Lebanese Forces in the north and on Mount Lebanon. I also reported this meeting to the commission. 'According to him,' I wrote to myself, 'The massacre was decided jointly by the political and military echelons of the Phalangists, with the aim of taking revenge and showing everyone "We are here and our power is here."'

In my testimony before the commission on 17 January 1983, I essentially stated the contents of the document cited above. After my testimony, I was asked to come for a separate interrogation by one of the committee members, Major General (Res.) Yona Efrat. He interrogated me for two hours in which he said the following:

'There are rumours about you, that in fact, at Arik Sharon's behest, you were the commander of an assassination unit in Lebanon.' (!)

I was shocked but controlled myself. I asked Efrat what the source of the rumour was, but he didn't answer my question. However, it didn't take me long to realise that the rumour came from Mossad. Later, I learned that it was Nachik Navot, then head of Tevel, who was responsible for Mossad's ties with the Phalangists. In his testimony before the commission, Navot said: 'Arik took Rafi Eitan, attached people from the General Staff patrol to him, and they carried out operations without Mossad's knowledge. Not only that, on the morning of the massacre in Sabra and Shatila, Rafi Eitan was seen around the camps.'

I said to Yona Efrat: 'There was no such thing. Get it out of your heads.' I explained there was a special team that focused exclusively on seeking to assassinate Yasser Arafat, under the command of Uzi Dayan, established by order of the chief of staff and with the approval of the prime minister and defense minister. I had provided intelligence to that team. I then gave Efrat a rundown of my actions in Lebanon, including my conversations with Shi'ite and Christian leaders. Efrat, whom I had known for many years, recorded my words, and I felt he believed me.

During the interrogation, Efrat asked me if I thought Israel had any responsibility for the massacre. Without hesitation I told him my opinion: if we have any responsibility for the massacre, then it is indirect, and falls entirely on Mossad, which was in constant contact with the Phalangists. It was Mossad's professional responsibility to know the Phalange leadership had decided on the massacre.

I was not called again before the commission. It is well known that in its conclusions the commission determined that Sharon had 'indirect responsibility' for what happened in Sabra and Shatila. I thought then and still do that this conclusion, which led to Sharon's dismissal, was a scandal.

Sharon admitted that the Phalangists entered the camps with his permission and with the approval of the chief of staff but asserted that he had no information and no basis to suspect that the Phalangists intended to massacre the camp residents. I want to emphasise that, contrary to the impression of the public, the report, although critical of Sharon, did not include a recommendation that he be dismissed.

I read the whole report and spoke to Sharon a few times afterwards and I can testify that until Begin dismissed him, it did not occur to Sharon to resign. I was very angry at Begin's decision, and believe it was an injustice to Sharon. I thought then, and still do, that the commission's conclusion about Sharon's indirect responsibility, and, perhaps even more so, Begin's decision to dismiss him, stemmed from political rather than legal motives.

Begin did not have to oust Sharon. As I mentioned, the commission of inquiry did not demand this, nor do I think there was public pressure here in this matter, certainly not when compared to the pressure on Golda Meir and Moshe Dayan to resign after the Agranat commission report (which also did not demand they resign). I would wager that Begin initially set up the commission of inquiry to 'deal with' Sharon, since Begin's resentment of Sharon mounted as the war progressed. He was dissatisfied with Sharon's conduct and his aggressive statements in Cabinet discussions. I think Begin hesitated for a day or two before dismissing Sharon, and that he did so under pressure from ministers and associates who had long wanted to get rid of Sharon. Their fear was that Sharon would succeed Begin, already in physical and mental decline. The massacre and the commission's conclusions provided them with the opportunity to eliminate the threat from Sharon.

Nearly forty years have passed since that war, and I am still convinced, as I was then, that it was an unfortunate necessity, a war of no choice.

To explain my views, I will first mention Begin's statement at the end of his meeting with Sadat in April 1982, less than three months before the war: 'And the land will be quiet for forty years.' It was a sincere and faithful expression of Begin's desire that peace with Egypt would spread throughout the Middle East. A few days later, a journalist contacted me and interviewed me about the issue of terrorism. Among other things, I told him, 'I anticipate a hundred years of terrorism,' adding that Palestinian organisations could not wage conventional wars, so they tried to achieve their political goals through terrorist acts. The next day, I grabbed the headlines in the evening papers, which highlighted the contradiction between Begin's statement and mine.

As a result, I was summoned to the Knesset's foreign affairs and defence committee to explain my remarks. I did not shy away from explaining my views. The Palestinian leadership at the time, namely Arafat, Abu Iyad, Abu Jihad, Farouk Kadumi and their ilk, worked tirelessly to bring all their organisations under one roof, led by Arafat. They sought to include even competing organisations, more extreme than Fatah, that had sprung up in Iraq, Syria, and elsewhere. In the decade after Fatah was expelled from Jordan in 1970, they had established themselves in Lebanon, at first in refugee camps in Tyre and Sidon and areas south of Beirut, and later entrenched themselves in West Beirut. They created systematic control, based on Fatah and a loose coalition with the rest of the organisations, which was united around the armed struggle against Israel, as stated in the Palestinian Convention. In all his speeches, Arafat called for the extermination of the 'Zionist entity', the State of Israel, and the expulsion of all its residents who had not lived in the country during the Mandate or were descendants of those residents, that is more than 80 per cent of Israel's Jewish population.

In this reality, 'Peace for Galilee' was a war of no choice. If Begin and Sharon had avoided war, those who came after them would have had to go to war to expel the PLO from Lebanon. Begin understood this. But Sharon was wrong in not preparing Begin for the possibility that the number of victims would be significantly higher than the IDF's forecast. It seems that, in private, Begin discussed this with Sharon, but Sharon's answers only increased the bad blood between them. Begin also resented the fact that at Cabinet meetings, Sharon confronted him more than once, and as described above, also deviated at least twice from his general guidelines.

In my opinion, we made two mistakes during the war, one at the beginning and one at the end, and both relate to timing. The war started too early. And without attacking West Beirut. If Begin had waited for that festering boil to burst, he could have won Cabinet approval to enter Beirut from the direction of Jounieh from the first day. The result would likely have been a far swifter war, with far fewer casualties.

At the end of the fighting, and after the evacuation of the PLO from Beirut, the IDF should have immediately withdrawn to the security zone in southern Lebanon, strengthened the Shi'ites there and left behind Lebanese rule, based on a complex coalition of all ethnicities. To his credit, the head of military intelligence, Yehoshua Sagi, pushed for an immediate withdrawal. It was Mossad that thwarted strengthening ties with the Shi'ites, and focused only on Pierre Gemayel's Phalangists. As far as I can tell, Sharon considered an immediate withdrawal and was leaning in that direction but the massacre in Sabra and Shatila disrupted the process and prevented him from carrying out a withdrawal.

When the fighting ended, Arafat and the PLO leadership moved to Tunisia, along with several thousand fighters. The rest – most of the battalions and brigades – were stationed in Yemen and Iraq, and a minority in Syria. This dispersion of forces continued until the Oslo Accords in 1993. In the meantime, the same fighters grew older, and started to raise families. The whole network got heavier and more cumbersome, and planning attacks against Israel or Jewish targets outside Israel become increasingly more complicated to coordinate. All this exacerbated internal divisions, leading the coalition under Arafat to crumble. The more militant bodies in Iraq, Yemen, and Syria became more independent from him, so that, in fact, only Fatah remained under his control.

The first intifada broke out at the end of 1987. Arafat had no part in its start. On the contrary, it took him completely by surprise. In my opinion, its eruption was our fault, or more precisely, it was the result of our failures. Israel wasted the 1970s and 1980s in internal divisions over territories occupied in the 1967 War instead of reaching a national consensus on the future of Judea, Samaria and Gaza along lines consistent with the proposed Allon–Galili Plan. Under the plan, Israel would have annexed about a third of the West Bank (about 2,000 square kilometres) and announced that it was amenable to any solution agreed on by the Palestinians for the rest of the territories.

At the end of July 1988, King Hussein announced that Jordan was abandoning all claims over the West Bank, so that its fate would be decided by 'legitimate representatives of the Palestinian people'.

On hearing his statement on the radio, I spoke with Sharon, then Minister of Trade and Industry. Together, we decided to try to move the government to apply Israeli law to Judea, Samaria and Gaza, in accordance with the Allon–Galili plan.

The next morning, I went to Prime Minister Yitzhak Shamir's office and briefly presented the main points of the proposal. Shamir listened, nodded and said, 'It makes sense, but I need at least seven votes from the Labour party. If Rabin supports it, I will go for it.' I immediately reported to Sharon, and he talked to Rabin. Sharon told me that Rabin 'bought' the idea, but refused to pledge support in the Knesset, saying that at most he and his friends would not oppose such a move, but would also not vote in favour.

Sharon met Shamir, and told him that he had consulted with Samuel Lewis, a former American ambassador to Israel who was in the country. Lewis thought that it would be difficult for the White House to oppose our plan. Despite this, Sharon sounded pessimistic. 'We have a problem with Shamir,' he said.

The next day Shamir informed us that he was rejecting our suggestion. That night I called his house and asked him why. His answer was short: 'Rafi, why not everything?' That is, why only the Allon–Galili plan, with only a third of the Judea and Samaria area? Why not all the territories?

The following day, 5 August 1988, I sent Shamir a personal letter stating, among other things:

> There are moments in the life of a nation where the sky opens with a narrow crack that must be entered as long as it is open. There are moments in the life of a nation whose leader must lead beyond the considerations and constraints of everyday life. Failure to do so costs future generations dearly.
>
> The proposal to apply Israeli law to the areas sparsely populated by Arabs in Judea, Samaria and the Gaza Strip is a necessary response to the situation that has arisen, and perhaps this is the last chance to apply Israeli law in a way that will forever prevent a Palestinian state. I will repeat: there are

> moments that a leader must lead, find ways and solutions to difficulties and act.
>
> Yitzhak! Now is your moment!

But it was a call in the wilderness. He did not respond and lost a moment that could have changed our history.

Meanwhile, in light of Arafat's meagre achievements, funding from Arab countries to the PLO dwindled. At the same time, corruption among its leadership was growing. In the Gulf crisis, which erupted in August 1990, Arafat gambled on overt support for Saddam Hussein. This position eroded Arafat's status in the eyes of Western countries. Saddam Hussein's defeat in the war with the American-led coalition left Arafat wounded, scarred and weaker than ever.

In the summer of 1993, when I first heard about the agreement with the PLO in Oslo, I was immersed in private business in Cuba. I asked friends in military intelligence: What happened? Has Arafat really changed? Their answer was: nothing has changed – not Arafat, not the Palestinian Convention, not the incitement against Israel and not the (anti-Israel) education of Palestinian youth.

I was very worried, and before the handshake ceremony with Arafat in Washington, I sent Prime Minister Yitzhak Rabin a letter warning him against bringing PLO members from Tunis into the territories, because it could wreak havoc on Israel. Rabin did not answer me.

On 13 September 1993, after watching the signing of the agreement between Israel and the PLO on television, I was anxious and perplexed. The same day, I filed a lawsuit against Yasser Arafat.

To my mind, the person most to blame for the Oslo Accord is Yossi Beilin (then deputy foreign minister), who dragged Shimon Peres, and then Yitzhak Rabin after him. To this day, I don't understand how Beilin managed to convince Rabin of the delusionary idea that allowing Arafat into Gaza would somehow convince Palestinian refugees from 1948 to relinquish the right of return and stay in camps.

Route 300

It is incumbent upon me to discuss in detail one affair in which I was involved, albeit from the side-lines, during my tenure as the prime minister's counter-terrorism adviser. I am referring what is known as the 1984 'Route 300 Affair.'

On the evening of 13 April 1984, I received an initial report at home that four Palestinian terrorists had hijacked a number 300 Egged bus travelling from Tel Aviv to Ashkelon. I immediately called my deputy, Gideon Mahnayimi, and we rushed south. To avoid endangering the passengers, the bus driver obeyed the kidnappers' instructions and continued south past Ashkelon to the vicinity of Deir al-Balah in the Gaza Strip, where Israeli police and IDF forces managed to cut him off and stop the bus.

When we arrived, the bus, with the hostages and terrorists inside, was standing at the side of the road. An IDF general staff team was present as were Brigadier General Itzchak Mordechai, Commander of Paratrooper/Infantry Forces, who led the operation, and Avrum Shalom head of Shin Bet, along with some of his men. Minister of Defense Moshe Arens arrived shortly after us. All of us met in the command post that the general staff unit set up in an adjoining field, and it was decided to free the hostages, with snipers aiming at the terrorists while troops stormed the bus.

During the operation, I stood close by, behind the unit storming the bus. A female soldier who was part of the unit raised her head while the snipers were shooting at the terrorists, was hit in the head and died on the spot. The bus was taken by the unit in two to three minutes. Two kidnappers were killed, and the other two were captured alive and taken for questioning in the command tent.

The purpose of the initial investigation, conducted by Shin Bet personnel, was to find out if the terrorists had left booby traps behind on the bus. Mordechai started to kick them while they were lying on the ground, face down, hands on their heads. They were fully conscious. Mordechai shouted at them and demanded to know if there was a booby trap on the bus, while continuing to kick them. But no one dies from such kicks. Suddenly Shalom turned to me and said, 'They should not leave here alive.'

I knew Shalom well from the Palmach and from the many years after that when we worked together when he was my subordinate. I knew there was no point in arguing with him. I did not have authority over him and I understood that anything I would say would fall on deaf ears. I said to my assistant, 'Avrum is up to something. It is better for both of us not to be here. It could end up in court. The operation is over, we have no role here. Let's get home.' We got in the car and drove away. The next day I received a routine report from military intelligence, which said that all four terrorists had been killed. It was not difficult for Mahnayimi and me to surmise that Shin Bet had executed them.

A short time later, the Route 300 Affair exploded, when *Hadashot* newspaper published a photograph in which two of the kidnappers were seen being led from the bus by Shin Bet security men. The two walked on their feet, and appeared frightened, but not injured.

Arens ordered the establishment of a commission of inquiry. Meanwhile, rumours circulated in the media that Mordechai had killed them. I met Mordechai even before the committee convened and reassured him, 'I know you're innocent.' In my testimony before the committee, I spoke only about what I saw with my own eyes. I mentioned that there was a 'violent atmosphere' in the command tent, but I didn't say a word about my suspicions regarding Shin Bet and didn't divulge what Shalom said to me.

Once it may have been possible to keep such incidents a secret, but by 1984 it was impossible. The committee did not succeed in discovering the truth, mainly because Shalom's representative on the committee, Yossi Ginossar, a very talented and very cunning man, did everything to deceive it. But some senior members of Shin Bet, who knew the truth, revolted against Shalom, who obliged everyone to remain silent. They did not keep quiet and turned to State Prosecutor Dorit Beinisch.

I do not know what went through Shamir's mind when he saw the photo published in *Hadashot,* but I have no doubt that contrary to Shalom's claim, the prime minister did not give the Shin Bet head prior approval to eliminate the terrorists, and he was not part of the cover-up by Shalom, Ginossar or the legal advisers of Shin Bet who advised those who carried out the execution.

What I write here is speculation, but I'm convinced I know what happened between Shamir and Shalom. I knew both of them, although Shalom more so than Shamir. I think Shalom called Shamir and informed him of the situation. He did not ask the prime minister what to do, nor would Shamir have told him. If Shalom had asked him, Shamir would have replied, 'Do what you think is right.' The rules in such matters are clear: the political echelon gives general instructions, the operational echelon deals with details. A prime minister would never give a specific instruction to execute terrorists who have already been captured and confessed, even if that prime minister was Shamir, former head of an operational unit in Mossad, and no stranger to executions. These rules were established in the early 1950s, and I was the one who drafted them. They still applied to the security services at the time of the Route 300 incident. The rile is that the operational echelon takes full responsibility if any operation goes wrong and embarrasses the government. The operational echelon does not have a superior on whom responsibility can be laid. The political echelon will do everything to protect the operational echelon from being personally harmed, but it will not accept responsibility because assuming responsibility in such a case harms the state's interest. Indeed, in private conversations we had after the affair, Shamir often asked me 'How could Avrum not have understood that he had to assume all responsibility?'

I have no answer to that question. To this day I do not understand what happened to Shalom. I do not understand why he decided to kill the terrorists, knowing that dozens of people who were not members of Shin Bet witnessed them getting off the bus alive and well; why he started a cover-up, and then tried to throw the responsibility upstairs.

As is well known, Shalom repeatedly claimed that Shamir gave him general permission to eliminate terrorists, and that Shamir also knew about the cover-up. When I asked Shalom why he did not tell the committee the truth and engineered a cover-up, he said he was afraid he would end up in prison. I don't think his assessment was correct. I am convinced that if Shalom had come to Shamir, confessed the truth and submitted his resignation, Shamir would have turned the world upside down to find a legal way to grant him – and the people who carried out the execution – immunity from prosecution. To my mind, Shalom handled everything wrong, from the order to kill the captured terrorists to the weaving of the tissue of lies before the commission of inquiry.

Later, in private conversations with me, Shamir confirmed that his policy was that 'terrorists should not be left alive', especially those involved in abducting hostages. However, he stressed that it should have been clear that this provision only applied to combat, and by no means to prisoners, let alone those that dozens of people, if not hundreds, had witnessed being taken off the bus, alive and walking on their feet. More than once he asked me, 'Why did Avrum not behave as you did in the Pollard affair and assume all responsibility?'

I can't answer this question on Shalom's behalf. I can only testify that, unlike Shalom, throughout my career in Shin Bet I never testified falsely in court, and never deceived my government, including in the Pollard Affair and all the investigations that followed. My instructions to those being investigated was: 'Tell the truth, each one his own truth.'

I certainly hold that there are certain circumstances, particularly when it can save lives by pre-empting an attack, where the treatment of terrorists requires methods not used in fighting other kinds of crimes. However, it seems to me that from the 1970s, particularly after the appointment of Avraham Ahituv as head of Shin Bet in 1974, the number of cases in which terrorists were tortured rose sharply. In that sense, it can be said that Shalom was the brilliant student who adopted the 'method' of his predecessor, Ahituv.

It has been more than thirty years since the Route 300 Affair, and I still occasionally ask myself why I was silent and left the scene when I knew what Shalom intended to do. I do not have a good answer. Sure, I can argue that I did not have the status of commander or supervisor over Shalom, a dominant and self-confident man. He might well have rebuffed me with contempt, and perhaps fear of this, more than anything else, caused me to shut up and retire. True as that may be, it is still not a complete answer to the question. In retrospect I regret being silent. It is possible that had I warned Shalom, and if, however unlikely, he had listened to me, the Route 300 Affair and the subsequent investigation, cover-up, Shin Bet revolt against Shalom, and his dismissal could have been avoided. On the other, I can take some comfort in the fact that the trauma following the affair benefited Shin Bet in the long term because if forced a thorough 'cleaning of the stables' from the lies and legal violations that clouded the service in the days of Ahituv and Shalom.

Chapter 27

Jonathan Pollard: Spying on the USA

The Pollard affair raised the question of why Israel, which has only a few friends in the world, dared to spy on its best and most significant friend. Behind the affair lies a century of Zionist history, in the course of which the Zionist movement faced many enemies but also won supporters, from the Balfour Declaration of 1917, to Britain's back-tracking on the Declaration to appease the Arab population in the region with the White Paper of 1922. There were the riots of 1929 during which about 140 Jews were murdered in Hebron, Jerusalem, Safed and other places, followed by a second British White Paper which severely limited the immigration and settlement of Jews in the area. Fighting between Jews and Arabs erupted again in 1936 and continued for about three years, during which 400 Jews were killed. In that period, the British determined that the area of Palestine they controlled should be divided into two states, Jewish and Arab. The Arab state, to be annexed to the Kingdom of Jordan, would receive 20,600 square kilometres (about 83 per cent of the total area), while the Jewish state would get the remaining 17 per cent – 4,840 square kilometres. This was accepted in principle by the Jewish community but rejected by the Arabs. This led to yet more concessions from the British, who in May 1939 issued a third White Paper in which they completely renounced their commitment to establishing a national home for the Jewish people in Israel, declaring that the Jews living in the country actually enjoyed autonomy, thanks to organisations and institutions such as the Jewish Agency, the Histadrut Labour Federation, the National Committee and so on and should not expect more. Immigration was even more restricted – this on the eve of World War II. The document stipulated that within ten years a binational state would be established in the country, which the Jews vehemently opposed, because it was clear that in view of restrictions on Jewish immigration, there would be a decisive majority of Arabs in such a state.

From these facts it should be clear that Zionists felt a sense of frequent betrayal early in their history from the country they considered their most important friend and it led to the insight that there are situations in which a friend may turn out to be an enemy. From there, it was a short route to the recognition that we needed to develop intelligence tools to spy on targets of all kinds, including friends who might turn on us. These tools began to be developed in the early 1930s. There were additional experiences of abandonment by friends. After Israel was established, the Soviet Union, which had provided us with abundant weapons during the War of Independence, soon became a declared enemy. In Israel's early years, relations with the United States were cool. In 1952, secret intelligence activities were carried out on American soil by Elyashiv Ben-Horin, a young diplomat at the Israeli embassy in Washington (who tried to recruit Arabs to spy on their countries). He was expelled and only strenuous efforts avoided a serious diplomatic crisis with the USA.

In the following years, the Americans refused to sell weapons to Israel, even though the Soviet Union sold large quantities of modern weapons to Arab countries, and in 1956 the United States cooperated with the Soviets in demanding that Israeli troops withdraw from the Sinai Peninsula. Relations with the United States became warmer only under President Lyndon Johnson (1963–9), especially after the Six-Day War in 1967, when the United States began to see Israel as a strong, stable, and democratic ally.

Israel experienced a particularly painful betrayal from France, its stalwart ally in the 1950s, when political, military and intelligence cooperation was very close. Ties included cooperation in 1956 in the Sinai campaign against Egypt and France's agreement to help Israel build a nuclear reactor in Dimona. The souring of relations between the two countries began in 1958, when General de Gaulle came to power in France. At first, however, he maintained friendly relations and even invited Prime Minister Ben-Gurion in 1960 for his first official visit to France. But in 1967 de Gaulle stopped France's military and technological partnership with Israel as part of a major political move aimed at developing closer ties with Arab states. On the eve of the Six-Day War, not only did he refuse to condemn the unilateral action of Nasser, but ordered an embargo on shipments of aircraft, weapons and military equipment to Israel – at a time when France was still Israel's main supplier of weapons.

The explanation for the Pollard affair – the recruitment of an intelligence agent in a friendly country – lies, therefore, in Zionist and Israeli history since the Balfour Declaration. Thus the answer to the question – how did we dare to spy against our most important friend, must be understood from an analysis of the history of nearly a century prior to this affair.

It is worth noting, however, that Israel was not exceptional in this respect. France, the United States, Britain and various EU countries – all of these and other countries have at one time or another created systems and tools designed to uncover covertly what their allies are thinking and planning.

Regarding the specifics of the Pollard affair, the facts and motives behind the decision to hire him, I will only mention one important fact so that the public knows: I was the one who gave the order to get Pollard out of the Israeli embassy as soon as he entered it. If we hadn't done this, the Americans – including the Jewish lobby – would have forced him out one way or another. Had we attempted to claim diplomatic immunity for Pollard, for even a moment, it would have created a grave diplomatic conflict between the two countries. It would not have prevented his arrest and would have jeopardised our chance of getting a commitment from the Americans – one which we received – to release him after no more than ten years in prison. For various reasons, the Americans did not stand by that commitment.

*

For years, Rafi Eitan debated between his desire to reveal to the Israeli public what happened behind the scenes in the Pollard affair and his sense of responsibility for the security of the State of Israel, a responsibility he saw as a sacred value, and to which he devoted his entire life. On Thursday 14 March 2019, lying on his deathbed at Ichilov Hospital in Tel Aviv, he dictated to his daughter, Yael Eitan-Gal, part of the above passage on the Pollard affair, and ordered the book's editor, Rami Tal, to destroy all previous texts he wrote on the affair, and complete the chapter at his discretion. He passed away nine days later, on Saturday 23 March 2019.

Chapter 28

Israel Chemicals

I finally parted ways with the Ministry of Defense when I resigned from Lekem on 1 April 1986. A month earlier, I had been appointed by Sharon, who was minister of trade and industry at the time, to the board of Israel Chemicals, a state company. By the end of 1985, in the midst of the Pollard affair, it was already clear to me that my time in the defence establishment was over. By that point, Sharon was batting around the idea of appointing me to a senior position in one of the state companies he oversaw. I submitted my resignation as head of Lekem at the end of 1985, but stayed on for a few months to dismantle the bureau and, on 1 April 1986, I was elected Chairman of Israel Chemicals by its board, succeeding Israel Sakharov, who was retiring.

I have no doubt that what motivated Sharon to offer me the position was his military credo that 'one does not leave wounded behind', and, after the Pollard affair, I was severely wounded, bleeding. He hoisted me on his shoulders when other politicians wouldn't touch me with a bargepole, for fear of an adverse American reaction.

The truth is that, in this regard, Sharon was no different from other politicians in that he provided employment to those who were loyal to him, and I had shown my loyalty to him in many ways over our long friendship. Sharon acted more systematically than others. He devoted a lot of thought, energy and political resources to 'arranging matters' for his loyalists, thus turning their loyalty into something on which their very existence depended. Nonetheless, I am certain Sharon would not have recommended me as chairman of Israel Chemicals if he did not think I was suitable for the position. Indeed, at Sakharov's retirement party, he put it thus: 'Rafi is a man of curiosity who likes to dig into every detail in any task he undertakes. He is an excellent manager and organiser, and, above all, he is honest and reliable.'

I knew it would take me two or three years to feel I was completely in command at Israel Chemicals. I do tend to delve into the details of any job and when I don't understand something I never pretend I do. I have the confidence, based on experience, that at the end, I will succeed in learning what I need to learn and succeed in the role assigned to me.

I mentioned earlier that chemistry was one of my favourite subjects and that in my youth, I considered studying chemical engineering. I devoted the month that I overlapped with Sakharov mainly to studying the chemical, industrial and marketing aspects of the company's chemical products. I perused my old chemistry books, but it was clear to me that a great deal had changed since my school days, both in scientific knowledge and in industrial applications. I purchased new books and devoted hours each day to studying them. Indeed, even at the first board meeting held under my chairmanship, the participants were surprised by my professional knowledge.

In 1986 Israel Chemicals consisted of the Dead Sea Works, a bromine company, a transport company, a phosphates, fertiliser and chemicals company, a desalination engineering company, a mining and operations company. Together, it was worth roughly $700–800 million. When I retired as chairman, the value had almost doubled to about $1.25 billion.

Within a year, I removed the CEO, who I thought was not creative enough, and with Sharon's permission, replaced him with Chaim Erez, a reserve general and a talented manager with first-rate organisational skills, who collaborated with me on my ideas and plans to expand the company's business.

With all its branches and subsidiaries, Israel Chemicals employed about 7,000 people. Every year it exported about 3.5 million tons of products. There was no lack of problems to tackle – profit-and-loss and liquidity issues plagued one subsidiary, marketing plagued another, and transport bottlenecks affected a third. All this weighed on the company's performance. Together with Aryeh Shachar, director of the Dead Sea Works, I assisted in the construction of the potash, salt and bromine ore conveyor project from the Dead Sea, some 400 metres below sea level, to the railway tracks in the Rotem Plain, 400 metres above sea level. About a year and a half into my tenure as chairman, I was able, together with Erez, to draw up a business plan for expanding the company. Our strengths were potash, bromine and its compounds, phosphates and special fertilisers.

While I was in my first year as chairman, Israel Chemicals' profit reached $30 million, in my third year it jumped to $80 million. This was partly due to reducing the number of employees, from 7,000 to 5,000 but mostly due to the acquisition of companies abroad, especially in Germany. It was not difficult to find potash, fertiliser or bromine companies for sale in the world. For example, there were only eleven companies in the world at the time that produced and marketed potash. There were no more than thirty specialty fertiliser companies in the world, and only three bromine companies. After mapping the world, we would make contact with the companies, directly or indirectly through agents, brokers and contacts. We did not shy away from failing companies if we thought we had a reasonable chance of turning them into profitable ones by streamlining them and integrating them into Israel Chemicals.

For example, near Cologne, West Germany, we acquired a fertiliser company on the verge of collapse at virtually no cost. Our advantage lay in a private port on the Rhine, which belonged to our subsidiary in the Netherlands, and saved us the transport costs that the German company paid. In Israel, we had much more modern production systems than the German company, some of whose machines were manufactured as early as 1910! We moved our equipment from the Negev to Germany, and instead equipped the Rotem factory in the Negev with even more sophisticated production systems.

We also expanded in Israel, in the field of transport, for example, becoming the biggest transport company in the country.

At the beginning of my tenure as chairman of Israel Chemicals, I was paid, according to the directive of the Government Companies Authority, only half of the usual salary for the chairman of a government company the size of Israel Chemicals. Despite this I worked full-time, from morning to evening, six days a week. Miriam and I had no doubt that the main reason for my lower pay, and perhaps the only one, was my involvement in the Pollard affair, and the fear of upsetting the Americans.

Of course, this situation seemed unfair to me, and I started negotiating with the finance minister, the Government Companies Authority and Ministry of Defense. As a result, even in 1990, at the end of my service as chairman of Israel Chemicals, my gross salary was NIS 16,000 (then approximately $6,000) per month, which was to say 85 per cent of the salary of a director-general of a government ministry at that time.

The Pollard affair continued to weigh on me in different ways. For example, when Colombian Defense Minister Rafael Samudio visited Israel in 1987, although I largely initiated and prepared the visit I was barred from attending official meetings on behalf of the state, lest the visit be tarnished in any way.

Furthermore, with legal proceedings still going on with the United States, I was asked not to leave Israel. Cabinet Secretary Eliakim Rubinstein suggested to Sharon that I resign from the chairmanship of Israel Chemicals so that Israel could tell the United States that everyone involved in the Pollard affair had been punished. Sharon defended me but as my wife put it in her diary: 'Arik does not leave wounded in the field, but he expects them to remember that.'

Indeed, Sharon protected me from those who wanted to get rid of me because of the Pollard affair, but in return he demanded a heavy price from me, which I could not in all conscience pay. Rows began between us even in my first year as chairman of Israel Chemicals and eventually led to my resignation from the position in 1990.

Sharon had been fighting for his political survival for years, and at the time I became chairman of Israel Chemicals, in 1986, was still suffering from the Kahan Commission report on Sabra and Shatila, which found flaws in his conduct regarding the massacre. There were those both within and outside his Likud party who strove hard to remove Sharon from politics, or at least severely damage his political power and status.

Sharon saw to it that I was appointed chairman of Israel Chemicals mainly because he saw me – rightly – as his supporter, acting much as other politicians did. However, those selected to head a state company are required by the Government Companies Authority to sign an undertaking to comply with the Government Companies Law, which states that regardless of who appointed him/her, the chair must act solely in the best interest of the company. When I signed this commitment, I meant it. I was, therefore, caught in a dilemma. Although I felt an emotional obligation to Sharon and wanted his best interest, I never considered prioritising his political interests over my responsibility to the company and to society.

One of the issues related to personnel. While I wanted to streamline operations with personnel cuts, Sharon did not want to see people in Likud strongholds in southern Israel lose their jobs. Another issue involved a 1989 government decision to privatise Israel Chemicals. Sharon supported this, but wanted his friend, Arie Ganger, an Israeli businessman living in the USA, to buy the company. I vehemently opposed this because I thought Israel Chemicals was an essential strategic asset which should not be transferred to private ownership.

The relationship between me and Sharon kept worsening. On 18 December 1989, I sent him a very personal letter:

> I decided to write to you, maybe it will help clarify matters. First know that in our relationship, I have a problem, and that is that when you are upset, or when I feel I have stepped on your toes, I clam up and bend. It's hard for me to confront you, and when it involves an issue of principle, I continue to stand

> my ground, but it is difficult for me to get into a face-to-face confrontation with you . . .
>
> It's my strength and my weakness. I have travelled down the political road with you and continue to walk with you. However, starting from that meeting about ten months ago where you aggregated supporters at a political crossroads, you attacked me in the presence of others on the subject of Kanafo [a case when I wasn't able to get one of his activists approved for work] and you actually said 'I'm done with Rafi.' You were frothing at the mouth and angrier than I have ever seen you.
>
> Since then, all contact has ended between us. You haven't invited me to any of your internal meetings . . . except for a technical exchange between us. I can't overcome this break between us, perhaps because of my personality. I've often thought, to tell you that you need to take into account how I'm built. On the one hand, I am politically loyal to you, in the present as well as in the past. On the other hand, I can't do things I don't believe in. And when a conflict arises, I am unable to overcome the gap unless you bridge it. When this happens, you immediately think and say it's at your expense. That's true, but it's the price you as a politician pay to his followers, and if you help me, I have no doubt our debts to each other will balance themselves out . . .

The letter went on to explain my position that Israel Chemicals should not be sold outright to a private investor and suggested that Sharon instead propose that a 25 per cent stake in the company be sold on the Israeli stock exchange and, after seeing the results, the government might consider selling further tranches on the exchange. I pointed out that this would be popular with his grassroots Likud supporters. The letter concluded on a personal note, with a plea: 'Please accept me as I am.'

Let me take a moment to explain my position about Israel Chemicals. It was among the country's most profitable state companies and those interested in buying included Shaul Eisenberg,

Arie Ganger, Mark Rich, Ronald Cohen and others. I did not disagree with the policy to sell government companies, including Israel Chemicals, but I strongly disagreed with selling to private buyers, whether local or foreign. I thought it should be sold to Israeli citizens through the capital market. It was my belief that any private entity that acquired the company would probably use bank loans to finance its investment, then use the company's profits to pay back the loan, rather than investing the profits in the company's development and growth. By contrast, selling company shares to the general public in the Israeli capital market would still allow state control, even with a minority of shares, and would ensure that most of the profits would not go into private pockets but would be invested in the development and expansion of the company.

Eisenberg and Ganger, the two leading candidates, mainly because of their close ties with the Israeli establishment, offered no more than $300 million for fifty-one per cent of the shares of Israel Chemicals, which was valued at $1.1 billion at the time. Eventually Eisenberg acquired Israel Chemicals (through his Israel Company) and mined Israel Chemical's profits to pay back the $100 million loan for the purchase rather than to develop the company. Indeed, in 2001 and 2011, Israel Chemicals' revenues from industrial products were still $1.5 billion, only slightly more than when I retired in 1991.

My chairmanship of Israel Chemicals ended twice in a way, the first time in a failed attempt by Sharon to dismiss me and the second when I chose to retire of my own accord. The first time occurred in February 1990. Sharon announced his resignation from Yitzhak Shamir's government on 17 February 1990, which was effective two days later. On 18 February, he convened a special meeting of the board of directors of Israel Chemicals behind my back, scheduled for 6.00 p.m. To make sure that I would not attend, his secretary called me and informed me that Sharon wanted to meet me in his office in Jerusalem – at 6.00 p.m.

I didn't know what he was up to, but I smelled something strange in the air. From Israel Chemical's small branch office in Jerusalem,

I asked two members of the senior management to let me know if there was anything I needed to know before I went into the purported meeting at the ministry. Indeed, the two called me at 6:45 to tell me directors were already assembled in Israel Chemical's boardroom for a special meeting. On the agenda: replacement of the chairman. In quick consultation with Israel Chemical's legal counsel, I sent the board the following message:

> I have only just learned of the convening of this meeting without my participation and the discussion of my dismissal. This meeting is illegal: A. The chairman is absent and B. According to the regulations of the Government Companies Authority, seven-day advance notification is required for meetings of this nature.

At the same time, I notified the minister's office that I couldn't make the meeting at the ministry for logistical reasons, and drove back to Tel Aviv. The next morning, after consulting those close to me, I filed a petition in the Supreme Court against Sharon, as minister of industry and trade, and against Shimon Peres, who as finance minister also had authority over Israel Chemicals.

The same day, I also called Attorney General Yosef Harish, and told him the whole story. He consulted with State Prosecutor Dorit Beinisch and got back to me in half an hour to say they were both convinced I was in the right, and that he intended to call Sharon and tell him that he did not have the authority to convene the board meeting nor the right to fire me as he had. As soon as 19 February, the Supreme Court issued a temporary order prohibiting the convening of a board meeting of Israel Chemicals.

The next day, Shamir sent me the following letter, apparently after discussion with the attorney general:

> Subject: Special meeting of the Board of Directors in accordance with Section 26 (b)
>
> On Tuesday 18 February 1990, the Minister of Industry and Trade ordered a special meeting of the Board of Directors of

> Israel Chemicals pursuant to section 26 (b) of the Government Companies Law, to discuss the issue of 'replacing the Chairman of the ICL Board and the election of a new chairman of the board of directors of the company'.
>
> Since the Minister of Industry and Trade who convened this meeting has ceased to serve in the government and in the coming days another minister will be appointed, I believe it neither fair nor appropriate for the board of Israel Chemicals to discuss this issue until the new minister of industry considers the matter and makes a decision regarding this.
>
> You are therefore required to remove from the board's agenda the discussion on the subject detailed above.

Sharon's retirement came into effect that day, and I cancelled the petition to the Supreme Court because it was no longer needed. Thus ended the 'first round' of my retirement process.

A week later, I convened a board meeting, detailed the whole story and announced my decision to retire as chairman in the summer. The board appointed the company's finance director, Victor Medina, to succeed me. During July we overlapped and on 1 August 1990, my retirement took effect.

To this day, I do not know why Peres, in his capacity as finance minister, agreed to Sharon's request to convene a special board meeting to dismiss me. Peres may have resented me over the Pollard affair, which clouded US–Israel relations for some time. Or perhaps Peres did not want to quarrel with him over me. To be honest, Peres had no good reason to take a stand in my favour.

At the time I resigned from Israel Chemicals, I was sixty-four years old and I thought I still had a chance to do something new in the next ten or fifteen years, something that would not be dependent on Israeli politics or Israeli politicians, especially not on Sharon. My four years as chairman of Israel Chemicals had served as the best possible school to learn about industry and business in Israel and around the world, and prepared me to do well in private business afterwards. I also met people who became my future business partners.

The rift between Sharon and I lasted about ten years, and we didn't exchange a single word during that time. In 2000, when his wife Lily passed away, I went to the funeral. Sharon's son, Gilad, approached me and asked me to shake hands with his father, who was standing by the fresh grave. We did so, and Sharon said, 'Come visit me during the *shiva* [the seven-day mourning period].' I went. We talked for a long time as if nothing had ever happened between us, and after that became as close as we were before.

Perhaps not exactly as close as before. I find it hard to believe that Sharon, who appointed me chairman of Israel Chemicals thinking I would always act in his interest and was disappointed when I prioritised the interests of the company, ever completely forgave me. But even when I fought with Sharon, I loved him. In 2001, when he ran for prime minister against Ehud Barak, I worked at his headquarters. In 2002, when he was thinking of running against Benyamin Netanyahu for head of the Likud, I again expressed my willingness to help him. I was his friend without reservations. On his side, I have no doubt there were reservations. When he became prime minister, I saw him in person only a few times. However, I did make suggestions to him, either by fax or through his aide Uri Dan, and he agreed with many of them. On political and state matters, there were practically no differences of opinion between us, but from the late 1980s until January 2006, when he had a stroke from which he never recovered, he never invited me to the meetings of his inner circle, known as the ranch forum, in which I had regularly participated in the past.

Chapter 29

Colombia and East Berlin

The chairmen of government companies are not civil servants, so they are permitted under Israeli law to engage simultaneously in private business as long this does not conflict with the interests of the government company they head. Throughout my tenure at Israel Chemicals, I did not abandon my private business interests.

With Yossi Langutzky, an expert geologist who worked in oil exploration, I established a partnership to provide security for PanAmerican airlines at major airports in Western Europe. We both agreed that due to the Pollard affair, my name should not be associated in any way, in writing or orally, with our company, which we called Kalanit. In May 1986, we received a contract to plan security for half a dozen of PanAm's airport facilities in Europe with a budget of about half a million dollars. We completed the plan within twenty months, including the recruitment of security personnel at the airports.

Whenever Langutzky travelled to the United States, I repeatedly warned him not to call me from there. I knew that the FBI regularly monitors all calls from the United States to the phone numbers of anyone on their wanted list around the world. I had no doubt that my number was on their list. But Langutzky was not careful and called me several times from the USA. So I was not surprised when the president of PanAm informed him that they had to stop working with us and indicated that this at the insistence of the FBI. I have no doubt that this was the result of the FBI learning that I was involved with Kalanit. PanAm paid the half million dollars it owed us, but refrained from implementing the second phase of the project – managing and overseeing the security of all PanAm flights.

In mid-1986, one of my old buddies from the Palmach, Haim Ben-Ezra, who had a company in irrigation and sewage-plant design that operated in Latin America, contacted me. He told me that he was friendly with Virgilio Barco Vargas, the Colombian former head of the World Bank, who wanted to run to be president of Colombia. Barco asked Ben-Ezra for advice on two issues: his personal security, and how the fight against terrorist organisations and guerrilla warfare in Colombia should be conducted. Ben-Ezra asked if I could help.

On the eve of the Colombian presidential election, I travelled – at my own expense – to Colombia with Ben-Ezra, and we met Barco. In our first meeting, I outlined some basic principles for dealing with terrorism and the drug trade, and for enhancing security for himself and those around him, including his immediate family members, against assassination or kidnapping attempts.

Regarding the insurgents fighting in the jungle, I urged him to buy planes and equipment made by Israel Aerospace Industries (IAI), as well as equipment and ammunition made by Israel Military Industries (IMI). When I returned to Israel, I met with IAI and IMI, and worked to promote deals with the Colombians. However, it was clear to me that even with the help of the latest equipment from Israel, the Colombian Army could not completely eradicate the underground jungle fighters. The jungle absorbs everything, and no matter how many bombs you drop there, guerrillas will manage to hide and emerge after the attacks. Therefore, I advised Barco to take a conciliatory approach to the underground organisations and told him, 'Do not persecute them, Instead, institutionalise them. Reach out to them, let them come out of the jungles. Try to integrate them into Colombian politics. Let them sit and talk in parliament. It's much better than uselessly chasing them in the jungle.'

As president, Barco adopted this advice, which he undoubtedly heard from others as well. The extremist FARC (Revolutionary Armed Forces of Columbia) guerrilla group did not respond to attempts at compromise, but the more moderate M-19 (Movement of 19 April) guerrilla group became a political party and stopped their guerrilla activities.

Langutzky managed the day-to-day work as security adviser to Barco. I was the strategist and travelled to Colombia once every two months, attending meetings of the Colombia general staff. I asked questions, I made suggestions, I was very active. Everyone accepted my presence as natural, since I was there as part of my position as senior adviser on security matters to the president of Colombia.

Barco was enthusiastic about a four-year programme I proposed to deal with three issues: personal security for himself, his relatives and assistants, and the security of his offices; reorganisation of Colombian civilian and military intelligence; and the supply of military and electronic equipment to the Columbia Army of about $230 million over four years. The equipment included Israeli-made Kfir fighter jets, Dvora patrol ships, missile ship renovations, and various sophisticated items of electronic equipment for military intelligence and combat units fighting terrorist organisations.

The first agreement concerning my work in Colombia was signed on 1 December 1986. I was appointed security adviser to Virgilio Barco, who was elected president about a month later. The agreement was on the basis of 'cost plus': every month I was required to submit an account of all costs incurred, plus a 20 per cent commission for me and Ben-Ezra.

The arms and equipment deal we signed with the Colombian government in December 1986 was for $230 million, with an entire commission of $14 million. My portion was $785,000 in promissory notes to be paid out between November 1991 and November 1997. Until the entire amount was paid, I joined a group known as Commando 183 – those Israelis who stay abroad at least 183 days in a calendar year to avoid paying taxes.

Barco, with whom I developed a personal relationship, died in 1997, at the age of 75. In 1999, Ben-Ezra and I decided to commemorate his memory in Israel. We contacted the Jewish National Fund and a forest was planted at our expense, near the Yitzhak Rabin Forest. We invited Barco's widow, son and daughter to the planting ceremony. In an emotional speech, his widow noted that many people had sought to be close to his husband while he was alive, and that only we, his Israeli friends, had acted to commemorate his memory after his death.

In late 1990, Max Mazin, head of the Spanish Jewish community who had in the past helped Mossad in connection with the immigration of Moroccan Jews to Israel, got in touch with me when he heard I had retired from Israel Chemicals. Mazin was a partner of the American businessman Mark Rich in a real estate company called Ron Investments, with a subsidiary, called Trips, which owned and managed a chain of hotels. They were seeking to enter the market in East Germany, at the time on the brink of reunification with West Germany. They wanted to buy hotels, office buildings and other real estate, mainly in East Germany, and perhaps in other Eastern European countries that were also newly free from the Soviet orbit and in the process of economic liberalisation. They suggested I become the representative of Ron Investments in East Germany. I accepted the offer. The contract we signed stipulated that my salary would be paid by Mazin's company, which was registered in Spain, and that Mark Rich would bear half the costs. I and my business partner, Elhanan Fess, decided to settle in East Berlin. Miriam and I rented an apartment in the eastern part of Berlin, where we lived from mid-1991 to mid-1992. We learned German. She was a better student than I was, although I learned enough to be able to read a newspaper in German.

An Israel Chemicals board member with connections in Berlin put Fess and me in touch with the head architect of East Berlin, who introduced us to the mayor of East Berlin and other important people, all of which helped us learn about upcoming projects in the city that could help us determine what assets might be worthwhile investments. The Berlin Wall was already down by then, but negotiations were still under way on the details of the unification of the two Germanies, officially announced in late 1991. Therefore, we conducted business negotiations with Communist government officials and the first contracts for property were signed with them.

Ron Investments signed several contracts for the purchase of hotels and other buildings in East Berlin and paid advance fees. But following the East German unification agreement with West Germany, the East German National Property Authority was established in late 1991, headed by someone who had previously served as head of the West German Chancellor's Office. I knew him from my time in the prime minister's office. I asked for a meeting with him, and he remembered me and immediately received me at his office in East Berlin. When I showed him our signed contracts, his face darkened and he said to me, 'Rafi my friend, you've thrown away your money on a losing bet!' It turned out that under German unification, the property authority was responsible for putting up East German state property for sale by tender. 'If you want, you can bid on the tenders. All the contracts you signed are null and void, but the authority will compensate you for all your expenses.' After negotiations with the authority, we eventually got back all our money – about DM 500,000, then worth about $350,000. Max Mazin and the Spanish partners refused to go to the tenders.

One person I got to know during my stay in Berlin, via my connections in the Jewish community there, was Markus Wolf, former head of the East German spy agency, the Stasi. I met him several times in Berlin, and then we met during his two visits to Israel. I also linked him to an American Jewish lawyer, who Wolf used when he was prosecuted in Germany. In an interview he gave to Israeli journalist Ilana Dayan, he mentioned that he and I had similar ways of approaching intelligence work. 'Both Rafi Eitan and I believe that one secretary in high places is worth more than a division of spies,' he told her.

Chapter 30

Fruitful Deals in Cuba

One night in April 1992, Ben-Ezra, my partner in Colombia, called me with a new proposition: to cooperate in managing orchards in Cuba and exporting the fruit to Europe. He explained that he approached me because I had knowledge of fertilisers from my time at Israel Chemicals, and some capital from my share of our business of brokering arms and military equipment to Colombia.

I did not hesitate for a moment to give a positive answer. I understand orchards – I grew up in them – and I also understand fertilisers. The other proposed partners had expertise in relevant fields, and the enterprise required a relatively modest investment. With some additional investors we established Gruppo BM, registered in Panama, and known as GBM

The relationship between Cuba and Israel is complex. Although Cuba has belonged since 1959 to the Communist bloc, which was led by the Soviet Union and hostile to Israel, Fidel Castro was sympathetic to Israel in the first years of his rule and wanted to cultivate ties between the two countries. Indeed, delegations of agricultural experts from socialist *kibbutzim* visited Cuba in Israel's early days. This was personally paid for by a Jewish German-born Cuban citizen named Ricardo Wolf, who was one of Castro's early funders for his guerrilla activities, and in turn was appointed Cuban consul in Israel after Castro's rise to power.

Cuba, boycotted by the United States, was highly dependent on the Soviet Union, but the disintegration of the communist bloc brought Cuba to the brink of an economic crisis that threatened its existence. To survive, Cuba was forced to liberalise its economy and allow foreign entrepreneurs to invest and to seek new markets for its produce. We were part of this new trend.

In June 1992, I visited Cuba for the first time. At first glance, it seemed to be a country in complete economic collapse. There were no buses in Havana, petrol stations were empty, electric power went out every few hours, most shops were closed or almost empty of goods.

Two weeks before we opened negotiations with the Cubans, we sent two agronomists to check out the orchard, which was about 10,000 acres, which had been designed and planted in the early 1960s, mostly with citrus trees, by experts from Kibbutz Gan Shmuel. Israel's total land dedicated to citrus at its height in the 1960s was never more than 250,000 acres, so it was a huge orchard by our standards and included the town of Jagüey Grande, with 80,000 inhabitants, at its centre. The two agronomists prepared a report with a comprehensive overview of the condition of the trees, the type and quality of the soil, the climate, the water, the methods of irrigation and cultivation, the expected crop, and the distribution of the citrus varieties grown in it – oranges and grapefruits.

Why did the Cubans think they needed a group of Israelis to care for the orchard? Good question. Until 1989, all Cuba's fruit exports went to the Soviet Union, by barter, mainly for oil. This included about a million tons of citrus fruit a year. Cuba still exported fruit to the Soviet Union in the early 1990s, but the collapse of the communist regime's systems meant that the Cubans received nothing in return for the fruit they exported. So they tried their luck in Western Europe but the fruit was packaged poorly and arrived in unsuitable condition for that market. Therefore, the Cubans were looking for experts and investors to teach them how to increase yields, improve their packaging, and market the fruit under conditions expected in the Western European market.

I was part of the GBM team that negotiated a multi-year contract with the Cubans, which was extended several times. Under the contract, the orchard, owned by Cuba, was managed and worked by

Cuban citizens. GBM funded everything requiring foreign currency, such as the purchase of tractors, fuel, fertilisers, chemicals, packaging materials, transport of the fruit to Europe and marketing expenses, with GBM receiving a commission for its outlays. GBM would market the fruit in cooperation with Israeli produce distributor Agrexco for a marketing commission. The contract allowed transparency, enabling the Cubans to review and audit all of our activities. Since that first contract was signed, we have worked with the Cubans fairly, honestly and transparently, significantly benefitting the Cuban economy. We've employed thousands of workers and made a significant contribution to training and coaching Cuban farmers and agronomists.

Initially, management of the entire system, in Cuba and in Israel, was placed on my shoulders. As early as June 1992, I brought packaging materials to Cuba and revamped their packing houses to sort, wash, disinfect, wax and pack the fruit properly in boxes imported from Israel.

I was impressed by the extraordinary enthusiasm of the Cuban youth who worked in the orchard. They reminded me very much of our youth after 1948. They believed in us, and were convinced that working with us allowed them, after three years of failures, to overcome the difficulties and export the fruit of their orchard. I and my friends' feeling was that we had revolutionary youth in front of us, with a fervent faith in the future of their homeland.

In October 1992 we exported our first citrus shipment, 2,000 pallets, from Cuba to Europe. The packing materials came from Israel, the packing houses worked under the guidance of our people. The shipment went to Antwerp and Rotterdam, where Agrexco handled the wholesale marketing system, a system of tenders between its customers, marketing chains, supermarkets and fruit and vegetable wholesalers. A year later, I left the active management of the business, and we appointed Sergio Zechariah Meisler, a Jewish engineer born in Brazil and a former marketing director of IAI, as a senior manager.

During this time, the Cubans still suspected that I was a spy We were well aware that we were under covert surveillance, that our letters and telegrams were read by the Cuban security services, and that our calls to Israel were subject to constant eavesdropping. It took them three years to believe in our integrity and that we truly were in Cuba purely to pursue a business partnership. Only after three years did they believe that I was right when I suggested planting new trees in about half the orchard because it would be cheaper than rehabilitating damaged stock.

It took four years for them to agree to let us manage the orchard as we thought it should be managed. But they did not stand in the way of our upgrading the fruit concentrate plant, which increased its yield from 4,000 tons per year to about 40,000 tons per year over the next decade. In practice, the professional management of the orchard eventually passed entirely to us.

I first met Fidel Castro in November 1993. We were presenting our products, primarily irrigation and fertiliser spraying systems from Israel, at a large industrial and agricultural exhibition in Havana. On the last evening, Castro personally presented awards of excellence, including two for our company, one for a fertiliser spraying system and one for drip irrigation. While I was on stage, receiving the second award, Castro approached me, then turned to one of his assistants who served as an interpreter, a man of Jewish descent named Avraham Mesikes, and ordered him: 'Arrange an appointment for me with him.'

In early 1994, I received the invitation. I got a phone call at my office and was invited that very evening, at 10.00 p.m., for dinner at Castro's office, together with my partners, Ben-Ezra and Meisler. I was not surprised by the time; it was known that Fidel Castro worked and ate late at night.

When we arrived, we were seated at a long table in Castro's dining room. Castro sat across from us, along with Prime Minister Carlos Laha and Minister of Agriculture Carlos Perez. The conversation was lively and lasted late into the night. I was very impressed with Castro, a tall man with a dominant presence, excellent memory and tireless curiosity. He demonstrated knowledge in a wide variety of topics, including the Middle East, and was well-versed in the details of our activities in Cuba. I pointed out ways to change agriculture in Cuba, such as using greenhouses for growing fruit and vegetables, pointing out that winter was the optimal time to grow these crops in open fields in Cuba, because there were fewer pests, and thus no need for pesticides. In contrast, pests proliferated in Cuba's humid summers, resulting in damaged crops and insufficient yield for local consumption. The problem could be solved, as proven by Israeli researchers, with extensive use of greenhouses along with a drip irrigation system that simultaneously also disseminated fertiliser and pesticides, instead of the outdated spray method used in Cuba. As Castro listened with great interest, I explained that the initial investment might seem large, but would pay off fairly quickly with higher yields year-round. Castro asked a lot of questions. When this subject was exhausted, he moved on to topics from Jewish history. I did not feel even for a moment that I was sitting in front of a dictator, and he treated me and my friends as equals when we asked questions and he answered. At the end of the meal, Prime Minister Carlos Laha, remarked to me, 'You are one of the few people that Fidel lets talk . . .'

In 1994, when the orchard was progressing to the satisfaction of both parties, I and my partners started a new enterprise, supplying Israeli-made greenhouses, complete with irrigation systems, for growing vegetables, based on my conversation with Castro. The project was highly successful, eventually growing to an area of 125 acres and led to our bringing about 500 Cubans to Israel to train in agriculture.

I looked around for other new projects and knew that few new office building had been built during Castro's regime, already in its third decade, and most existing buildings were falling apart. Some 600 foreign companies operating in Cuba were housed in 'abandoned property', houses and villas left behind by the rich who fled when Castro came to power and rented by the government to local institutions and foreign companies. It seemed to me that constructing office buildings for rent, mainly for foreign companies, would fill a need – and offer new investment opportunities.

In 1995, I and my partner Sergio Meisler met with the chief architect of the Havana municipality, who also chaired the district planning and building commission. We discussed the idea of building a complex of office buildings. He listened to us and showed us the city master plan, pointing out potentially suitable locations. After various discussions, we decided to focus on an area of about 75 acres owned by the city in the new Miramar district. The plan was to build a complex of office buildings with malls in the centre of the complex, surrounded by a series of hotels.

We chose as our strategic partner, Baruch Habas, a veteran and experienced entrepreneur and contractor, who had built malls in a number of Israel cities. One of his associates, Zvi Enrique Rosenberg, spoke Spanish and conducted the negotiations with the Cubans. Under a contract reached in 1996, the project involved a 51 per cent stake in a construction project in Havana for a Cuban group which controlled all the abandoned real estate in Havana, and 49 for us, GBM-Miramar, which was GBM with Habas. Although the majority stake was Cuban, it was stipulated that the project management would be entrusted to the Israeli group. The area was leased to us for fifty years, with an option for another fifty years, covered 20 acres and provided for the construction of eighteen buildings of six to seven floors.

We needed $14 million to finance the construction of the first two buildings, complicated because the American boycott of Cuba meant most large international banks refused to provide loans for projects in Cuba. Eventually, we obtained lines of credit from a medium-size Dutch bank, from Israel's Bank Hapoalim and from a few Spanish banks, and invested some of the profits from GBM.

Construction began in early 1996, with Cuban subcontractors. Only aluminium windows, air conditioning systems, elevators, doors and communications were brought from abroad, first from Israel, and later also from Canada. At the end of 1997, the construction of the first buildings was completed, and by the beginning of 1998, all the offices in them were rented out, for $4 million a year. By 2004, all six planned buildings were completed, each with a commercial area of 10,000 square metres, as well as a parking lot. The ground floor of each building was designated for retail use. These six buildings are one of the best deals our company has made.

In construction, the Cubans only gave the land and did not invest a penny, but they made good money. The Cuban government was very pleased with our activities, so much so that I am convinced the success of the project was what prompted Castro to extend an invitation to meet us in November 1966, when we were due to see Minister Carlos Laha and give him a detailed report on the orchard and construction projects. He told us Castro would host the meeting at his residence.

When we arrived, Castro was waiting for us in the courtyard of the palace, opened the limousine door himself, beckoned me with his hand, and when I emerged from the car, approached me and asked me, through an interpreter, 'Tell me, did you help the South Africans detonate a nuclear bomb?'

I was taken aback a moment and then answered: 'Mr President, Fidel, do you believe I will give you an answer to such a question?' He smiled and did not repeat the question.

The intimate meal with Castro was attended by three members of our company, the prime minister, the foreign minister and an interpreter. The atmosphere was very pleasant, and this time, too, Castro turned the conversation to Judaism. His questions were many and detailed, indicating a genuine interest in the subject, so much so that I wondered if he believed he might have some Jewish ancestry. During the entire conversation between the two of us, which lasted and lasted until 4.00 a.m., he addressed me by my first name, Rafi, and I reciprocated by calling him Fidel.

We spoke also about the Middle East. Castro had many questions, about the Palestinians and Arafat, about the prospect that the Oslo Accords would succeed in bringing peace, on Syria and Lebanon.

Without mincing words, I told him, 'Arafat is a swindler and a crook who must not be believed.' Fidel just listened, did not argue or try to contradict me. We also talked about American policy, about technological innovations and biotechnological developments. Most of the conversation took place between the two of us, and only when it revolved around the construction project and the cultivation of our orchard did my friends also take part in it.

Our company continued to expand in Cuba, setting up a shipping line to get produce to Europe, and establishing subsidiaries that deal with construction and with the sale of agricultural-related products such as fertilisers, chemicals, tractors and irrigation systems. We also established a communications subsidiary called GBM Communication, which sells hardware and software, mostly from Israeli companies, to develop and maintain Cuba's communication networks.

In all these businesses, I always insisted that all original GBM partners be partners in the subsidiaries as well, both for moral reasons but also because GBM acquired an impeccable reputation with the big banks that opened credit lines for us as well as with the Cuban government. Cuba has ranked us first among all the foreign companies active in Cuba in terms of the trust they have in us, our honesty and our contribution to the Cuban economy. We have never cheated them. They know this and appreciate it. Outside of the tourism business, we were for years the second largest foreign company in Cuba in terms of the scope of our activities there.

Our contract management of the large orchard expired in 2009, and we decided not to renew it, mostly because I and my partners were getting on in years. Furthermore, I was a government minister at the time, and could not devote time and attention to business in Cuba. But GBM remained in Cuba, providing consulting and contracting services, and also partnering in various agricultural initiatives. We draw an annual dividend from our business in Cuba, and our relations with the Cuban authorities continue to be excellent. I visit Cuba once every six months.

Chapter 31

The Pensioners' Party

In late 2005, ahead of the seventeenth Knesset elections, scheduled for March 2006, Sharon left Likud and founded Kadima, along with Ehud Olmert . One day I was called by Nava Arad, a former Knesset parliamentarian from the Labour party, who was very active in asserting the rights of pensioners, and in 1996 had formed a party called Gil, which advocated for senior citizens but did not receive enough votes to win a seat in the Knesset. I knew her and appreciated her persistence in trying to improve the lot of senior citizens. She asked that I suggest to Sharon that he give her and a close associate of hers two realistic places on Kadima's list to the Knesset. I spoke to Sharon who was positive about the idea but in January 2006, he had the severe stroke, from which he never recovered, and Olmert took his place at the head of the party. As a result, Nava was given forty-second place on the Kadima list, her associate Yaakov Ben-Yizri, who headed a pensioner's organisation, was given forty-fifth place. Polls predicted that Kadima would not get more than thirty-five seats. In other words, they were not given realistic places.

I convened a number of the leading advocates for senior citizen rights, and suggested that given their ranking in Kadima, they should run as an independent list, without favours from anyone. They were positively inclined – if I stood at the head of the list. Without hesitation I agreed even though we had only two days left to submit a list to the Central Election Commission.

Because Gil had existed as a party and had remained registered, the process of re-activating the party was easy. Moshe Sharoni, chairman of the Haifa Municipality Retirement Association, had used part of his budget to pay the annual fees to keep the party registered. Arad, Ben-Yizri and I went to Haifa. There we were joined by Yitzhak Galanti, who headed an organisation that represented retirees from Israel's electric company. He took us to meet Sharoni. We all sat down with Sharoni, explained to him that we wanted to re-activate the party and would be happy to give him a high place on the list of candidates for the Knesset. Sharoni did not hesitate for a moment and signed the necessary forms.

We returned to Tel Aviv and all met the next day. I set three conditions to my participation as head of the list:

- I would not fund the party myself. I would give my share, but they would have to raise the rest of any necessary funding. I would not deal with financial matters.
- If we only got one or two seats, I would resign within six months. I felt I would not be able to do anything substantial with just two seats.
- If internal arguments broke out – I would decide matters and have the last word.

They agreed to all the terms, and we submitted the list on time.

Gil turned out to be the big surprise in the elections to the seventeenth Knesset, garnering seven seats, defying predictions it might get one or two. I was less surprised than the others. I did not expect seven seats, but thought we might get three or four.

It was not due to me that we won seven seats in 2006, or that we crashed in the next elections in 2009. We were a bubble party, a passing phenomenon. A pensioner party does not have a stable electoral constituency it can build on. Most senior citizens vote for the parties that they voted for in their younger years. Furthermore, for the most part, retirees do not focus on their narrow interests. They are interested in everything that is happening in the country, they have long-formed opinions about security, the economy and social matters. When they go to the polls, they ask themselves first and foremost what their country needs, not what they need. In this context, it is worth noting that at least three of the seven seats we received did not come from retirees, but from people aged 20–50, who voted for us as a protest against Finance Minister Netanyahu's economic policy, which hurt the elderly, or as an expression of despair and anger against Israeli politics in general and corruption in particular.

With seven seats in my pocket, I could get Olmert to give me any job that came to my mind. Olmert expected me to demand a senior economic portfolio but in our first meeting I told him: 'We want one of our people to be minister of health and we want the establishment of a ministry for senior citizens' affairs.' This is how I turned the retirees from a party into a government office. I was not a brilliant politician, but I put the issue of senior citizens' welfare on the agenda. I set up a government office whose entire business is to assist them.

Our first year in Olmert's government was a huge success. Together with Ben-Yizri, who was appointed Minister of Health, we achieved, among other things, expanding the types of drugs offered as part of the national health-care system, lowering the charges on medications, increasing retirement benefits and benefits to those in poverty and diverting more funds to care for the elderly. I became Minister of Pensioner Affairs. In this position, I discovered that there were fifty-three different organisations of Holocaust survivors operating in Israel, so I centralised the care for all survivors under one roof in my ministry and procured a budget to advance their interests.

In September 2008, Prime Minister Ehud Olmert announced his resignation, and Tzipi Livni, who succeeded him as chairman of Kadima, was asked to form the next government. In her negotiations to try and form a government with Labour, she drew up an agreement that I realised would take away all the influence I had gained by virtue of my seven seats, including relinquishing the Ministry of Pensioner Affairs. Although the ministry would not be abolished, no law I might propose would be submitted by the government to the Knesset unless it was approved by the Labour party. Of course, I could not accept that. I called Livni and told her so.

A few days later, she called and told me that if I failed to accept the agreement and join her government, she would not be able to form a coalition, resulting in new elections. I suppose she thought that because the polls showed that new elections would not be good for our party that I would cave in, but I didn't. The next morning, she informed President Shimon Peres that she could not form a coalition.

That same day, Bibi Netanyahu and Gideon Saar showed up at my house, proposing that I join the Likud party in the run-up to the upcoming elections. I declined, explaining that while I personally sympathised with the Likud, all the members of my party came from the Labour party who would not join Likud, and that they wanted to operate in an independent party.

In the run-up to the eighteenth Knesset elections, I debated whether to run at the top of the Gil party list. I did not like the petty conflicts and incessant intrigues that were part of life in the party. Finally, mainly due to a sense of responsibility, I agreed to head the party again. But the polls were right: we received about 17,000 votes, far too few to win even one Knesset seat.

Chapter 32

My Political Vision

I know the Jewish–Palestinian conflict intimately. I was born into it, I grew up in its shadow, I have dealt with it – in various forms – for most of my life. I have accumulated more than enough knowledge and experience to understand what is possible and what is not, what can be done now and what should be postponed, what is likely to happen – or will not happen – in the future, and, most importantly, what is needed to ensure Israel remains a Jewish and democratic state.

We and the Palestinians need to go our separate ways. I mean by unilateral action initiated by Israel, one that is not dependent on negotiations and does not involve consent, because consent will not be reached in the foreseeable future. Negotiations are always desirable, but we should not hang our hopes on them. Not in this case. I do not believe in displacing Jews from their homes or in removing Arabs from their lands.

Israel will not be able to continue to exist as an occupying state. It will not be able to bear the label of an apartheid state. International pressures, unremitting and ever stronger and more intense, will not allow it. I have lived on this land long enough not to dismiss international pressure, and to understand that it has consequences. Israel does not have the legitimacy – today, in the past or in the future – to occupy a population, fence it in, set up barriers against it, restrict it and bear down on every aspect of its daily life, not even when all this is done for security reasons. The security arguments, although justified in themselves, don't hold if they require constant repression. Israel has the legitimate right to defend itself. There is international recognition of this right. The oppression of millions of Palestinians cannot be justified by security needs. Therefore, the line that should guide us is that Israel is not occupying, but defending itself, and this should guide the course of action we take and the course we reject.

We must leave most of Judea and Samaria unilaterally. I emphasise, most of it, not all of it. The territories we evacuate, we should evacuate completely. They will remain in Palestinian hands. They will be able to establish a state there, with all the usual institutions, including an army. I do not feel threatened by the military that such a state would establish. I am also not bothered by the possibility that Hamas will control it in this country. I do not see Hamas, with all its rockets, as a real threat to our existence. My assumption is that the Palestinians will be smart enough and sufficiently life-loving to prevent Hamas from controlling the territories that will be evacuated, but that is already their internal business, and even if this assumption is wrong, it does not change the course of action I propose.

We must keep the Jordan Valley in our hands, but not invest in settlements beyond the existing ones. Let us not overwhelm the region with population. Those who live there can stay there, Jews and Arabs. No one will be evicted, no one will be uprooted, no one will be enticed to leave. The areas of the Jordan Valley inhabited by Palestinians will remain as enclaves under Israeli security control. Our security control in the Jordan Valley will prevent any Palestinian state established in the territories, no matter who controls it, from joining the army of any Arab state to the east. Our security control in the Jordan Valley will separate the Palestinian state from the other Arab states, and that is the only measure we can take to guarantee our narrow land strip. I do not forget for a moment that if we return to the 1967 borders, which is more or less what I am proposing, there will be parts of our country, where there will be a mere 14 kilometres between our eastern border and the Mediterranean Sea. However, we must also maintain a focused grip at strategic points on the eastern ridge over the Jordan Valley, so that we can watch and prepare in case of need.

Have we taken from the Palestinians territory that they say belongs to them? We need to listen to their claims, and if they are just ones, we must offer them a fair replacement – square kilometre for square kilometre. Yvette Lieberman has spoken about giving land in Wadi Ara to a Palestinian state if and when such a state is established, in exchange for areas with dense Jewish settlements. I don't rule this out, but I find it hard to imagine that Israeli Arab citizens will want to become Palestinian citizens. If I am wrong, and they do want to do so, this should be made possible. There are other areas, though not large, that can be offered as compensation to the Palestinians. If the barriers to population and land exchange are insurmountable, fair compensation can be offered in other ways: financial support, building a passageway between Gaza at one end, and Judea and Samaria at the other, at our expense. Practical, not ideological.

What remains in our hands from the territory occupied in 1967 will be considered as a temporary holding, retained solely for security purposes until better days come, when negotiations on permanent agreements become practical and desired by both sides. It is a process that will evolve, and evolutionary processes take a long time, so there is no point in standing with a stopwatch and setting unrealistic deadlines.

I call the separation I envision and have been trying to promote for many years a 'mosaic separation', because it leaves Jewish enclaves in Palestinian territory and vice versa. In the enclave areas, whoever on both sides wants to evacuate will be able to leave and receive compensation. Those who express a desire to stay where they are, will be able to stay, but must accept whatever is required to live in such an enclave, Jewish settlements within Palestinian territory will be surrounded by a fence with access roads to and from the State of Israel and settlement blocs.

As stated, we will hold the territories that remain in our hands solely for security reasons, not religious ones. The approach is practical and can be summarised as follows: the amount of territory we must take from the Palestinians for our security does not allow us to demand from them the signing of peace agreements and the 'end of the conflict'. For their part, they cannot guarantee our safety. We do not believe them, and we have solid reasons not to believe them.

At best, shifting to a mode of coexistence with us will permeate their consciousness very slowly until it crystallises. After all, they are in no hurry and believe that time is in on their side. Even if they do not say so openly, in their hearts they believe that in the future, a matter of two to four generations, the Jewish state in the Land of Israel will not survive. What will happen to the Jews? It doesn't mean that the Jews will be thrown into the sea, but they will become a minority in this country, a minority without national rights, only religious ones. The Palestinians have said this often enough for me to believe them. In this matter, Mahmoud Abbas is no different from Arafat. He explained his decision to reject Olmert's proposals, which went further than any other Israeli proposal, by saying that 'Olmert is unable to fulfil his obligations because his rule is coming to an end . . .' This is a ridiculous, if not idiotic, argument. If he wanted a peace agreement and an 'end to the conflict', he would have taken what Olmert offered, and not worried about Olmert's ability to stand behind his commitment.

The disengagement from Gaza led to Hamas taking over the Gaza Strip. I believe that the friction between Hamas and Israel will continue for years, but in the end the instinct for life will prevail. Gaza residents will learn to cooperate. Separation requires them to cooperate, to talk, even for purely essential needs. There is a dialogue between Israel and Hamas. It is disrupted by hostile actions to which we respond with disproportionate force, but over time a relationship will be formed between the two enemy sides, who live side by side and talk only when they must. Neither of them need recognise the other, but neither should they kill each other. The daily dialogue that will take place will concern their essential needs: how many trucks of food will enter today, how many trucks will enter tomorrow, how will the cargo be transferred, how will people leave, how will they enter, who enters, who leaves. This will happen not only in Gaza, but also in the territories of Judea and Samaria if Hamas rules there, because they have no choice.

I believe the process I am outlining here could lead to peace agreements within a few decades. They will no longer be an occupied population. They will not see us before their eyes in everyday life. We will not stop them at checkpoints, we will not require certificates, we will not enter their homes, we will not walk around their yards, we will not go up on the roofs, we will not impose a closure or curfew. We will indeed hold joint economic initiatives with them, we will employ them within Israel, and this will give rise to a dialogue between the two peoples, who, although forced on each other, have to learn to live with each other.

I do not consider my suggestions generous, just or moral, but they are practical and realistic. And that is the best we can do, as long as the fundamental situation stays at it is, and I don't see it changing in the foreseeable future.

As mentioned earlier, there was a break in my relationship with Ariel Sharon between 1990 and 2000, which was renewed after his wife's death. In 2004, when Sharon was prime minister, I first learned of his intention to withdraw from Gaza. He invited me to his farm in the Negev two or three times and presented his plan to me. His reasoning was that over the long term it was impossible to hold on to isolated Jewish areas in the heart of an area with a hostile Arab population. He also said he intended to make a similar move in Judea and Samaria.

He managed to carry out the first phase – an Israeli withdrawal from Gaza and the evacuation of the Gush Katif settlements. He did not manage to carry out the second phase – the evacuation of the isolated settlements in Judea and Samaria – due to the massive stroke he suffered. To me, this is a tragedy that will reverberate for generations. I have no doubt that if Sharon had stayed in power for another two or three years, he would have implemented the second phase. He was the only one who could have carried it out, and our situation would be much better today (2019) if he had.

My parents were on the Left – adherents of Ben-Gurion's Mapai party. I turned right. All my adult life I supported settlement in Judea and Samaria. Even when I served under Prime Minister Yitzhak Rabin during his first term, I supported the settlements. I was always close to the leadership of the settlements, but I have never had the illusions which those among them have that there is some magic way to reach a Jewish state that will rule all of Judea and Samaria, and the Palestinians there will be citizens of a foreign state – Jordan – and vote for the Jordanian parliament.

In this context, I recall the discussions that took place in the Knesset's Foreign Affairs and Defense Committee in 1977–8, in which I took part as Begin's counter-terrorism adviser. Weizmann and Sharon, respectively defense minister and agriculture minister at the time, had bitter debates about the settlements. Weizmann argued that Jewish settlements should only be established where there was a close connection with Israel's pre-1967 borders. Sharon's position was to settle everywhere, to make separation impossible. At one of the meetings, I wrote a note to Sharon; 'Arik, Ezer is right.' But he could not be convinced, and continued to argue for spreading out the settlements. His position changed only in 2001 when he became prime minister. So much so that in 2004, I found myself sitting across from him in his farm, and he was trying to convince me that separation was best for Israel.

In 2007, I served as Minister of Pensioner Affairs in Olmert's government. For various reasons, the issue of the property of the Jews who were forced to leave Arab countries following the War of Independence and moved to Israel, came up. The relevant material was concentrated in my office, since most of them were senior citizens by then. I approached Livni, then foreign minister, and Olmert, and told them, 'The refugees – both Jews and Arabs – must be compensated with money. But no refugee will be returned – neither ours nor theirs.'

The conversation evolved into an in-depth discussion. I told Olmert, 'There is no chance you will reach an agreement with [the Palestinians] at this stage. They can't sign an agreement with you.

It's not that they don't want to, they just can't do it for a long list of reasons that Mossad, military intelligence and Shin Bet have analysed much better than I could. I am just quoting them. So, Ehud, let's do what Arik understood needed to be done and wanted to do: evacuate and separate now. Take the space you need for security purposes and give them the rest. Do not ask them for anything in return.'

Olmert did not accept my advice, continued negotiations, reached an agreement in principle with Mahmoud Abbas, but when the time came to sign, as is well known, the Palestinian leader refused to do so.

Netanyahu heard this plan from me in 2009, in the first month of his return as prime minister. He heard it again a few more times, not just from me. At one point, he even asked me for a proposed map. I suggested to him, in writing, to set up a team that would examine in detail the various options for separating the populations in Judea and Samaria.

In response, I was invited to a meeting with Yossi Cohen, then head of the National Security Council, later head of Mossad. He told me that the prime minister was interested in hearing details. All this was in 2014. Nothing came of it, and Netanyahu did not adopt the idea.

While I was a student at the London School of Economics, I began to formulate a global vision, based on an understanding that the world needs to move from leadership of individual nations to collective, global leadership. I thought that the threat of nuclear weapons would accelerate inter-state cooperation and that within fifty years a global leadership would be established, which I called a 'world government'. Obviously this did not happen.

The European Union was established in 1993. I saw it then as a first step in the direction of establishing a global leadership. I did not see fighting terrorism as part of this, because terrorist incidents were not of a magnitude to demand global attention. But the combination of terrorism and nuclear threat on the one hand, and the development of cyberspace communication on the other will eventually bring about such global forums.

In 1982, I said that another hundred years of terrorism awaited us. I then referred to our conflict with the Palestinians, but the Jewish–Palestinian conflict does not threaten world peace. What threatens world peace is a nuclear weapon in the wrong hands. The horror scenario of nuclear weapons falling into the hands of uncontrollable fanatics has kept me awake since the early 1950s. Until a 'world government' is established, only sovereign states can be trusted to suppress terrorist organisations operating in and out of their territory. Therefore, world peace is severely endangered by failed states that do not have a strong central government, bound by accepted international laws and arrangements. These are the countries where terrorist organisations thrive, and which pose the greatest potential danger to the world. Terrorist organisations that previously operated without a territorial base have been exterminated: the Japanese Red Star, the Baader-Meinhof in Germany, the Red Brigades in Italy. This is how it has worked for years. You deprive terrorist organisations of their territorial base and uproot them. As long as ISIS controls territory on the Syrian–Iraqi border, it will prosper. When the Assad regime, due to the determined efforts of Russia, Iran and Hezbollah, took control of ISIS territory, this murderous organisation weakened and almost completely disintegrated.

In order to eradicate the bases of terrorism, two things need to be done: to establish sovereign states that bear responsibility, and to strengthen them with united international forces aimed at eradicating terrorism. What is important here is the unity of purpose, because behind every such multinational force, are the countries that contribute troops, and each such country has its own interests. What can prompt the United States, France, Germany, Britain, Canada, Australia, China, Korea, Japan, to unite on this front with the aim of attaining peace and economic prosperity? It is clear to me that occasional terrorist attacks here and there will not prompt the required unification of interests. However, a nuclear threat may indeed. A nuclear weapon that falls, God forbid, into the hands of a terrorist organisation will prompt a unification of interests. A terrorist organisation that controls territory and maintains the appearance of a state may lay its hands on an atomic weapon. Only awareness of such a threat will unite the international system for unified action to make sure that no land on the planet falls under the control of terrorists.